PRAISE FOR
ALWAYS CRASHING IN THE SAME CAR

"Matthew Specktor's *Always Crashing in the Same Car* is going on the shelf with *Play It as It Lays* and *The Big Sleep* and my other favorite books about LA. I'm not sure what it is. A memoir-essay grafted onto a psycho-geographic travelogue of the weirdest town to be from? All I know is I couldn't stop reading it."

— **JOHN JEREMIAH SULLIVAN**, author of *Pulphead*

"Haunting, powerful, riveting, unforgettable–I could go on (and on) about Matthew Specktor's astounding new book about failure, writing, Los Angeles, and the movies. With scholarly rigor and tenderhearted sympathy, Specktor excavates the lives of artists forgotten (Carole Eastman, Eleanor Perry), underappreciated (Thomas McGuane, Hal Ashby), and notorious (Warren Zevon, Michael Cimino), while always circling back to his own benighted Hollywood upbringing. This is an angry, sad, but always somehow joyful book about *not* hitting it big, and I've never read anything quite like it."

— **TOM BISSELL**, author of
Magic Hours: Essays on Creators and Creation

"In Hollywood, according to Brecht's famous formulation, there was no need of heaven and hell; the presence of heaven alone served the unsuccessful as hell. But Los Angeles has always been full of commuters on the congested freeway between both camps. They are the subject of Matthew Specktor's continuously absorbing and revealing book, itself nestling in the fruitful terrain between memoir and criticism."

— **GEOFF DYER**, author of
Out of Sheer Rage: Wrestling with D. H. Lawrence

ALWAYS CRASHING
IN THE SAME CAR

Published by Tin House, Portland, Oregon

Distributed by W. W. Norton & Company

Library of Congress Cataloging-in-Publication Data

Names: Specktor, Matthew, author.
Title: Always crashing in the same car : on art, crisis & Los Angeles, California / Matthew Specktor.
Description: Portland, Oregon : Tin House, [2021] | Includes bibliographical references.
Identifiers: LCCN 2020057479 | ISBN 9781951142629 (paperback) | ISBN 9781951142636 (ebook)
Subjects: LCSH: Specktor, Matthew. | Authors, American—Biography. | Los Angeles (Calif.)—History—20th century—Biography. | Los Angeles (Calif.)—Intellectual life—20th century.
Classification: LCC PS3619.P437 Z46 2021 | DDC 813/.6 [B]—dc23
LC record available at https://lccn.loc.gov/2020057479

First US Edition 2021
Printed in the USA
Interior design by Jakob Vala

www.tinhouse.com

always crashing in the same car

ON ART, CRISIS & LOS ANGELES, CALIFORNIA

MATTHEW SPECKTOR

TIN HOUSE / Portland, Oregon

For K, whose life was beautiful anyway

CONTENTS

One life was never quite enough for what I had in mind.

—SEYMOUR KRIM, "For My Brothers
and Sisters in the Failure Business"

I

monkeybitch

introduction

These are the picture people.
Do not blame them too much.

—F. SCOTT FITZGERALD, *Notebooks*

THERE'S A CERTAIN sort of person one sees all over Los Angeles, the kind you'd rather stare at, perhaps, than know. These people—you've seen them too—are elegant, compact, and possessed of a bland perfection, a vegetable grace. You barely notice them, not because they aren't visually striking— on the contrary—but because they seem to lack credible flaws. Their bone structure, their carefully tended hair and stubble, their laughter. If you were the type who was inclined to judge such things, a casting agent or just a garden-variety asshole, you'd probably be able to tell what was which and who was most likely to succeed on the basis of these attri- butes (for these people are almost all, in one sense or another, actors), but me? All my life I've viewed such specimens with confusion. Gliding past in their cars, hanging on the terraces and patios of outdoor cafés, hunched over laptops, scowl- ing, in the back booths of restaurants or lolling—in pairs, in quartets—drinking green juice, drinking matcha tea or iced cortados, giving off the air, always, always, always, of ease, of success, of industry, of hope, of readiness, of the absence (see the yoga mat, the keys, the sunglasses, the well-thumbed copy of Stanislavski's *An Actor Prepares*, or *Save the Cat!*) of all visible signs of difficulty.

Such people once filled me with envy: the sad pangs of an ugly duckling sentenced to waddle among them. Later, the feelings they stirred were ones of resentment, and competition. But it is only recently, after a long struggle with my own ideas of "success" and what these people might be aiming toward, that I have begun to pity them. To look at them now feels like looking at a photograph of soldiers headed to war, or one of those spammy internet pages that purport to show images taken on the precipice of calamity: the instant before the shark bites or the bear lunges, or the foot slips fatally from the ledge. This morning, I slalomed through a crowd of them on my way to get coffee, my hips brushing up against their shoulders, glancing down at their sunstruck, symmetrical, self-enclosed faces, the narcissistic flowers of Beverly Boulevard, innocent, every last one, of what wind was coming to destroy them. By the time I made it back to my car? I was in tears.

◎

Some time ago ("in my younger and more vulnerable years"), I suffered a kind of crash. "Suffered" may be a grand and heroic word for it, considering the quantities of a more profound misery in the world, but, nevertheless. I found myself loose, at large within the city where I'd grown up, from which I'd departed in a nervous panic at eighteen, and to which I'd only recently returned. *Hollywood.* Los Angeles contains so many sub-quadrants, most of them having nothing in particular to

do with the movies, but "Hollywood"—which is as much a notion as it is a neighborhood, one that permeates the actual city
like a gas—is where I'm from. My childhood home may have
sat in Santa Monica, a sleepy suburb by the sea, but my family resided in Hollywood as surely as anyone ever has. Which
place is to many folks still a metonym, a symbol of all that is
shiny and empty and attractive and awful in American life, all
that is stupid and all that is—we can't help it—irresistible to us,
pulling as it does with the hopeful energy of sex. To me, growing up, this city had been the precise opposite: a glamourless
desert, a hall of mirrors where I was unable to escape my own
unfortunate reflection. All these roads and avenues running
nowhere beneath the green palms, leading me back inexorably
to my own perceived limitations. Surely there was something
the matter with me. How could I dislike my own hometown
so much? I'd ejected myself with all the force of a hairball, fled
east to college in Massachusetts, west to San Francisco, then
east again to New York City. I'd been elsewhere for a long, long
time, and now that I was home, probing along the margins of
my native place the way you would at an abscessed tooth, with
tenderness and care and a gnawing fascination . . . I fell in love,
though to this day I cannot quite say with what. Maybe it was
just the thing about Los Angeles that claims everybody, eventually: weather, buildings, loveliness, light. Or maybe, I'd fooled
myself again. Having expatriated myself from the city for so
long, and having insulated myself for a while by marriage, one
that had recently ended, I was coming to it now as an outsider,
and for the same reason so many do: as a sucker, hoping against
some very steep odds for "success."

"I'll take it."

My voice echoed sharply off the walls of a small but empty room, the acoustics of which—wood floors, high ceiling—made it feel slightly larger: just big enough that I might not feel for a while the potential for confinement.

"OK, great." The landlady, a gnomish, leathery-looking figure with the straw-blond hair of someone thirty years her junior, smiled. "I'll draw up a lease." She leaned over, conspiratorial, and whispered, "Y'know who used to live here? Cary Grant."

"Really?"

"You know who else?" She beamed. "Al Pacino."

I stared at her. There was no way of knowing if either of these things was true, if she was serving up local folklore or if (as she pulled a cell phone from her pocket and showed me a number she insisted was Pacino's) this landlady was in fact a little bit nuts. But in a way it didn't matter: Los Angeles is full of such apocrypha. This apartment was just a ghost crib, a launching pad toward a greater, more hopeful future.

"Cool," I said, as I followed her outside. "I'll try to honor them both."

The place I'd landed was at the stone center of Hollywood's mythological grid: the head of the Sunset Strip, the intersection at Crescent Heights that shears off into Laurel Canyon on one side and toward Beverly Hills and the beach if you gaze straight ahead, at the twisting road that winds past the Chateau Marmont and a million other landmarks—the Whisky a Go Go, the Roxy, the Polo Lounge, and the Beverly Hills Hotel. *Hollywood*. If you picture it, apart from its fabled hillside sign *this* is what you see. If you're attuned to this place, its history and poetics, you think of all the things that have happened along this very street, or in the canyons that branch directly away from it: John Belushi OD'ing on a speedball in one of the rooms at the Chateau; Jim Morrison kicked out of the Whisky forever for unspooling the oedipal psychodrama of "The End" an obscenity too far; Arthur Lee of the great sixties band Love, himself stoned immaculate between Clark and Hilldale, his band collapsing in a fog of drugs and money problems; the Manson murders; farther west, the O. J. murder. If you wanted to, you could map the entirety of Sunset Boulevard, all twenty-one and three-quarter miles of it, exclusively in terms of mayhem and collapse, chart it as purely as the stations of the cross. For a place so synonymous with hedonism, this city sure seems to arrive at one bummer after the next. And for a place so gilded, so enamored—again, still—with stardom, it sure does seem to cradle more than its fair share of failure, of oblivions both natural and man-made.

Perhaps I was simply obsessed. We've all seen the movies: Norma Desmond, beckoning for her close-up, in Billy Wilder's indelible portrait of a faded silent screen star, *Sunset Boulevard*; Jake Gittes and Philip Marlowe, the great PIs of, respectively, *Chinatown* and *The Long Goodbye*, both endlessly chastened and infinitely bruised, shivved up and knocked out for the simple sin of curiosity. (I picture Roman Polanski playing a small-time hood in his own *Chinatown*, sliding the tip of a switchblade inside Jack Nicholson's nostril. "You know what happens to nosy fellas, huh? No? Wanna guess?") Los Angeles might be a place for those who ask no questions to thrive. In this it is like every other place. But for those who wonder, who voice even the most basic existential concerns—*What the fuck am I doing here? And why?*—this city is a sticky wicket.

What *was* I doing here? I'd left, I came to realize, for reasons having everything to do with failure (my mother's, as an unhappy screenwriter and an abusive alcoholic, whose career collapsed under the weight of her own disappointment and rage; my own, as a son trying to please a hypercritical talent-agent father, one of the early architects of Creative Artists Agency whose tall shadow fell across the film industry; LA's, maybe, in its inability to live up to what I once thought a city should be), and with my own hopeless desire to transcend it. I'd wanted to be a writer. Leaving aside that this was a dubious, romantic, at once trivial and ridiculous ambition—at least the way I wanted it then, it was—it seemed somehow out of true with what this city was about. Bret Easton Ellis, who grew up three years ahead and five miles away, told me once, "I associated literature with the East. My goal was to find a college, get through four years, then make the move to New York." Same here. LA was for idiots and movie producers, people who didn't even read. And if my interest in literature, as I understood that term at seventeen, marked me out also as a pretentious jerk, I nevertheless knew what I *didn't* want to be: a hack, a sellout, a (I can feel my adolescent self fairly cringing with disgust) *screen*writer . . .

Flash forward (or "cut to," whichever cinematic crutch you prefer) twenty years. I've settled in now to this apartment in West Hollywood on Hayworth Avenue, next door to the Directors Guild of America, thirty yards maybe from the Strip. It's beautiful, this place (whether it was ever really

Cary Grant's or Al Pacino's or anyone else's), small but beautiful: a Spanish-style building with a courtyard and pink tiles, terra-cotta mosaic outside and hardwood floors within, french windows on either side so when I open the place up at midday my apartment is a sieve for light and wind, and even—no joke—the occasional hummingbird who trembles on the verge and then flits in, flits out. There is a fireplace, but who needs it? The apartment is a studio, just one rectangular upstairs room with an ell consisting of kitchen and then bath, but it'll do, for now. By day, it's an aerie, the live-work space of my dreams.

By night? A different story. The windows fold shut, the Murphy bed comes out of the wall, and the room becomes a prison, my riot cell, the roof beneath which my preschool-age daughter is not sleeping. A few miles away she rests inside the home I have vacated to my wife (a banker, she can afford the mortgage, as I suddenly cannot) and her boyfriend/coworker, of whom I try not to think too much. I pace, I swelter. I harbor my grudges. I labor, a little fruitlessly, on a novel, and I contemplate the looming Writers Guild of America strike that has slowed hiring around town—a (cough) mid-level screenwriter such as myself barely stands a chance—but which also absolves me of having to contemplate the crappiness of the last thing I've written, a script so lousy I wish I could bury it in a vault at the bottom of the sea. I drink. I surf Craigslist and, in these days before Tinder or Bumble, flirt and have occasional sex with strangers. I wake up in the middle of the night to pee and wade into the bathroom clutching a broom with both hands, preparing to smash the enormous palmetto bugs that will scurry the moment I hit the light. I flail blindly. More than once, I hit the mirror above the sink. Which cracks and then eventually shatters, so I have to replace it on the cheap.

◎

1448 North Hayworth Avenue was the address. Directly across the street, and visible when I leaned out the southward-facing windows, was 1443, the complex I knew had been occupied by the English-born gossip columnist Sheilah Graham, chronicler of Hollywood's original "golden age" six and a half decades earlier; in fact, it was in her living room that F. Scott Fitzgerald dropped dead on December 21, 1940. That date, the twenty-first, happens to be my own birthday, and it happens to be the birthday attributed to actor William Holden's character in *Sunset Boulevard*, the hack screenwriter Joe Gillis. ("I like Sagittarians," Norma Desmond says, when Joe tells her when he was born. "You can trust them.") It is also the date on which John Keats, a poet who may have mattered to F. Scott Fitzgerald more than any other, wrote a letter to his brother in which he coined the notion of "negative capability," which he defined as "when man is capable of being in uncertainties, mysteries, doubts, without any irritable reaching after fact and reason."[1]

1448. 1940. Arcane dates and numbers, fragments—as everything comes to seem in time, or at least everything seemed to me, then—of the vanished past. Was it fate that I'd become

---

1. The dating of this is in some places disputed. The internet dates it the twenty-second of 1818, but my Oxford edition of the letters dates it the twenty-first to twenty-seventh of the year before.

that thing I'd once upon a time most despised, or that I'd washed up on the margins, where these bits of trivia could collect and start to feel meaningful in all the most cryptic and uncomfortable ways? I scrubbed my face in the kitchen sink. I brushed my teeth and spat out the window. I developed questionable habits, in avoidance of the room that was full of smashed bugs, but also in observance of perverse superstitions. Failure is a pattern of mind, but it is also, when we are close to it, delicious. It pulls a lot harder than success, which is more like a surfboard or a set of skis: the object of a wobbly, always temporary, mastery. I leaned out those south-facing windows a lot in those days, farther than I should've, because it would've afforded me a bizarre and profound fascination to know I could see *in* to the room where Scott Fitzgerald died. Occasionally I crossed the street and crept over the lawn, always imagining I was going to get called out for—interloping, I guess, the mortal sin of casing someone else's apartment complex. The Hayworth Chateau, as it was once rather too grandly called, looks now much as it did then, much as it had in photographs taken several decades earlier: unprepossessing and gray, a boxy, vaguely Tudor-seeming structure with a mansard roof carved into eight apartments. If mine seemed cheerful from the outside, all sun-splashed courtyard and butter-colored walls, this one seemed not ominous but retiring, tucked back a bit from the street.

I couldn't see into the unit where he died from the lawn. The window was drawn with a thick white curtain.

◎

I was obsessed with Fitzgerald, who'd once represented to me, as he had to so many, everything hopeful, everything gilded, bright, and beautiful. The publication of his first novel, *This Side of Paradise*, made him famous almost instantaneously. Its initial printing sold out in three days. Fitzgerald, celebrated progenitor of the so-called Jazz Age—the term he is said to have invented—whose own prosperous twenties corresponded with those of the century: the writer was twenty-four when that book appeared in 1920. On the wings of his success he spent the subsequent decade living in New York City, in Great Neck, and then, with his talented, gorgeous, schizophrenic wife Zelda in tow, in Paris, Rome, and Antibes. They "[looked] as though they had just stepped out of the sun," Dorothy Parker recalled of her first meeting with Scott and Zelda. "Their youth was striking."

To me too. At fifteen, I sat out on the terrace of my father's divorce pad in Malibu and read *Tender Is the Night* for the first time. I couldn't help but mistake my own view for the one Fitzgerald offered of the French Riviera: the same "bright tan prayer rug of a beach," same "ripples and rings . . . through the clear shallows." Not exactly, perhaps, but to my fevered, wishful adolescent mind it wanted to be, just as *I* wanted to be Dick Diver, and later Amory Blaine or Nick Carraway, those figures who, like Fitzgerald himself, begin in hope but end in disillusionment or worse. At the time, those disastrous ends served only to make the beginnings more attractive. On my father's patio, I basked in Sunday sunlight and read, gazing down at the dazzling Pacific at the bottom of the bluffs, following the cars as they shot off down the Coast Highway toward Zuma, the Malibu Colony,

Paradise Cove, warming my bare feet on the terrace's pink brick. *They looked as though they had just stepped out of the sun.* I stared at the author's jacket photo. His open, friendly, Irish-leaning face resembled my own. By the time I stood up and stretched, firing a clove cigarette to set the seal on this experience, my die was cast. I knew what I wanted to do with my life.

Much later, I'd hear there was another story: that of a gifted American novelist who blew his talent and then flew to Hollywood where, desperate for money, separated from his wife who was confined to a sanitarium back East, he descended into hackwork, into screenplays so crummy that (unlike those of his peer William Faulkner, whose alcoholism didn't prevent *him* from doing quality work for the movies) they were never even produced. This is the other story of F. Scott Fitzgerald, the one in which, no longer popular the way he'd once been, his fame evaporated as rapidly as it had come on, the writer came to LA and washed out, the way people, and writers in particular, so often do. He left behind a fragment, a partial novel some said might have offered redemption if he'd been able to finish it. But alas, or so I was told, he came up short, and died the sorry ruin Hollywood, even more than anything else, had made him.

◎

Which of these stories was true? At fifteen, too, I'd read Fitzgerald's famous 1936 essay "The Crack-Up," in which he'd offered his maxim that "the test of a first-rate intelligence is the ability to hold two opposed ideas in the mind at the same time, and still retain the ability to function." He'd painted himself as someone who failed that test: as a fragile, alcoholic mess whose best days—whose *only* days, really—were behind him.

Were mine? Sitting in my apartment, staring over at that place in which my first literary inspiration had died, I couldn't help but wonder, and I couldn't help but start sifting my own history for clues. "Hollywood" offers not just promises but distortions: one person's grab at immortality is another one's pulverizing defeat; the promise of a limitless, impregnable success seemed just as useless as that of an irremediable failure. Life is lived in the wide gap between these things. And yet . . .

All my life I have been fascinated by those figures whose status—not their work, which frequently has as much claim to greatness as that of those better known, but their status— is faintly marginal: artists whose careers carry an aura of what might, also, have been. Those who failed, those who faltered, those whose triumphs are punctuated by flops or by periods, often lasting years, of obscurity. "Marginal" is a misleading word, insofar as these artists, the ones who swam upstream through the silver age of Hollywood, many of whom I discovered in adolescence, were too often white, and framed within a context, that of the industry's long-standing racism and exclusion, that is itself distorting. Those great figures who bucked the system or were shut out of it entirely, filmmakers like Billy Woodberry and Charles Burnett, Kathleen Collins and Gordon Parks, were unknown to me until later, and put the lie to the industry's definitions of "success." But that summer, as I sought to find my balance, as I sifted through the ashes of my marriage and the origins of my ambition, I began a process of returning to those artists (writers, directors, an occasional outlier in the form of an actor or musician) whose work had formed me, or would: a series of felicitous encounters with people who, no matter how idiosyncratically they arrived at my door, all seemed to have something to say about these questions of failure and achievement, and how Hollywood—by which I really mean America—treats its artists. Together they make a strange, and decidedly limited, constellation, but those limits—of gender, of race, of class and identity—make up themselves a part of the lesson I would spend the next few years learning. Eleanor Perry and Carole Eastman were never exactly household names; Tuesday Weld and Warren Zevon were largely so, while Tom McGuane, Hal Ashby, Michael Cimino, and Renata Adler were famous, at least in the capitals and on the coasts. All of them represented, one way or another, creative ideals I held when I was younger: romantic (although in some cases also practical) images of what an artistic triumph, and what a capitalist or a characterological disaster, might look like. To re-encounter them in midlife was bracing, but it offered a necessary, and useful, clutch of information. Once upon a time the very notion of a "great American novel" was defined, contentiously and inadequately, by Fitzgerald's *The Great Gatsby*, but while we're only just getting around to dismantling the structures that would have allowed such a narrow definition in the first place, the book itself remains, shot through with problems—reflective of the racism and antisemitism that are inseparable from the nation's history too—but worthy all the same of our attention. I might say as much for the writers and artists here: their flaws are obvious (even when they are not, as in most of these cases, those same flaws), but their rewards are substantial. All of them deserve a bit more sustained appreciation than they've received. And each of them might illuminate, in different ways, what it means to be a person: how to square one's desires, one's dreams and disappointments, with the act of being a citizen of the world.

◎

I bought a copy of *The Last Tycoon*. It remained, for some reason—perhaps just the obvious one of reckoning with that corner of Fitzgerald's experience I had been unwilling thus far to reckon with inside my own—the only book of his I hadn't read. It was unfinished, left incomplete at the time of his death, and so he had written portions of it, I imagined, on this very block where I now lived. It occupied his mind as he shuffled from his own apartment, on Laurel Avenue, to Sheilah's place these few streets away. As he walked along Sunset Boulevard, past Schwab's Pharmacy and the Garden of Allah, that fabled apartment complex he'd lived in himself when he first came to Hollywood in the thirties, his mind was humming with it. All those portraits and self-portraits of him as a "cracked plate," a washed-up and feeble alcoholic who'd "[mortgaged himself] physically and spiritually up to the hilt," turned out to be in-accurate, or half-accurate: the book is as vital as anything he ever wrote.

> *You can take Hollywood for granted like I did, or you can dismiss it with the contempt we reserve for what we don't understand. It can be understood too, but only dimly and in flashes.*

Fitzgerald gives these words, on the novel's first page, to the young Cecelia Brady, the improbable avatar—a college student, the pampered daughter of a film studio executive—who serves as narrator, but the book's real object isn't Cecelia at all but rather Monroe Stahr, the dynamic man with whom she (and perhaps Fitzgerald too, after a fashion) is in love. Stahr is based, transparently—unmistakably—on Irving Thalberg, the legendary head of MGM Studios who'd steered that company through its golden age in the 1930s. Thalberg was, if anything, a more romantic figure than any even Fitzgerald himself had managed to dream up: a "boy wonder" who ascended to power at an impossibly young age and then died, of congenital heart failure, at thirty-seven. Handsome, dashing, above all decisive, it was Thalberg who furnished the words Fitzgerald put into Stahr's mouth, who spoke them to the writer when he'd first come out to visit Los Angeles in 1927.

> *"Suppose you were a railroad man," he said. "You have to send a train through there somewhere. Well, you get your surveyors' reports, and you find there's three or four or half a dozen gaps, and not one is better than the other. You've got to decide—on what basis? You can't test the best way— except by doing it. So you just do it."*

These words, spoken by Irving Thalberg to Scott Fitzgerald in the MGM commissary during a brief chance encounter and then repurposed, a dozen years later, into dialogue for *The Last Tycoon*'s protagonist, must have hit Fitzgerald hard. Writers are vacillators, living and dying—and, y'know, *both*, often enough,

at the same time—on the strength of their capacity for inde-
cision. The executive power of a man like Thalberg was the
power required to write a novel. It was also the power that
had bedeviled him during his recent years in Hollywood as
Fitzgerald had labored under unsympathetic or backstabbing
producers to write botched drafts of films like *Winter Carnival*
and *Three Comrades*, films that, while not terrible, bore little of
his own stylistic imprint in the end. His morale had suffered.
His sobriety, tenuously achieved when he'd arrived in LA to
stay in 1937, had buckled. And it was men like Thalberg (not
Thalberg himself but savvy, sharp figures like Walter Wanger
and Joseph Mankiewicz, industry veterans who knew better
than to let a writer's feelings get in the way of making a movie)
who'd bedeviled him. *Mankiewicz*. Or, to use Fitzgerald's own
nickname for his nemesis—the producer who'd fired him from
a movie immediately after reassuring him, via telegram, that he
would do no such thing—"Monkeybitch." This was the root
of his misery, the person who obstructed his creative impulses
and decided, instead, to take things another way. You couldn't
blame Fitzgerald for hating the people who kept him, in his
view, from succeeding in Hollywood. But you might be a little
surprised to find he had decided, in the end, to make this same
type of man the sympathetic center of his final novel.

◎

Monkeybitch. Was this what had bedeviled me too? I hadn't
experienced much success in Hollywood, or anywhere else for
that matter—I'd written things, none of them published or

produced—but I didn't blame anyone else for it. I blamed myself, restless memory, restless mind, whatever it was in me that
couldn't get comfortable where I was, that insisted, against both
common sense and evidence, that I'd be happier somewhere else,
once the future (what future?) had conferred recognition upon
me. Never mind that this feeling has another name, entitlement,
or that my own willful obliviousness to it constituted a further
crime. I was restless. I was unhappy. My wife—soon to be an ex-
wife, as we prepared to file our divorce papers—had responded to
it in a practical way: by having an affair. I didn't exactly blame her
for that (how could I? I'd been insufferable), but when I thought
back over our demise, lying there in the dark at 1448, I couldn't
help but find myself filled with rage, and regret. *Monkeybitch.* The
word rang in my head, its very unsettling nature, too ridiculous
to be an epithet, too furious to be anything else, inflaming me
further, until I couldn't sleep. For Fitzgerald, just a nickname, a
tag hung on a person he resented. For me, a mantra, concentrat-
ing my self-loathing into a pinpoint of perfect disgust.

Outside, the fronds rattled. The moon hung over the courtyard, weirdly bruised, huge and ugly like a thumb. I could hear
the palmetto bugs scurrying, or thought I could, in the kitchen
and in the bath. The jilted lover's condition: that paranoia that
turns the world sickly. Perhaps it is the Angeleno's condition
too: all those jilted husbands looking to retain the services of
the great film PIs—Mr. Marlowe, Mr. Gittes—in order only to
prove what they already know.

Nights like this: too many of them. Nights I woke and
poured myself a drink, or prowled down the Strip to the Chateau, there to stare at the soldiers, diamond-bright martini

glasses lined up atop the bar. How many people had murdered themselves in this room? How many glasses, soldiers, would I knock down, myself? Enough to remember I was nothing like my mother? Or enough, alas, to forget?

◎

Who did I want to become? The question stuck to me, too, in the daylight hours, when I wasn't plodding along Sunset Boulevard tracking down Fitzgerald's old haunts like the Garden of Allah (now a McDonald's) or Schwab's Pharmacy (then a Virgin Megastore, itself in the process of closing). The last script I'd written, an assignment offered in the waning days of my marriage, I'd leapt at the way a starving dog leaps at a chicken nugget held aloft, but now I couldn't even think of it without cringing. Who did I want to be now? I drove to Encino, to the ghost shell of the place Fitzgerald had occupied over there for a while on Amestoy Avenue, now paved over by the 101 Freeway. As if this would tell me.

"What do you do, Dad?"

My daughter's voice rang out sometimes, in the hollow bucket of my apartment, now that she was old enough to be curious.

"What do you do when I'm not here?"

Afternoons, I had her in those days. There was no place for her to sleep, and so my ex would pick her up after dinner. We'd play and read, or sometimes watch cartoons; take walks down to Santa Monica Boulevard, where we'd get frozen yogurt. Sometimes we'd wind up back here and while I took a moment to catch up on an email, she'd ask me again: "What do you do?" I never quite understood whether this little chant of hers was a professional question—like, she understood her mother went to work in an office where I did not—or an existential one. It sounded like a song.

"I make things up."

"Yeah?"

"Like—for TV, or the movies."

It sounded so flimsy, said out loud, but she seemed to accept it. I knelt down next to her now: my V! She had my ex's fairness, and, I hoped, her practicality, although it was too soon to know about that.

"Oh."

I placed my palms on her shoulders. The sound of her breathing was enough to make me happy. But I felt, too, such pulverizing shame. *I make things up?* It's a weird thing, maybe, to wish one's child—a child that young—to be proud, but I did; selfishly, I did. She appeared mildly crestfallen.

"Come on. I'll make you dinner."

She followed me over to that L-shaped kitchen. "I make things up," I heard her whisper: testing it out for herself. It sounded better when she said it: she was three years old.

◎

In those days I couldn't even pull it together to do that much. Instead, I studied Fitzgerald's final testament, and tried to figure out where it all went wrong. In *The Pat Hobby Stories*, those pieces he wrote grubbing for pocket money between assignments in Hollywood—fees that couldn't touch what he'd made at the height of his popularity a decade earlier, when he was making four grand for a single story in the *Saturday Evening Post*—the protagonist in each is a hack screenwriter, a man whose hapless efforts to restore his own dignity (by stealing a younger writer's ideas; by blackmailing a studio executive; by sneaking a pretty actress into a premiere) all seem to end in disaster. But in *The Last Tycoon*, these efforts are gone, replaced, instead, by a stoic resignation, what might be called wisdom if it were not, too, so anguished and so sad.

> *He wanted the pattern of his life broken. If he was going to die soon, like the two doctors said, he wanted to stop being Stahr for a while and hunt for love like men who had no gifts to give, like young nameless men who looked along the streets in the dark.*

Hear the urgency in those lines, the assertion? That must have been him, Fitzgerald, begging to become not just the somebody he once was—the popular author whose novels were everywhere, instead of the forgotten man who used to duck into bookstores on Hollywood Boulevard and astonish the shopkeepers who'd thought he was dead—but the nobody he'd been before that, the nameless young man from Minnesota who was too poor, once, even to win Zelda's heart. *He wanted the pattern of his life broken*. Don't we all, at one time or another? And don't we all wish we could achieve this, even for a moment, without having to grapple with death? Fitzgerald described Stahr, in a letter to the magazine editor Kenneth Littauer, as "over-worked and deathly

tired, ruling with a radiance that is almost moribund in its phos-
phorescence." He'd given his protagonist the same congenital
heart problems Irving Thalberg had, the ones that had indeed
killed him a few years earlier, and he'd given Stahr too some of
his own exhaustion. But the core of that character remained his
desire, the wish to become someone else.

> *Writers aren't people exactly. Or, if they're any good, they're*
> *a whole lot of people trying so hard to be one person.*

This observation is offered by the novel's Cecelia Brady, but
it's clear enough Fitzgerald was talking, equally, about himself.
(To Stahr, the author donated a more hard-boiled assessment:
"You writers . . . get all mixed up and somebody has to come in
and straighten you out," he lets the studio boss say. "You seem
to take things so personally, hating people and worshipping
them—always thinking people are so important—especially
yourselves. You just ask to be kicked around. I like people and
I like them to like me but I wear my heart where God put
it—on the inside.") That's me too. The people in this book are
all those I would like to be, might prefer (in some cases) not to
be, cannot help (in all cases) but to be, or at least to understand.
They have brushed up against the hem of the motion picture
business, or, like Fitzgerald, passed through it to another side,
found a way to embrace a machinery that was the engine, too,
of their own destruction. This machinery spreads through the
tangible city of Los Angeles. There is no way to live here without being, in some way, touched by it. Even if that "touch" is
only the coldness with which it—America—ignores you.

Staring out the window at 1443, I pictured him moving across the lawn, on his way to see his lover, Sheilah Graham. I pictured him inside the apartment, eating a chocolate bar and listening to the radio, Beethoven's *Eroica* playing on the morning his own alcohol-saturated heart simply—stopped. I pictured him before that, moving through the great, atrial systems of his last unfinished novel, the ones that showed the workings of a movie studio so tenderly and with such loving particularity, the minutiae of the very thing that had eaten him alive.

He was a flawed man. "Flawed," perhaps, does not begin to cover it, given that in his alcoholism he surely—I knew a thing or two about this—had generated suffering in those who stood close to him, inflicted pain and humiliation. But he was a kind man, a generous man, sending money he barely had back to the sanitarium in Asheville, North Carolina, to support his wife, writing letters, thoughtful and affectionate ones, to his daughter, and to Ernest Hemingway, whose talent he had endorsed from the beginning. There was something of the ghost to him even when he arrived in Los Angeles for the first time. Budd Schulberg, who would immortalize a certain version of Fitzgerald in his portrait of "Manley Halliday," the alcoholic protagonist of his book *The Disenchanted*, described him thus: "There seemed to be no colors in him. The proud, somewhat too handsome profile of his early dust-jackets was crumpled. . . . The fine forehead, the leading man's nose, the matinee-idol set of the gentle, quick-to-smile eyes . . . he had lost none of these. But there seemed to be something physically or psychologically broken in him that had pitched him forward from scintillating youth to shaken old age." So he was, and I looked for him everywhere, for a while. I looked for him in West Hollywood, in those early days of exile that followed my separation. I looked for him in Malibu, where he'd lived for a period, and in Encino. I searched the glittering air, hovering over the Pacific. I searched the desert scrub, the blasted tan practicalities of the Valley, and the collapsed dreams, the vanished palaces of the Sunset Strip. I looked, the way I must have once looked for my own mother, who was very much on my mind those days, and everywhere I did, I came up empty.

Would it have consoled him to know, after these years of obscurity—like the booksellers he visited, even the studio heads who hired him sometimes needed to be reminded, first, he was still alive—that his work would outlive him? Probably not. What is the point of being loved in absentia? And what is the point of loving someone else who is missing? What is the point of loving the air?

He was alone when he died. His friends had betrayed him. Hemingway, who'd repaid Fitz's practically slavish worship of his gifts by condescending to his "wasted" talent, depicted him in *A Moveable Feast* as an anxious, simpering toady to the rich. Dorothy Parker, his friend for twenty years, with whom he'd gossiped in New York and holidayed on the Riviera, squinted down into Fitz's casket and pronounced him a "poor son of a bitch." These people, as gifted as they were, were not Fitzgerald's betters. They were his peers. And if they viewed him, after the fact, with pity or disdain, imagining the world that had claimed him—*Hollywood*—was somehow beneath their station, or that they'd survived it themselves out of some moral or intellectual superiority, they were mistaken. To Hemingway, three weeks before he died, Fitzgerald wrote to congratulate his friend on the success of *For Whom the Bell Tolls*, saying he was going to read it again and throwing in some warm words for *To Have and Have Not* for good measure. He was kind, and these people, his "friends," well, they fucked him. Because that's how they do it: they stab you in the front and then a few times more in the back for good measure. "Poor bastard." Shaking their heads as they walk away, zip up their flies, whatever defilements they may have added while Fitzgerald lay bleeding out on the floor. "Wanna go to Musso's, wanna go to Spago?" Turning to one another, their future fellow victims. "Let's go grab a drink."

First-rate, Scott. There was no more first-rate intelligence than yours. Because what two ideas are more opposed than the impulse to save yourself and the one that makes you want to grind yourself to dust, to drown yourself in gin and set your house on fire? And if this town could do that to *you*, friend, then imagine, just imagine—holy shit!—imagine what it might do to me.

II

polish star

eleanor perry
and frank perry

To hold a pen is to be at war.

—VOLTAIRE

THIRTY-EIGHT STEPS from where I lived was the Directors Guild of America, which sat on the corner of Hayworth and Sunset and which had once upon a time housed one of my young life's grimmest scenes. Thirty-eight steps, drunk or sober; thirty-eight whether I hopscotched or staggered, slouching away from the place where I'd decided to spend my forty-second year, away from my work ("work") in search of a distraction: a drink, a burrito, a meeting with a person I would inevitably disappoint. I'd pause for a moment to rest my hand on the low marble wall that ran alongside the building, staring up at the brownish, cylindrical structure of mauve-colored granite with burgundy accent bands. It looked a bit like an inverted wedding cake, or, as one of the architects wryly noted, like a stack of film canisters. I laid my hand on that wall, which seemed always cool—even in the midday sun, its heat was more like dry ice—as a kind of superstition, a charm against a disaster that had already happened. Decades ago, my mother had written a movie, and after she'd dragged me, at fourteen, to a screening of that movie, she'd gotten so disconcertingly plastered she'd peeled off with friends and abandoned me in this building's lobby. That night, unable to reach my dad, I'd hitchhiked home alone to Santa Monica and wondered if I'd ever forgive her. These days, I was more understanding, more sympathetic to her plight—indeed, we'd recently resumed talking, a year or so earlier—but I couldn't help but wonder: If my mother had never written that movie, would I have chosen differently for myself? Perhaps I would never have written any screenplays to begin with, and thus would not have found my-self motivated by so much loathing and contempt.

Self-loathing, and self-contempt. I sometimes wonder if there's any other kind. Los Angeles retails these feelings, and to have grown up here—lounging under palm trees, staring out at the swimming pools so blue and unconsoling, my teenage heartbeat rabbity with cocaine and disgust—is to be intimately acquainted with an intolerable self-image. My mother knew it. She had grown up here just as I did, and I know now that when she wrote that movie, she felt as I in time would: reluctant to be prostituting her talent by writing a film to which she held no profound personal connection—the job was just a contract rewrite, of a prison drama called *Love Child*—and indeed reluctant to be writing a film at all. There may have been additional reasons for her to feel that way, reasons that might, even, have precipitated a full-scale meltdown one night inside the Directors Guild building, say, ones of which I might have been ignorant at that age, but a predominant one was that she preferred literature. As do I. For people who grew up in the shadow of the movies, neither my mother nor I ever really *cared* about them that much, not the way we cared, at least, for books. Later that may have changed—I know for me it did, and that my mother and I spent hour upon hour when I was in high school watching old movies, irrespective of whether she was drunk or sober, all the same—but in the beginning, for her as for me, was the word. "What makes Iago evil?" "For a long time I used to go to bed early." "My mother is a fish." These sentences, like so many others, were internalized by the time I was barely clear of puberty. They amount to a strand of my DNA.

◎

What makes Iago evil? This sentence, as dear to my mother as any in all of literature, is the first of Joan Didion's *Play It as It Lays*, a book that, when I first read it at fifteen, seemed to fan out a picture of the life I decidedly did *not* want to live. (Had my mother lived it? Had she, like the book's Maria Wyeth, ever "made a list of things she would never do"? Had she never carried a Yorkshire in Beverly Hills, balled at a party, done S-M? I never asked.) When I was fifteen, this book cast its monolithic shadow across my life—or rather, in its illustration of a suffocating emptiness of which I was already, sadly, a little too aware, it seemed to describe a set of terms and conditions I was desperate to break; it was more like a lease than a novel—and so I stuffed it in a drawer. I didn't revisit it until, a decade or so later, I caught a rare screening of the 1972 film adaptation at a revival house in San Francisco. I was mesmerized by it, not least by Tuesday Weld's turn as Maria Wyeth, the shots of the collapsing actress firing a pistol as she guns a yellow Corvette across the Nevada desert, then filing her nails as she winds, later, up La Cienega Boulevard in town. The script was written by Didion and her husband, John Gregory Dunne—their second screen collaboration of what would be many, after 1971's *The Panic in Needle Park*—and the film was directed by Frank Perry.

◎

Frank Perry. The name dropped into my mind like a pebble lobbed into a well, trailing a few feeble, unrelated associations—my childhood best friend was a Perry, as was V's then-favorite singer—before vanishing altogether. The seventies were full of underappreciated auteurs, filmmakers whose modestly masterful bodies of work, or whose rare freak successes, crested the surface every now and again only to disappear. Beyond the Altmans and Ashbys, the Coppolas and Scorseses, beyond the Cassaveteses and Friedkins and De Palmas and Lumets, there exists that whole other caste—Martin Ritt, Richard Rush, Claudia Weill, John Flynn, Robert Downey *Senior*—whose films might not be discussed quite enough even by heavy-duty enthusiasts. Frank Perry, I surmised, was one of these. And so I forgot about him, until my memory was jogged a few years later by another revival screening of Perry's most nearly enduring movie, *Diary of a Mad Housewife*, which, like *Play It as It Lays* and like his adaptation of John Cheever's short story "The Swimmer," rarely ever screened and never seemed to be available when I browsed the racks of dodgier outlets (Kim's Video, in New York; Vidiots, in LA) that might have had bootleg DVDs in stock. It wasn't long before I forgot about him all over again . . .

Until one afternoon I found myself at the Iliad Bookshop in the Valley, a place where I could brush off my distress about work, about the looming WGA strike, about divorce, about a worrisome issue with my mother, which I'll come to, to spend the day browsing the aisles. Iliad is the quintessential used shop: whirring fans, torpid cats, that silence—punctuated by throat-clearings, coughs, the occasional squeak of a footstep—through which readers and collectors stalk their prey. This silence has largely faded from Los Angeles: you don't hear it in Barnes & Noble, or at Book Soup, at Skylight Books or Eso Won, but now as then you can drive out to the intersection of Chandler Boulevard and Cahuenga and enter archival time, that yellow-lit, musty-smelling corridor that is the closest thing to intimacy you can find in the commercial arena. During the period I lived at 1448, I spent whole days there, days with tired eyes and aching feet and an itching throat. What was I looking for? Like any decent bibliophile, I'd know it when I found it; I'd find it without even knowing I needed it, until that moment when it fell into my hand. I passed over a lot of great books in those days, either because I already owned them (I remember a particularly beautiful hardcover of James Baldwin's *Another Country*), or because I wouldn't know I needed them for a few years yet (Elizabeth Smart's *By Grand Central Station I Sat Down and Wept*); I searched fruitlessly for a number of books—John Hawkes's *The Lime Twig* was one—they never seemed to have, and which weren't even difficult to find online. But I wanted them from Iliad: lightly pencil-scuffed, dust-jacketed, underpriced. In a sense to shop at Iliad was like playing the slots, an ultimate loser's pastime. I played not to win but to fail; so I could aim my car back over the hill to my roach-filled apartment, then come back again to do it the next day.

Eleanor Perry. Who, exactly, was that? I must have passed by the single copy of her novel, *Blue Pages*, a dozen times; maybe I was reaching for something else—Walker Percy? James Purdy?—when it fell into my hand: chunky (but not *too* chunky), nondescript, its bone-white cover hatched with blue and gold stripes. There were no blurbs, only a taut excerpt on the back cover, a few lines indicating this might be a story about divorce. I think I clutched it because it looked like the sort of book I would've seen on my parents' shelves when I was a boy, like Judy Blume's *Wifey* or John Irving's *The 158-Pound Marriage* or Leonard Michaels's *The Men's Club*, one of those chronicles of midseventies conjugal torpor that lived on every other suburban shelf. It looked like comfort food. What better way to shake off one's own sense of incompetence and despair than by reading about the ennui and distress of the previous generation? I tucked the book under my arm, then went to ring it up. It wasn't until I got home that I noticed the bio on the dust flap: "Eleanor Perry is an acclaimed Hollywood screenwriter whose credits include . . . *Diary of a Mad Housewife.*" Above this a photograph of a sharp-eyed, patrician-looking woman with a low-slung beehive. I liked the look of her, a real cool customer, even as my heart sank. Novels by screenwriters—*career* screenwriters, people who've spent their lives writing for the movies and then decide to switch horses—are rarely very good, just as there are many novelists whose attempts to write persuasively for the screen are hopeless. Obviously, there are exceptions, but for the most part people who are good at scene construction (dialogue, skeletal or absent description, brief, staccato action punctuated by the POUNDING of melodramatic DETAIL) tend to suck at the rest of it: observation, meditation, the staging of human consciousness in ways that are fundamentally interesting. I noted that Eleanor would likely have held some relation to Frank—it seemed improbable a film would have two unrelated Perrys working as screenwriter and as director—and tucked in, reluctantly.

◎

Vincent and Lucia Wade are the names of the couple depicted in *Blue Pages*, a male director and a female screenwriter, the woman older than the man, the man announcing in the book's opening scene that he no longer loves the woman. The novel is told from her point of view, alternating sections in first and third person. The former describe the writer's adventures in Hollywood after her divorce—she is writing a western, a female-centered cowgirl drama on which she is credited as co-producer, but is endlessly stepped on by her male peers—while the latter depict, in a way that is clear-eyed but tender, pointy but never merely cruel, the origins of Lucia and Vincent: how the writer fell in love with an animated, charming, overweight man who looked like Balzac ("with his plumped-out cheeks and rolls of chin and shaggy hair and beard"), who ate Fig Newtons in bed even as he swore he would never leave her. This Lucia, the younger Lucia, is no fool: she (like Eleanor Perry herself) has been married once before, to a conventional-sounding man in Cleveland, Ohio; she (like Eleanor herself) has a thriving life as a New York playwright. She has no real need for a love affair, for this puppyish importunate man, even as she rides alongside him in a taxi uptown, thinking of her childhood, her mother's preparations of strawberries and cream.

> *Now she stares through the taxi window at the dark empty avenue, loose dirt and papers blowing along the gutters, an overturned trash can, plastic bags of garbage piled like sandbags against the window of a coffee shop, a lighted telephone booth covered with graffiti, its broken instrument askew on its cord. She is almost a middle-aged woman, neither good nor bad, who doesn't believe in God, her father and mother have long ago waged their wars and parted, and too many times these days the strawberries taste like damp cardboard.*

Reading this passage, homely but intimate, concrete in a way that feels specific, somehow, to the writer's own experience, I was ashamed of not knowing the facts, not knowing that the best work of Frank Perry—everything before *Play It as It Lays*—was in actuality the work of Frank and *Eleanor* Perry in tandem. Eleanor wrote their first movie, 1962's *David and Lisa*, based on a case study by the psychiatrist Theodore Isaac Rubin, and then, in order, *Ladybug, Ladybug* (1963); *The Swimmer* (1968); a trio of TV movies in collaboration with Truman Capote; and, finally, *Last Summer* and *Diary of a Mad Housewife* (1969 and '70, respectively), which together form the core of Frank Perry's admittedly modest reputation. From the sound of it, Eleanor didn't much care for Didion's *Play It as It Lays* (during the argument that kicks off *Blue Pages*, Vincent brags about some film rights he's recently acquired, for what will be his first film free of Lucia. "You didn't even like the book!" he snaps, to which she responds, "I admired the writing—I didn't like the heroine. She seemed so paralyzed, so numb . . ."), but she, and Frank, had created a substantial body of work before that. So why hadn't I heard of her? Perhaps the reason was obvious, down simply to the institutional and overt sexism that has been such a part of Hollywood's history from the beginning, but it seemed a shame, and even a crime, that her husband's name was familiar to me, but Eleanor's was not. If the work was good enough to be remembered at all, then why shouldn't it be remembered as hers?

◎

You hear the one about the Polish starlet? She fucked the writer! Everyone knows that Slavophobic joke—everyone in Hollywood, at least—but no one ever comments on the other things that are wrong with it: Why does it assume a "starlet" and not a "star"? Is it because a man would never be dumb enough to sleep with the writer? Why is the writer, at least in the coarse tellings of the joke with which I grew up, assumed to be a man himself? Never mind the bigotry, the joke is crummy for all sorts of reasons. But—once upon a time, a man (half-Polish, it turns out, and an agent rather than an actor) *did* fuck the writer, who happened to be my mom. To hear her tell it, he fucked her in more than one way—in the way that agents and executives are said to do in Hollywood, figuratively as well as literally, and well, the net result was . . . me. Who grew up to be a writer, and a whole other woman's mistake. The story of my parents' marriage, to which there is of course more than one side, is a separate matter, but reading *Blue Pages*, I couldn't help but think of my mother, whose cool literary intelligence was ill matched for my father's hard-driving dealmaker's vitality, but who must have been drawn to him just as Lucia (Eleanor) was drawn to Vincent (Frank). It's almost always a mistake to conflate an author's life with her characters', but the meticulous parallels between the Wades' filmography and the Perrys', the precision of Lucia's childhood memories and geography, even Vincent's physical appearance (Frank indeed looked like Balzac, almost disconcertingly so), all this squares with the idea that *Blue Pages* is, at least, a roman à clef. And if I squint hard enough, I can recognize my parents in Eleanor's fine-featured, northeastern cool (like hers, my mother's familial roots were in Cleveland), and in Frank's walrus-y, egotistical charm (didn't all white suburban men, at least the kind who drove sports cars and who took up running to combat their middle-aged paunches, the hard-charging coastal types, look a bit like Balzac in the seventies?). I can certainly recognize the casual brutality, and the grotesque masculine vanity, the site-specific manners of a late twentieth-century Hollywood divorce.

◎

I saw these things in myself too, as I sprawled on the ratty gray couch I'd rescued from my house on Vista Grande Street in West Hollywood, the house I'd shared with my ex, and which now skewed crooked on the floor of my otherwise nearly vacant apartment. There was the bed that folded out of the wall; there was a small desk and a rickety shelf that held books and CDs. The rest was empty space, puddled with sunlight and a scattering of my daughter's toys; a copy of *The Very Hungry Caterpillar* and a pair of tiny luchador masks I would slip over her small finger and my own before allowing her to beat me, to her boundless delight, at thumb wrestling. I stared into that blank space and contemplated it, the mystery of Eleanor Perry, just as I contemplated that of my own divorce, my own vanity, and my sense of daily loss. Like Eleanor (Mach 1), I'd married a straight arrow, a woman from the Northeast. Like Eleanor (Mach 2), I'd been replaced, left for a man who wasn't much younger but who was emphatically more dependable. As I say, I wasn't able to blame my ex—I'll call her N—for this. When I thought over the catalog of injuries I'd inflicted with my inattentiveness, my self-occupation, my typically, boringly masculine absorption with work and tendency to moan about it, I wanted to leave me too. I'd been just as bad as Vincent Wade, in my way, just as convinced of my own unassailable importance. And if there was nothing to be done about that, about the demise of my marriage, at least, I could still think and learn of other people's. I could still train my sight upon an artist who might have been overlooked the first time, upon the life and work of Eleanor Perry.

◎

They came out of the theater, she and Frank both. Eleanor had cowritten a series of suspense novels, five of them in all, with her first husband under the shared pseudonym Oliver Weld Bayer, as well as a stage play called *Third Best Sport*. The latter had made it all the way from Shaker Heights to Broadway, produced by the Theatre Guild in 1958. Frank had been a theater rat from the beginning: at fifteen, he'd worked as a parking lot attendant at the Westport Country Playhouse, then hustled his way up to become an associate producer and a stage manager at the Theatre Guild himself, making a hundred and fifty bucks a week. That's where he met the then-married Eleanor. I can picture it: she, born in the shadow of the First World War, married to her intellectually active but rather staid husband—an attorney and would-be writer—bored out of her mind when she looked across the theater one day and saw Frank. Who must've seemed as his character does in *Blue Pages*: volcanic, impetuous, intense. With his ink-dark hair, downward-drooping mustache, and heavy-lidded, deep-set eyes, he would have seemed to her alluring in a way her husband was not. And he would have found her irresistible in her elegance, intelligence, and accomplishment: she was sixteen years older than he was, and one of her novels had been made into a movie, 1945's *Dangerous Partners*. Even from the beginning he could sense her quickness of mind, the ease with which she could snap together a convoluted noir plot like a puzzle. They were working long hours, endless hours of rehearsal, watching the play's star, Celeste Holm, master her part as a corporate bride who wreaks havoc at a dull convention. Eleanor must have wanted to wreak a little havoc of her own, but when Frank came on to her, she waved him off.

"I'm too old. You're too young, rather. It'll never work."

"I'm twenty-eight."

"Yeah, and I'm forty-five," she said. "I'll be fifty before you know it."

"You'll be dynamite at fifty." He had a fat kid's bluster. "Hell, you'll be approaching the beginning of your prime."

Eleanor smiled. She knew a line when she heard one, but she didn't mind. She liked his energy, and she was sick of being a Cleveland housewife. She and her husband had two children, but both were college-age now. Did she need to continue this masquerade? Proximity with Frank led to the moment of crisis, some evening when they were alone in the theater after-hours or staggering up Forty-Ninth Street in the cold. *Third Best Sport* opened in New York in December, on New Year's Eve's eve. Maybe he took her arm one night as they were leaving, or maybe—Frank certainly loved to eat, as he loved to smoke and drink—it was one evening over pasta, wine, cigarettes, espresso, when he leaned across the table and planted one on her. You know how these things go . . .

◎

I knew how these things went too. In due course, I'd discover exactly how they did, how that dream of infidelity became the real thing. But for Frank and Eleanor, it was soon much more than that: collaboration, not just romance. *David and Lisa* was the first: Eleanor had read a case study by Theodore Isaac Rubin about two emotionally disturbed teenagers, a boy who couldn't stand to be touched and a girl whose rhyming word salads were indicative of a split personality. It was a natural adaptation for her; before she'd written stage plays, Eleanor had earned a master's degree in social work, and she'd written short skits that had been published and produced by various psychiatric associations and mental health organizations for children. But what did they know about making movies? Not even enough to know there were things you needed to know. Frank was so green that—the story goes—he turned to his producer on the verge of shooting, nodded at his camera, and asked, "How do you make this contraption work?" They raised the budget, all $183,000 of it, by hitting up family and friends. It was the first era of American cinema when such was possible. In 1959, John Cassavetes had financed *Shadows* out of his own pocket and cast it with novices and theater people. The film claimed to be an improvisation, and it won the Pasinetti Award at the Venice Film Festival. It must have electrified Frank—most likely more than it did Eleanor, who would have found it energetic but underbaked—with its wobbly handheld camerawork and its Charles Mingus score. He wasn't the first director to wade in over his head, and he certainly wouldn't be the last.

David and Lisa was, to the surprise of nearly everybody, a hit. Like Cassavetes's film, it premiered at Venice, and it won an award for Best First Work. Frank would eventually find himself nominated for an Oscar for Best Director, as the film grossed over $1 million in its first weekend alone, and the Perrys were instantaneously in demand. Considering Frank's inexperience, it's a stately and collected directorial performance. Compared with Cassavetes's riotous street poetry, the film is patient, quiet, and centered very deliberately on its actors, and on the equilibrium between them. The Perrys would make better, bolder movies than this, and Eleanor, too, would grow more attuned to the possibilities of cinema, but *David and Lisa*'s screenplay is equally assured. Through her career, Eleanor's scripts would tend to run long (the shooting script for *David and Lisa* was almost 170 pages; industry standard is closer to 120), but the films themselves somehow remained models of economy. She saw her role as akin to that of an interpreter, whose primary duty was to remain scrupulously true to her source material, and seemed to lack the galvanizing egotism of her masculine peers. In interviews and in letters, in the notes appended to *Trilogy*, the published version of the three scripts she adapted with Truman Capote, one sees this. "When we say an adaptation is good we can mean that it is faithful to the book and has all the virtues of the book," she writes in the preface to *Trilogy*. While she goes on there to note the counterpoint—that any film needs to be judged, first and foremost, independently—I cannot help but wonder (this, too, reminds me of my mother) whether her modesty didn't work against her. If along with her talent came a corresponding impulse toward self-erasure.

◎

Success went straight to Frank's head. At least, if the portrait of Vincent in *Blue Pages* reflects him, it did. Even after the commercial failure of their next film, 1963's *Ladybug, Ladybug*, a stark, paranoid drama set against the backdrop of the Cuban missile crisis, Frank remained intransigent, stubborn about what he wanted to do next and with whom.

"I don't like it," he said, after Eleanor had handed him a short story she'd just read in the *New Yorker* one afternoon in the summer of 1964.

"Why not?" They were in their apartment, Eleanor on the couch, he, pacing and pontificating.

"I don't think it's a movie. You think it's a movie?"

"I do."

"Nothing happens!"

Eleanor smiled. "Everything happens."

The story was "The Swimmer," and for a while Eleanor might have been the only one who saw its cinematic potential. Rumor had it Cheever himself wasn't eager to let the film rights go. He didn't want Hollywood to fuck it up, his elegant, strange, phantasmagorical story about a man's decision to swim home across the Connecticut county where he lives, flailing drunkenly from swimming pool to swimming pool. Of all the films the Perrys would make, *The Swimmer* is by far the most improbable, the least literal; on the page the story's protagonist is plainly delusional, and the slow turning of its landscape from summer to decay signals Neddy Merrill's psychological collapse. How was that supposed to show onscreen? But Eleanor wrote Cheever a letter, and together she and Frank went to see him in Ossining.

"We see it as a tone poem." They worked him over as delicately as they would Truman Capote a few years later, with Frank maybe even using the very line Eleanor gave Vincent Wade in *Blue Pages*. "Extrapolate it, but not *violate* it." We'll need to expand on some things, they assured him, but there wouldn't be any radical changes to the story.

Charmed, the writer let them have it. Eleanor wrote the script on spec, for no money. With luck, they'd be able to get a studio interested.

By now this was no longer a given. Frank may have been nominated a few years back, but since then they'd been scuffling. After *Ladybug, Ladybug* failed, Eleanor had adapted one of her old plays, *Toys and Fictions*, for the actress Jennifer Jones, but that fell apart when Frank turned argumentative with Jones's husband, the mogul David O. Selznick. For a while they'd gone to Italy in an attempt to hustle up a project with Marcello Mastroianni; then Eleanor wrote another script called *February*, but this, likewise, fell apart. There were other things—a proposed adaptation of Dostoevsky's *The Gambler*; a version of Steinbeck's *The Winter of Our Discontent*; the producer Elliott Kastner approached her about writing a treatment based on Raymond Chandler's *The Long Goodbye*, the idea that would blossom, almost ten years later, into one of the greatest films of the seventies[2]—but there was no money. They were living in an apartment at 40 Central Park South, around the corner from the Plaza Hotel, a few blocks east from Eleanor's old place where they started. Until they got a movie off the ground, they were pretty much in Dutch. Occasional script fees from the studios were all that kept them alive. Eleanor's script for *The Swimmer* finally went to the producer Sam Spiegel (*On the Waterfront*, *Lawrence of Arabia*), and if he didn't quite get it either—what was with all these damn

2. Kastner's original intention was for the Perrys to write and direct, and Cary Grant to star. It's hard to argue this could possibly have been better than the Leigh Brackett–scripted, Robert Altman–directed version that starred Elliott Gould, but it sure would have been interesting.

swimming pools?—he thought that maybe, just maybe, he could get the movie made . . . with the right star.

The right star. In this case, he thought of Burt Lancaster, who had the perfect background: he was bookish, literate. As a working-class grandson of Irish immigrants to New York City, he probably appreciated the nuanced touches of class consciousness Eleanor had brought to the script. Amusingly, Lancaster did not know how to swim. But he was willing to learn in the service of the part. And while production was to be delayed after Frank found himself needing to recover from a heart attack he'd had in London—he may have been on the near side of forty still, but he smoked like a maniac and drove himself as ferociously as such egotists tend to—principal photography began on *The Swimmer* in the summer of 1966.

The Swimmer is a strange film. It was the first time the Perrys had worked with an all-out Hollywood star, an experiment neither one of them would repeat for a while, and their first film to be shot in color. It boasts an obtrusive Marvin Hamlisch score and a sometimes-garish sense of montage—an odd sequence in which Lancaster's Neddy Merrill gambols across a field with a younger girl in tow—but the movie gets better as it goes, as it twists from a quirky Connecticut pastoral to the deeper, more dramatic confrontation between Ned and an angry neighbor; Ned and an isolated boy in an empty pool; Ned and his pissed-off creditors. Finally, between Ned and his former mistress, played, excellently, by the actress Janice Rule, who'd replaced the originally cast Barbara Loden.

These scenes and others, such as a collision with a pair of nudist neighbors under gathering thunderheads, bear all the

Perrys' hallmarks: a dry wit and a fine emotional clarity, a subdued intelligence that lets the actors' performances carry the day. Cheever's story is just ten pages long and compressed: Eleanor re-sequences the encounters and expands their delirious elision into full-blown scenes, adding ones that aren't in the story at all to allow additional themes, like the very racism and classism of that WASPy Connecticut in which it is set, to shine through. The performances, from Lancaster's on down, are exemplary. Aside from whatever glop that feels ladled on from a studio perspective—that loud, orchestral score is really distracting—it's a fascinating film, one that feels pregnant at every turn with the psychedelia that was to erupt onto the screen, and into American popular consciousness, over the next year and a half. But the experience wasn't seamless, and the result isn't entirely the Perrys' either. Possibly over the question of Janice Rule—the director had really wanted Loden—Frank clashed with Lancaster, clashed above all with Sam Spiegel, clashed with nearly everyone until he was fired, and replaced by a series of directors who came in to do patchwork. In the end, it was Sydney Pollack who delivered the finished film, reshooting the Loden scenes as well as a pivotal one with Janet Landgard. Sam Spiegel, who'd pushed for the advent of a happier ending besides, took his name off the movie. Even if *The Swimmer* ultimately holds up, and it does, as one of the better cinematic portraits of American WASP rot ever committed, the experience was something of a mess. It was not a happy one from either Perry's perspective.

◎

They were right back where they started: word of mouth on *The Swimmer* (which wouldn't be released until 1968) was so bad Frank couldn't buy a job, but Eleanor stuck by him. When Elia Kazan asked her to adapt his novel *The Arrangement*, which Kazan would direct, she turned him down. She and Frank were a team. And so, they found themselves in Rome, trying to corral Mastroianni again for another movie when *Life* magazine sent Eleanor a book to review, the book that would change everything. If *The Swimmer* was the fevered delirium of suburbia in decline—a noted inspiration, much later, for the television series *Mad Men*—then Sue Kaufman's *Diary of a Mad Housewife* was the chronicle of that decline from the inside out: *Mad Men*, if January Jones's Betty Draper were the protagonist of that show, with her husband Don nothing but a condescending, insufferable satellite.

Eleanor had long been a sharp critic. Writing about Christina Stead's blistering, underappreciated novel *The Man Who Loved Children* in 1965, she called the book "a snare, a magnet, a Pandora's Box that you can circle around but not ignore." (Anyone who's ever read it knows how well that description nails the book's queasy, terrifying allure.) In her *Life* review of Kaufman's similarly themed *Diary*, sardonically headlined "Angry Mom Revolts, Writes Book About Dad," Eleanor noted that the book would likely be viewed as "'a woman's novel' whatever that may be," but that it was really "a woefully hilarious book about men." She loved it. And knew, right away, that it would make a brilliant film.

She wasn't alone. The book was a hot property—there were other bidders—but the Perrys optioned the book out of their own threadbare pocket, while Eleanor took on a side gig writing a pair of teleplays, based on Truman Capote stories, just to keep them afloat. At which point things get a little fast and furious. As Eleanor sat down to rattle off *Diary*, a producer named Sidney Beckerman sent them a novel called *Last Summer*, by Evan Hunter. Not for the last time their jury was split. Frank hated it. (According to Eleanor's divorce deposition, he literally threw the book across the room.) But Eleanor jumped at the chance to write that too. The legendary producer Robert Evans, at that time head of Paramount Pictures, offered Eleanor a hundred and fifty grand for her *Diary of a Mad Housewife* script, which he wanted for himself, but she refused. Frank would direct it, or no dice. They were running out of money, so Eleanor took a quick gig writing a film called *The Lady in the Car with Glasses and a Gun*, a psychological thriller set in France. Frank begged her to quit futzing around with *Last Summer* and to let go of *Diary*. A hundred and fifty large was money they could use!

"Baby, come on!" You can imagine the argument, can't you? You've had a version of it yourself. One of them prowling and pacing while the other—Eleanor—stood, unmoved. "Can't you let it go?"

"What are we supposed to do, Frank? Just throw it away?" Eleanor lit a cigarette. They were there in that borrowed apartment they'd taken in Paris so she could write *The Lady in the Car*. "You think we should let Evans just swoop in and steal it?"

Frank wheedled and pled, but Eleanor stuck to her guns, until Allied Artists agreed to put up the money for her to write *Last Summer*, and for Frank to direct it if they liked the script.

It took her four weeks. She sat in that apartment and banged it right out, the easiest any script had ever come for her. And so, thanks to Eleanor, the Perrys' two best movies—the best either of them would ever manage, together or apart—came together.

◎

I knew something about this. N had picked me up too. While I was regularly employed scratching out rewrites on the low end of the WGA pay scale for the classics arm of a studio, even as I slogged through draft upon draft of a complicated, ultimately unpublishable, novel, she carried more of the burden than I did. I wasn't paying a full half of the mortgage on WGA minimums. But: she believed in me. I believed in her also. I'd been the one carrying more than half of the rent while she was in grad school. Wasn't it supposed to be that way? There are no villains, in this portion of our story. I wrote until my fingers bled; spent hours on the phone with my coproducers, and with the head of our studio, for a film I'd written, an adaptation of a prestigious Australian novel, to which various actors attached themselves at different times: Guy Pearce, Kate Hudson, Adrien Brody, Peter O'Toole. A windfall would come, the moment everyone said yes at the same time. I woke up with the baby, diapered her, bottled her. N was off before dawn, keeping time with the New York markets. We had, for a while, a partnership. Like a pulley system, in which the gravity of one could abet the rise of the other.

"Remember, we have that thing tonight."

"Which thing?"

I flashed back to this, while I was reading *Blue Pages*: an exchange that had occurred one morning a few years earlier, while V was still an infant.

"Dinner."

"Oh right." I lay on my side, watching N get dressed: her silhouette, darting around our bedroom like a fish. It was dark out still: all I could see was her outline, poised for a second before the dull pool of a standing mirror in the corner. "With—"

I could never remember her colleagues' names: certainly not at 5:00 AM, but often not at midday either.

"Yeah." I could hear her smile somehow, as she turned and came toward me. "Them." She brushed her lips against my temple, then grabbed her purse off the door handle. "Five thirty, at Roku."

"Oof," I mumbled. "Senior citizens' hour."

But I didn't mind. I lay there in the dark, listening to her footsteps in the living room, the car starting outside, then pulling away. A partnership, right? The latest draft of my script, one of God knows how many, lay open on her nightstand. This was how it worked. (But why couldn't I remember her business partner's name? Was it because I hadn't been listening?)

No villains. Not yet.

◎

Last Summer is a pitiless movie. Shot on Fire Island in the summer of 1968, the film is about three teenagers: two men, and one young woman, played by Barbara Hershey. The air is fraught with late-adolescent sexual tension: the two boys meet the girl on the beach, in the act of rescuing an injured seagull. There's no tenderness in this: brutality, and erotic competition, bubble along the surface from the movie's first frame. Parents are basically absent. The children wear white, and their creepy, Aryan natures are highlighted throughout. This is not a summer romance; it's *Lord of the Flies*, in which the prime instigator happens to be a woman. Another girl—awkward, homely Rhoda, played by Catherine Burns—stumbles into the triad. The games become crueler. Eventually . . . well, you can imagine. Hershey's Sandy goads the boys into something terrible. Or maybe they goad themselves. The movie ends upon an act of violence, of sexual terror. Sun flickers across the salt marsh, the dunes. Nothing is resolved, nothing is explained.

Last Summer remains, I believe, the Perrys' best film. Eleanor would maintain it was the finest script she ever wrote. It shares with *Midnight Cowboy* (likewise released in 1969, and likewise released with an X rating) a sexual frankness, and a blunt, bleak view of the too-often transactional nature of human behavior. The movie is excruciating to watch, and also hard to see—not only has it never been licensed for an official DVD release, the one known 16 mm print in circulation is housed in the National Film and Sound Archive of Australia—but it's insanely rewarding even in the grainy extralegal streams that offer the easiest path to viewing it these days. It was a modest commercial success, and a lavish critical one. But it was nothing, in the latter respect, compared to *Diary of a Mad Housewife*.

When did it begin? Not the production of *Diary*, on which principal photography commenced in January 1969, in an apartment at 135 Central Park West, but the disintegration that would unknit their marriage and their creative partnership alike. The Perrys were offered real money at last: 400K, in sum, for writing and directing, a quarter of which was paid to Eleanor up front. This probably didn't help. Eleanor had been floating them for a while now—even as Frank was filming *Last Summer*, she took still another assignment, an adaptation of Max Frisch's *Homo Faber* proposed by the actor Anthony Quinn—but now she was in the chips. After *Diary* was shot, but before its release, Frank slipped off to Spain to shoot a western called *Doc*, written by Pete Hamill. According to Eleanor's later deposition, the experience was a mess: Hamill had never written for the movies before, and Frank was ready at one point to pull the plug on the production before Eleanor stepped in to rewrite the script under a pseudonym, for no credit—never mind that she had no great interest in westerns—only to have it taken back by Hamill and rewritten again. Somewhere in here, perhaps, in the antechamber preceding their greatest success, those months when *Diary* was still in the can, while Eleanor was rich and Frank was flailing, it happened: the rupture from which there was no going back.

First, however, *Diary*. It is the film for which the Perrys are best remembered, and it was a massive hit. It lingered in theaters for an entire year, with lines stretched around New York City blocks. The film spoke to its moment, and if it is, inevitably, a little dated, its clearheaded feminism holds up. The silent scream of a Manhattanite named Tina Balser (played, with an astonishingly dry wit, by Carrie Snodgress) caught between the numbing pomposity of her socially ambitious husband, Jonathan, and the even more numbing self-absorption of her lover, a famous writer named George Prager, the movie nails the East Coast establishment affluenza of 1969. The film is about the insufferable egotism of men, and how Tina's implicitly vivid internal life is actively withheld from them in an act of passive resistance. This resistance was debated (some thought it was *too* passive), but when one watches it now—after years in which the best one could find was a crummy transfer on YouTube, it is finally on DVD—the effect is clear, and Snodgress is utterly magnetic. *Diary* is a gas from end to end, even as it concludes ultimately on a note of irresolution, one of those exhilaratingly ambiguous bummers (like the concluding moments of *Midnight Cowboy*, or like those of *Shampoo*, and of *The Graduate*) that manage to delight us, still, all these decades later.

They delight us. Did they delight Eleanor? Did she channel any of her growing exasperation with Frank into her portrait of egomaniacal George Prager, that swaggering jerk (played by Frank Langella) who puts Tina's hand on his crotch at a party and tells her *this* is what she really needs? Sue Kaufman's novel is in first person, and it's witty and alert, a book well deserving of rediscovery. But Eleanor's script uses no voiceover, no monologue. There's just the patient, wry drip of Snodgress's performance (she was nominated for an Oscar), bringing her deadpan, withering attentiveness to life.

◎

Picture this: a car parked on Ocean Avenue in Santa Monica at twilight. It's late 2005, maybe early 2006. The air is cold. A couple, a man and a woman, leaving a dinner, a very boring dinner, with one of the woman's work colleagues. The man yawns. He can barely keep his eyes open, though it is not yet seven at night. There is a baby at home, a sitter. Tomorrow morning the woman will need to be up before the sun, and the man will wake when the baby does. He is exhausted, uncomfortable, a little ashamed even of the car they are driving, a battered Toyota Scion. Most of her colleagues, including the man they have just had dinner with, drive Beamers and Mercedes, cars that, like everything about them, fairly drip with wealth, privilege, and an air of adult responsibility. The man is aware this isn't important, that the car you drive is an irrelevancy, at best, but he feels, in moments like this, like a person who has arrived at a black-tie function in bathing trunks. He stares at the Ferris wheel, glittering above the Santa Monica Pier; the moonlit Pacific, undulating down below the bluffs.

"That"—he belches, tasting the aftermath of soy sauce and wasabi—"that was one of the most boring meals I've ever endured. You owe me one."

"I know, right?" The woman laughs. "Thank you for taking one for the team."

"No problem." (And it isn't a problem, because the man admires the woman. He admires, among so many other things, her drive, her intelligence, her energy, her wit, her willingness to just go pedal-to-the-metal to succeed.) "Just—do all of your colleagues have to be such normies? That guy . . . d'you think he's ever smoked weed? Has he ever seen a band that wasn't playing at the Coliseum? Was he born in a Lacoste diaper?"

She laughs. At least, as I remember it, she does. *I know, right?* The other man and his wife, the opposing couple (we'll call that man, for the purposes of this narrative, R), are on their way home to *their* baby, their sitter. For all I know they are vivisecting us, the wife turning to R and saying, "She's nice, but her husband is a little . . . off, isn't he? Smart, maybe. But he's too full of himself. I'd hate to be married to that."

I will come to think of this moment a lot. The silence that followed my own dismissal of R, N's good-humored (I'd thought) agreement. Our bodies settling on the cheap upholstery of our car, our bodies stuffed with sushi we could hardly afford either, since our mortgage was expensive, and N wasn't earning anything like Investment Bank Money. She was a trainee, a new hire, a year at least away from making the sort of coin people in her business could, and did, take home. The ethics of working in finance weren't even a full-fledged question to me yet—we were a few years away from the mortgage crisis—and N's job (which had nothing to do with subprime derivatives anyway; she worked in what was euphemistically called "private client services") seemed a little nebulous, the kind of drone capitalism you could practice by contorting, but not necessarily dissolving, your own principles. But by the time I turned the key in the ignition, poor R, that lantern-jawed cipher, whoever he was exactly, had completely evaporated from my mind.

◎

Polish star.

Who was the fool in my relationship? Who was the schmuck, the moron, the patsy? Was it me, or was it N? (*She slept with the writer!*) In my experience, it's hard to tell which role is whose. I felt like a fraud—even bumbling through those dinners, those work events where I was at best exotic and at worst irrelevant, to these people whose job was to juggle the well-stropped knives of the world economy, I recognized myself as a cliché: not just the writer, engaged with the questionable relevancies of art, but the *struggling* writer, unproduced and unpublished, bitter, boring, and dull. I was, just on the underside of forty, a failure. My parents, my wife: all of them could see it, that moment when an earlier, confident promise had curdled into something darker; the recognition that I wasn't going to be what I'd always hoped to become. Most men fortunate enough to confront this question in the first place were Jonathan Balser: confident, too confident, in their success and ambition. Others were George Prager: riding the wave of their bachelor sexuality, too busy banging starlets Polish or otherwise to notice the clock on the wall. Me? I felt like I was going to throw up just because the bill had arrived at a Santa Monica sushi restaurant. I was the nexus where nothing turned itself inside out, where a masculine privilege—even just the privilege of thinking one's modest talent could mean anything—collapsed in upon itself. And my real crime was being too oblivious, too blind and too stupid, to wonder what N thought of any of it. To ask her, as I surely should have, *Don't you just get sick of me? What do you need? Is there anything I can do to make your life better?*

◎

Frank gave Eleanor a Cartier goblet inscribed, "Your vision, your talent, your guts, my love always." The object was to commemorate the success of *Diary of a Mad Housewife*, which, thus, he acknowledged as belonging to Eleanor. She made it happen, the success that, at long last, had settled upon both of them. Their next movie was going to be an adaptation of a Joyce Carol Oates novel called, fittingly enough, *Expensive People*. His own directing fee alone was now almost as much as they'd gotten paid altogether, both of them, for *Diary*. A costly trinket like that goblet he could afford. On talk shows he was a little less generous. The groovy Tinseltown director of a hot film that put down social-climbing squares like the Balsers. He felt like it was his beat to go out there and admit he didn't really believe in marriage or monogamy, sentiments that may have been in the air at the time, but which were still news to the mortified Eleanor when she tuned in to watch him, the Hollywood superstar suddenly appearing, alone on TV. Still, he was playing to the crowd, right? He may have mouthed a few similarly hip sentiments around her at parties ("I don't believe in affairs while shooting, but afterwards, anything goes"), but it wasn't *real*. He wasn't cheating on her (was he?); this was just the sort of thing you said when you were passing a joint around the dinner table up in the Canyon. You had to, you know, be a man, a Hollywood man, not some uptight little New York ninny who got the vapors whenever Jack and Warren showed up and started talking about pussy.

Success makes nobody kinder. There was never any recognition, any award, any paycheck, any honorific or yacht or private plane or compensation that made a person more deserving or *better* than he or she was before receiving it. Because empathy is a product of lack, of yearning and suffering and absence, and of the recognition that you don't, in fact, "deserve" any better than anyone else does, no matter what you've done or won or been awarded. If Frank became a jerk inside the marriage, well, you go cash a check for seven figures and see if it makes you feel like a kinder, nobler human being. You may feel like you deserve it, but that's just the money talking. Trust me, it is.

Still, Frank and Eleanor were together. In interviews and magazine profiles, they were droll and affectionate, just like all the other Hollywood power couples—Taylor and Burton, Mel Brooks and Anne Bancroft, Joan Didion and John Gregory

Dunne; they talked with only a bare hint of stringency. "I honestly don't feel that the marriage in [*Diary*] is at all like ours," Eleanor told Guy Flatley in 1970, while acknowledging that hers and Frank's was a little offbeat. "They say you're supposed to work out all your neuroses in your first marriage, so that you'll be marvelous in your second marriage," she said. "*Second* marriage? I should live so long!" Frank quipped.

Hunky-dory, then, right? *Your vision, your talent, your guts, my love always.* In *New York* magazine, the Perrys interviewed one another, and Eleanor pledged her devotion to film as "a director's medium," and when Frank asked if there was conflict for her in being a writer and a spouse, she said, "Oh, for God's sake, if you want a button sewn on, I'll sew on a button. If you want a script written, I'll write a script." The tension was there, but in Eleanor's mock exasperation, and presumably mock submissiveness as well ("If you'll let me stop living it and start writing it," she snapped, when asked if the shooting draft of their next film would be ready in time for its pending start date), there is still evidence of affection. And now they'd made it. They were ready to cash in, creatively and otherwise. *Expensive People* was good to go. The contracts were drawn up—they were ready to start shooting in September 1971—and Frank had already set his sights on a project that would follow that: the adaptation of *Play It as It Lays* that Eleanor, indeed, was not crazy about ("While I respected it very much . . . it was essentially about the emptiness of life in the film colony and about the meaninglessness of existence," she said in her deposition), but which was a hot property. Sam Peckinpah wanted it; Mike Nichols did. And Didion, who was no fan of *Diary* herself (per Eleanor, she "hated" it), didn't want to sell it to Frank. Who flew to LA alone to woo her, just as he and Eleanor had gone out to Ossining to see Cheever.

December 1970. The city was quiet; Frank had gone away. Eleanor was out walking her dogs when she ran into Didion's in-law, Dominick Dunne, on the street.

"How's Frank?" Dunne asked her. "I'm gonna see him in LA next week. We're scouting locations."

"For what?" *Expensive People* was set in an imaginary Michigan suburb. There were no LA locations involved.

"For *Play It as It Lays,*" Dominick said, baffled. "What else?"

Was this when it dawned on her? In the atomic silence that might have followed that disclosure, Eleanor gazing off at the chaos of yellow cabs, carolers, strangers in scarves trailing along the margin of the park. Maybe it was a mistake. She ran home and called Frank in LA and he denied it. "No, no, baby, Nails"—this was his nickname for her—"of course not. *Expensive People* comes first. You haven't even written *Play It as It Lays* yet."

Ah, but. Those contracts, for *Expensive People*, weren't signed—they'd been sitting in the Perrys' agent's office for weeks—and Eleanor did not know that Frank had approached Universal about backing out of the picture, citing "strains" in his creative relationship with Eleanor. His *creative* relationship. He wasn't copping to anything else.

◎

A hot autumn day in Los Angeles. Indian summer, the grass dry beneath my feet as I traipse back in from my studio, the un-air-conditioned shack where I do my writing. I've had a breakthrough. I can hear the soft rasp of the lawn under my Converse—like fingertips raked across stubble—as I head inside, wanting a cocktail, wanting to talk to my wife, wanting to pick up our daughter and talk with her about her day, to kiss her Popsicle-stained face. It's late 2006. We bought this house, a three-room hutch in West Hollywood, near the height of the real estate bubble: its value has basically plateaued. I open the french doors, stride into the living space, which is like a tiny barn. N is over by the front door, glancing through the mail.

"You'll never believe it," I say. I am eager to share whatever it is that's happened to me in my studio (that part is lost to me now), whatever it is that makes me feel this is *it*, I've got it, eureka, my creative—and thus, hopefully, financial—bacon is saved. *We're* not in trouble; *I'm* in trouble. My basic sense of competence is threatened. N, sifting through whatever bills are stacked in her hand, reminds me of this just by being. She looks at me, blond hair flashing, her face, pale and pretty, revealing nothing at all.

"We need to talk," she says.

◎

It is almost impossible, isn't it, for these moments to be free of cliché. A better writer, a more eloquent human being, would've forced N to say something else, even if he had to misremember her actual words to do it. But no. Eleanor had the same problem. "Please don't leave me," Lucia begs, then immediately thinks, "*I'd cut my throat before I'd write a line like that!*"

Alas, these bad movies are all the same. They involve the same cruddy dialogue, the same need and callousness and pleading. The same guilt. Also, generally, the same dreary betrayals. In Eleanor's case, there was a magazine journalist, a writer who'd grown tired of churning out profiles, who'd been hanging around, one of Frank's new protegees: maybe he'd mentor her into the movies. Barbara Goldsmith was her name. She and her husband had sat next to Eleanor and Frank at a party.

It's always there in plain sight: the knife, the blunt instrument, the person (usually) with whom your spouse betrays you. I do not remember, either, exactly what I said when N went on to tell me she "[had] feelings" (what a euphemism!) for R. (*What kind of feelings? Sensitive, chaste, romantic ones?* I did not ask for any such clarifications.) I believe I laughed out loud, because I suddenly and intuitively understood it was my duty to play the jerk—it might make this easier for both of us— but really, also, because I *felt* like a jerk; because I had been played, because I was not kind, because I had been inattentive to someone who'd loved me—she did, she had, for a lot longer than I deserved—and I frosted that cake now by acting contemptuous, at least for a moment, of her choice.

"Really?" I remember I said this much "*Him?*"

Ah, R. Tempted though I was to beclown him, to turn all my own insecurities loose upon the blank screen of his personality, or what little of it I'd been privileged to see, he wasn't the heavy. I knew that even then. It was my own foolishness, my self-absorption, that had led me to this point. And nothing that I said or thought or did would mitigate how much it hurt.

Eleanor, too, hurt. She gave her deposition in May 1971, and she and Frank agreed to terms for their separation on July 12. There were issues around the economics of it. The collapse of *Expensive People* at Universal was going to be harder on her than it would be on Frank. He already had his next picture lined up—*Play It as It Lays* would go, instead, in September, same fee—and she? Eleanor was left to twist in the wind. Barbara Goldsmith was younger than she was, the same age as Frank, and would soon appear as the director's other half in magazine profiles, glowing by his side in their renovated kitchen, where it was said they served up snazzy morsels of California cuisine for their pals like Roy Lichtenstein, Tom Wolfe, and (who else?) the Didion-Dunnes. In time, Barbara's career would outshine Frank's: her nonfiction book on Gloria Vanderbilt would sell a kajillion copies just a few years later, and others—on Marie Curie, on the suffragette and spiritualist Victoria Woodhull, on the Johnson & Johnson pharmaceutical empire—were similarly lauded. So it wasn't like he'd just leapt at a bit of arm candy. But Eleanor, well, she was talented, sure . . . no one could deny she'd written a few good movies. But who was she, really? Wasn't the real star in the relationship Frank?

◎

Expensive People was never going to happen. Even though she'd keep slugging with it for the better part of a decade, Eleanor went off instead to write a feminist western, called *The Man Who Loved Cat Dancing*. The result was dispiriting: despite her being a producer on the picture, the movie was taken away from her, as the script was rewritten, and then, during a two-and-a-half-month writers' strike in 1973, Eleanor, being a WGA member, couldn't even cross a picket line to watch rushes with her coproducers on the lot. She wasn't even allowed to take her name off the film! In a 1974 recorded interview with the critic Arthur Knight, Eleanor disparaged the experience. ("Alas," she sighed, before the movie's title was even out of the interviewer's mouth, "I could not believe that *my* name was on that picture.") As Frank's Didion adaptation flopped—he moved on to do an odd little psychological study called *Man on a Swing*, and then a low-key western called *Rancho Deluxe*, with a script written by Thomas McGuane—Eleanor's career was in a muddle. The myth says that she was never the same, that she, of course, was no good without Frank. Which isn't true, even if the produced legacy isn't really enough to prove it. There was a television movie, *The Thanksgiving Treasure*, in 1973, for which she won her second Emmy, and then silence. She kept writing—an adaptation of Alix Kates Shulman's novel *Memoirs of an Ex-prom Queen*, which she could never get off the ground; a take on Graham Greene's *A Burnt-Out Case* for Otto Preminger—but there was little result. In 1979 she told an interviewer she had a half-dozen unproduced features and eleven teleplays just sitting there. The problem was always the same: men, or more specifically, the way men failed to understand stories about women. *Memoirs of an Ex-prom Queen?* Forget about it, she was told, as she went from meeting to meeting. Streisand's too old, Liza Minnelli's no prom queen, and who else can open a movie? No one. The reasoning was insipid, but worse, I suspect, was a narrative that began to adhere to Eleanor herself. She was, y'know . . . a *feminist*, this reasoning asserted. A troublemaker. A person bent on making "progressive pictures." In an anecdote that would come to define her career almost as much as anything she ever wrote, she attended the 1972 Cannes Film Festival and was arrested by the gendarmerie for defacing a billboard; she'd decided the three-titted she-wolf decorating the advert for Fellini's *Roma* was not to her liking, and climbed up a ladder with a bucket of red paint. ("I adore Fellini," she told the cops. "But this ugly distortion of the female anatomy is a humiliating offense to women everywhere.") It was the type of thing that, had a man done it, would've been written off as a conqueror's hijinks—like swimming naked in a hotel fountain, being loud and drunk in a theater lobby—but here? It had the force of a Gesture.

What were the words she had hanging above her desk at home? Voltaire: "To hold a pen is to be at war." All her life, well before Hollywood, she knew this. All those suspense novels, those plays she'd "collaborated" with her first husband to write? All those stories she'd written with Frank—*for* Frank: all those battles had been hers. And so, exasperated by her encounters with Hollywood, and with men she'd carried over the abyss of their own limitations before they received credit for what was in large part her work, she sat down to write her testimonial. A novel. Doesn't every serious writer need to produce one eventually? It was time, at last, for Eleanor to write hers.

In the triumphalist version of this story, that novel, *Blue Pages*, is an unacknowledged masterpiece, the equal of anything Joan Didion or Eve Babitz ever wrote. Sadly, this is not quite the case. *Blue Pages* is a very good book—crackling, amusing, suffused with Perry's unsparing intelligence, sharply evocative of mid-1970s Los Angeles and Manhattan—but it's no pinnacle. It should certainly be in print, but for all its accomplishments one can't quite celebrate it as the realization of a first-tier writer's vision. So (considering how many "very good" novels there are in the world already, considering how many greater literary injustices there are to be righted and how relatively few trees), why remember it? Shouldn't we train our attention somewhere else?

Perhaps. But Eleanor's story (which bears such a striking resemblance to that of "Lucia Wade," in *Blue Pages*) is worth knowing, as representative as it is of the experience shared by a whole generation of women. Like Rita Mae Brown's *Rubyfruit Jungle*, like Nora Ephron's *Heartburn*, like *Memoirs of an Ex-prom Queen*, and indeed like *Diary of a Mad Housewife* itself, *Blue Pages* interrogates the uncertainties and convulsions, the liberations of a world no longer defined by the expectations of men. Which isn't to say the book was met with open arms, as Eleanor surely knew it would not be. ("If Saul Bellow or Philip Roth complains about his relations with women, that's OK— they're writing a novel," she said. "If a woman does it, it's 'hell hath no fury.'") There were those who, predictably, wrote the whole thing off as score settling, or who dialed in a little too closely upon its gossip value. Certainly, her ex-husband wasn't impressed. "I haven't read it," Frank sniffed in the pages of *People* magazine, while snidely grumbling about alimony and allowing Barbara Goldsmith to dismiss Eleanor as "an injustice collector."

The thing is, there's nothing particularly furious about it. Disappointed, maybe. Calmly, dryly exasperated, and gimlet-eyed—often lethally so—about the people, almost all of them male, who surround Lucia Wade: the lippy producer who overrides every creative decision she makes on the feminist western she is writing; the fraudulent urban cowboy who hits on her even as he is rewriting her script into oblivion; the dumbass New York tycoon; the preposterous "Arnold Rivers," who sticks her with the check at the end of every date and then dumps her, asking if she'll remain "a friend of my heart." There are others, of course, characters based transparently on Frank (Vincent), on Truman Capote and/or John Cheever (an alcoholic Brahmin named Quentin Moore, who steals a screenwriting credit after Lucia adapts a pair of his stories), on Otto Preminger. But there's no hostility or righteousness, nor even much in the way of caricature or distortion. I grew up in this world, this world of hustling producers and loudmouthed assholes, people who'd say things like "EST convinced me I've been living a pea-soup existence," or who might have been described like this:

> *Philip was a perfect example of the affluent, middle-aged, permanently tanned boy-men in the "business," a type that usually gives me eye trouble. They glitter. Their silvery hair, shampooed with high-protein conditioner, glitters, the blinding caps on their teeth glitter, the gold bands on their Piaget watches glitter and their shoes, made by Lobbs in London, glitter.*

If this seems broad to you, a little crisp and on the nose, you never met my father in 1979, nor any of his well-coiffed, mirror-fixated peers. The image of Frank (OK, "Vincent"), with his weight yo-yoing, his ego ballooning after the success of their hit movie *Somersault* (modeled on *Diary* but named, rather, after the first, never-produced script the Perrys ever wrote together), drunkenly belittling Lucia before he kicks her to the curb . . . well, it might strike certain readers as burlesque, I guess, but I remember my own parents' divorce in 1981, and I remember my mother's telling of it too. That story, my mom's, was a little self-serving, and so might mine be, when you come down to it, but Eleanor's has a ring of accuracy, of fairness. That, of itself, is a rare enough quality to make it worth one's time.

◎

I went recently to the Margaret Herrick Library to view Eleanor Perry's papers. Given that there isn't very much about the novel online, or, other than a few 1979 reviews, much about its genesis and reputation, I wanted to find out what I could. The editorial notes on her first draft of *Rough Cut*, as the book was first called, were light: mostly cuts, to allow the present-tense story—of Lucia's life after Vincent—to run a little swifter and power the narrative ahead of the flashback sections that describe their marriage. The book was summarily re-titled (*Blue Pages* refers not to melancholia but to the color-coded revision schema for a script; "blue" pages were the writer's first, but almost never the final, revisions); it was teased, several times, on Page Six in the *New York Post*; Liz Smith, a friend of Eleanor's, ginned up a little featherweight "feud" between Eleanor and Capote, who was gracefully bitchy, but didn't actually seem to take the novel's portrait too hard. Engines were revved over its tell-all nature. *Blue Pages* was respectfully reviewed, as outside the gossip pages, it was treated like any other serious novel, and aside from a few caveats about its alleged acidity, was warmly received. It was a Book of the Month Club selection. It sold well.

Once upon a time you could publish a novel—you could direct even a modestly successful commercial film—and wind up profiled at length in the pages of *People* magazine. To some extent this remains the case, as Hollywood still rewards even its lesser lights disproportionately, but sifting through Eleanor's papers, a thick folder stuffed with mostly glowing reviews and clippings from magazines and regional newspapers around the country, I found myself marveling at what was once the formidable cultural reach of an artist few people, today, have heard of. I wondered, too, what she might have produced next. There is a running start—about seventy-five pages—toward another novel, provisionally called *An Old Wife's Tale*, but for whatever reason she never finished it. Maybe she ran out of time: the pages are undated. But as I riffled through her papers with gloved hands, sitting in a carrel in Beverly Hills, I couldn't help but think of my mother, whose own career was truncated along not-dissimilar lines, and I urged myself to slow down, to savor those pieces the most that offered a bit of her life's grain: a smudge of what looked like ash on the bottom of an envelope; a scrawled, half-legible annotation in the margin of a script. Confronted with even her minor fragments—correspondence, unproduced screenplays, treatments and ideas—I felt protective of Eleanor, as if I were treading somewhere I ought not to. This was a writer who'd been ill-used by others, in some sense, all her life; what right did I have to go tromping through her archive? Another man, putting her good material to rough ends.

◎

These were, I suppose, her emeritus years. Active in Hollywood, working—she got paid for all those teleplays, regardless—she lived in her apartment on Central Park South and schlepped out to the coast as necessary. She hosted a screening of *The Stepford Wives* for "opinion makers" (Gael Greene, Betty Friedan) on the Columbia lot in 1975; she wrote articles for *Vogue* and *Mademoiselle*; plotted a return to theater by writing a stage adaptation of Sheila Weller's novel *Hansel and Gretel in Beverly Hills*. She lived alone. A *Washington Post* profile from 1979 described her apartment as furnished in a "contemporary" style: glass coffee table, abstract art, books, books, books. She claimed to have a line she attributed to Gore Vidal—"When I hear the word love, I reach for my revolver"—tacked above her desk alongside the Voltaire. She lived a gregarious life: she summered on Martha's Vineyard, had dinners in the city at Elaine's; her phone rang constantly. When friends came to lunch, she served them smoked trout, *pâté maison*, chiffon cake with orange sauce. In the afternoon, she stood in the sunlight that flooded her windows and looked down on the Paris Theater eleven stories below, at the lines stretching around the block for the hits of 1979: *Kramer vs. Kramer*, *All That Jazz*. Movies she could have written, perhaps. Perhaps.

I do not think she was lonely. The articles about Frank—always the same: he was thinner, he had a young wife, he'd never been happier—surely amused her more than anything. Her dogs, Anatole and the beloved poodle, Lulu, basked at her feet, and the pair of Emmys she'd won for television writing glimmered on the mantel. She wrote letters, the way we used to, corresponding with a man from Shaker Heights named Robert Newman, her first love. (His cousin was an actor, a famous actor: in her 1974 interview with Arthur Knight she'd belittled a few of his movies, *Butch Cassidy and the Sundance Kid* and *The Sting*, for their coded homoeroticism. Why couldn't men just *make* movies about getting it on, for God's sake? Why did they have to pretend?) With Robert, she discussed literature: the novels of Machado de Assis. Was this what she'd wanted all along? She ate, lived, and breathed literature (it's in the scripts, where characters bicker about Proust); she idolized Colette; with her daughter she begged to differ on writers she had trouble with: Jane Austen, Flannery O'Connor. The latter was a surprise. Born Jewish—Rosenfeld was her family name, before she became Bayer—Eleanor in fact once contemplated a conversion to Catholicism. According to one who spoke later, at her memorial, the rationale was simply, "If it's good enough for Graham Greene, it's good enough for me."

She fell ill. (Had she achieved, finally, what she'd wanted? To be a novelist? Was she like my mother, merely condescending to write for the movies? I don't think so. Her love for the cinema, and her saturation in it, sparks even within *Blue Pages* itself. She loved Truffaut and Lina Wertmüller; wrote as effusively to Sidney Lumet—after *Network*, which she admired—as she did to Cynthia Ozick.) She fell ill, having quit smoking too late. She estimated that it had taken her fifty thousand cigarettes just to get through *Blue Pages*. She underwent treatment for cancer and then, as she was preparing for a trip to Italy, to Montecatini Terme to celebrate her daughter's fortieth birthday, she collapsed and had to come right back to New York City.

Fall 1980: barely a year after *Blue Pages'* publication. It is spooky, and a little impertinent, to describe the intimate circumstances of another person's death, a person not quite famous enough to rise to the standards of biography and who (let's face it) deserves a little privacy in this regard. Don't we all? She was in the hospital for a month, and when she came home, she was frail. She asked her daughter to guide her around the apartment, so she could look at her own life as if from the outside.

"Stop here. Look." She gestured at the shelves, the art. "Look."

Surveying the books, the mirrors, the flowers, the dogs—Anatole and Pansy, now, who'd replaced Lulu—she appeared, at long last, to be satisfied.

"It looks as if a fascinating woman lives here," she said.

Morphine, for the pain. She died at home on a Saturday morning in early spring—March 14, 1981—and she did it the way we all do: uncomfortably and, even for the witnesses who are present, if we're lucky, unknowably. In the *New York Times* her daughter described the artifacts she left behind: typewriter; hairbrush; small cloth angels, cherubim, hanging on the wall above her bed; the embroidered flower on the nightgown she was wearing when she died. There was also a notebook, filled with jottings about a New York City mystery novel she'd intended to write.

◎

Who was she?

I wondered this, as I sat on my couch and finished reading *Blue Pages* for the first time, in my apartment at 1448. I thought about Eleanor, and I thought about N, whose feelings for R were a mystery. How long before she told me anything did they start fucking? The forensics of their relationship remained unclear. I studied the jacket picture of Eleanor Perry—smiling faintly in her black dress, she looked a little like my maternal grandmother, herself only a decade older than Eleanor—and my thoughts drifted to my mother, and then back to N. "Feelings" for R. Our life together had been fatally euphemistic, toxically polite all the way to the end.

Sun splashed on my hardwood floor. The light was spiking at the end of the day. Did she get what she wanted (Eleanor; N, I supposed, was having it)? Was her failure in Hollywood—if "failure" is indeed what it was—merely a matter of leaving behind an incomplete legacy, one that had been truncated by divorce? Or was the real failure, the greater one, what happened when you got exactly what you'd wanted, Frank's failure: the kind that left people as ego-mad grotesques? I stood up to stretch my legs, walked over to my french windows to close them. It was getting cool, now, in the early evenings. Traffic swished along Sunset. I closed my eyes to listen, that surf-like sound I have always loved, that to this day can bring me back to childhood's most peaceful, languid hours. (What did Eleanor love? Couscous, hardware stores, green apples, Bobby Short singing "Losing My Mind" at the Carlyle, Elaine's at eight thirty, the first hour at a party. Cigarettes after swimming; that was better, even, than after sex.)

My telephone rang. It took me a moment to notice it, since it hadn't been ringing much these days. I fumbled for it over on my desk, that old Nokia flip I carried a little reluctantly. I do not exactly remember—it's funny that I don't—whether the afternoon I finished reading *Blue Pages* was the same in which my mother called to bring me her news, or if it was a few days later. I told you that we'd recently begun once more to speak. I remember the summer was fading, that the light outside had that bronze, autumnal cast, and the palms shot up out of the building's brick courtyard, reaching up into the dimming air.

"Hi, Mom." My forehead pressed against the window's glass; my thin reflection shadowing me inside it; my line of sight, blocked by the condominium complex rising on the opposite corner, strained toward the Laugh Factory, Greenblatt's, where my parents used to buy their prosciutto and champagne for parties, the Chateau: landmarks of my childhood. My breath, mortality's pale footprint, fogged up the glass. "What did the oncologist say?"

III

the intervals

carole eastman

I am much too bluely contused.

—CAROLE EASTMAN, "Poems"

MY MOTHER WAS calling from the Pacific Northwest: a
town called Edgewood, just east of Tacoma, to which she'd re-
moved herself nearly twenty years earlier. When her screenwriting career ended, she'd pulled up her stakes and bought
a house on a lake, where she now lived in a kind of splendid
isolation: the end of a cul-de-sac, with a view of water and
geese. *Edgewood.* I pictured her there, tall and drawn at the
living room window, staring out at the concussive circles drawn
by rain, always rain, on the lake's surface.

"What'd she say?"

"Not good." She exhaled sharply. It was a sound she used to
make while smoking, but—not now. "Stage four."

"Oh." I shut my eyes for a moment. As if this was going to
accomplish anything. "Oh shit."

"Do you and V want to come up for Christmas?"

"Yeah," I said. Christmas was a few months away yet, but
still. "Of course."

I kept my eyes shut, thinking back to an evening that had
occurred between us, decades earlier.

"You're drinking too much," I'd said then.

When I was sixteen, I'd once tried to force a conversation. I'd walked into our kitchen, where she was sitting alone, and put the facts on the table.

"Mom, I really think you should stop—"

"You little cocksucker." A bottle came whistling by my head, exploding against the wall behind me. "You shit. What do you know about what I should do?"

My mother had stopped drinking several years ago now, but that night, she was so plastered she could barely walk. She sat at the butcher-block counter in our old house in Santa Monica with her vodka and lit into me.

"You fucker. Everything's been given to you, you little shit. What right do you have to complain?"

That night, I stood there and took it. My mom's drinking was rarely violent. Most of the time it was subtle, an introspectiveness—she'd sit at this same table, reading or doing a crossword puzzle—that hardened into a silent trance. I'd only just realized a few weeks before that the glass of "ice water" she'd sit with was nothing of the kind.

"Shut the fuck up! Get out of here! Don't tell me what I need to do!"

Well? Vodka dripped from my hair, and my ear, where she'd almost clipped me. Her nightgown was peach-colored; the window above the sink was open, and I could hear the hydraulic hiss of a neighbor's sprinkler system. Smoke from my mother's cigarettes hung in the air, vague and suggestive. Evidence of a battle I might have thought was just beginning, but which, instead, was already lost.

"I'm sorry, Mom," I said now.

There was so much more to say, and I had no idea how to say it. Our relationship had mended, but never really healed. For a period of more than a decade, throughout my twenties and early thirties, my mother and I hadn't spoken at all. Now we stammered and hesitated, our voices crowding against each other to blot out an intolerable silence.

"You'll come up for Christmas?" she said.

"Yeah, of course," I said, too quickly. "It'll be wonderful to see you."

But I simply didn't know, really, if this last sentiment was true.

◎

Everything I learned about literature, and about film, growing up—and everything I learned, much later, about forgiveness—I learned from my mother. Even during that period in which we were not speaking, I would sometimes receive a package in the mail of books and occasional VHS tapes or, later, DVDs. Opening these packages, and lifting out whichever of her own fresh favorites my mom had sent me—Dawn Powell or Richard Powers, Stanley Donen's *Two for the Road* or Elaine May's *A New Leaf*—I would be reminded of the person I'd known in happier, more lucid times, the one who'd lead us both to Dutton's on book-buying sprees or take me, all the time, to the movies. On weekend mornings or after school we'd hit up the revival houses, the Fox Venice Theater on Lincoln Boulevard, the Monica Twin, the Nuart, the Vista, or she would cue up the Betamax to record things on the Z Channel, LA's

legendary proto-cable network, and together we would watch
her now-problematic faves: Woody Allen's early comedies, Polanski's *Chinatown* and *Knife in the Water*, Coppola's *The Conversation* and Pakula's *Klute*, Godard's *Weekend* and Antonioni's
Red Desert. (She was, of course, a permissive parent. How could
she have been otherwise?) It wasn't necessarily a deep education, more an induction into the sixties' and seventies' greatest
hits, but at fourteen, or sixteen—my mother was always a little
ahead of the curve that way—I found the experience incendi-
ary. Teeing up Sidney Lumet's *Network*, she'd pour me a glass
of wine and we'd get drunk together, and we'd rewind the scene
to shout it in unison: "I'M AS MAD AS HELL AND I'M
NOT GONNA TAKE THIS ANYMORE!" Or sometimes, in a
more melancholy mood, she'd break out a tape of another film
she loved, much quieter in its approach, its script less noisily
oracular and more introspective, called *Five Easy Pieces*.

◎

Five Easy Pieces. But what could I have made of that movie
when I was fifteen, no matter how subversively kicky it was
to watch with a loaded parent? I remember taking note of a
scene, because it was my mother's favorite, in which Jack Nicholson's Bobby Dupea attempts to order a side of wheat toast in
a roadside diner and is thwarted by an officious waitress who
tells him this basic dish is not on the menu. Eventually, he
breaks down and tells her he would like a chicken salad sandwich, "no mayonnaise, no butter, no lettuce," and that he would
like her to hold the chicken, as well. "You want me to hold

the chicken, huh," says the prickly server, and Nicholson thus delivers the riposte that makes the scene: "*I want you to hold it between your knees.*" My mother, in retelling this scene, would always embroider it a little ("I want you to spread the chicken salad between your thighs"), but the basic point was the same. My mother loved the anti-authoritarianism of it. As did I.

◎

Not long after I graduated from college, my mom made her break for the Pacific Northwest. I say "made her break for" because it seemed exactly the sort of landscape into which you could vanish: forbidding and cold, all narrow straits and towering conifers, hemlocks and Douglas firs. I'd visited her there just once, before she rebuffed yet another of my entreaties for her to get sober and we had our big falling-out, and we'd taken a drive through what she referred to as "Carver country," that part of Washington State where the great American short story writer had lived and only just recently died. (I kept hoping we'd catch sight of his widow, Tess Gallagher, on the street, or in one of the town's few restaurants or its bookstore. Port Angeles wasn't very big.) That was all I had come to know of it, and once my mother and I stopped speaking, I never visited again. It felt as if she had just disappeared, vanished inside that gorgeous but unnerving landscape, all frigid-looking water and doomy-feeling trees.

That landscape dominates *Five Easy Pieces*. The latter half of it was filmed on Vancouver Island, BC, and even its story evokes those same frigid lines. In it, Bobby Dupea (Nicholson at his most charismatic, caddish, volcanic: this was the picture that broke him out as a star) goes home, reluctantly, to visit his ailing father, and there finds himself confronted with the very frigidities he has spent his life trying to escape. Bobby—Robert Eroica Dupea, to give him his full name—is a flaming asshole, and also a musical prodigy. He has a sister named Partita, a brother (somewhat comically confined to a neck brace, which hinders his own violin playing for the time being) named Carl, and a father who, despite having been rendered speechless by a recent stroke, looks at his son with such loathing and contempt that it's obvious why Bobby had to get the hell out of there to begin with. The movie is about wasting your talent, about hating the expectations placed upon you so much you'd just as soon set yourself on fire as make the slightest move toward fulfilling them. A movie, in other words, about failure. No wonder my mother loved it. And, in a strange way, had almost seemed to be living it in reverse. Her side of my family had once had money. Her great-grandfather, a man named Amasa McGaffey, was a lumber magnate, one of the wealthiest men in New Mexico before a small plane he was piloting was struck by lightning. His survivors quickly pissed their inheritance away. My mother grew up in solid middle-class comfort—one could not call it wealth—in Santa Monica, but by the time she was an adult, her own mother was living in a mobile home, which she parked in places like Victorville and Barstow, places much like the dry, desert Bakersfield in which we first meet Bobby. According to my cousin, with whom she still spoke, my mother was now doing the thing Bobby Dupea spends the entire film refusing to do: playing piano, I was told, for as many as six or seven hours a day.

My mother was a failure, if that's how you care to view it. Even when she'd managed to commit a significant amount of her time to a practice over the years—modeling, acting, painting, fiction writing, screenwriting, ballet, and now, classical piano—she'd shown a tendency to walk away before any real reckoning of her talent could take place. That didn't make her untalented; it simply meant she was afraid to be judged. Many people feel this way, and there is a sense in which the only meaningful metric for "success" is not recognition, or publication, or congratulation; it is perseverance. Talent is merely an invitation to work. But Bobby Dupea takes a different route. He just tells his incontestable genius to go fuck itself. He doesn't even try, mostly because the exercise of his gifts would be so costly—would require subjugation to his family's will, and by extension to his own fathomless self-hatred—he cannot afford to. Damned if you do, damned if you don't. Or in the immortal words of Bartleby: "I would prefer not to."

◎

I hadn't thought much about *Five Easy Pieces* for years, before the afternoon my mother called to inform me her cancer had spread, but I found myself now drifting back to it. My feelings that afternoon were complicated: I set down the phone and wept, but I was stunned by the things I did *not* feel. I loved my mom, but I shook with a sense of absence, a sense that because she hadn't operated in my life as a "mother" for so long, I would have to grieve not just her loss but the very absence of that loss. Would I miss her? Yes, but I would also miss that feeling

I'd had for a long time of not missing her at all. Mourning an abusive parent is difficult, as we all know, and I wanted to go back to those things she had loved, in the hope they might bring me closer to her. I opened up my Netflix queue (this was the primitive Netflix era, in which they merely rented DVDs) and ordered *Five Easy Pieces*.

◎

The film might strike one today as a time capsule. It feels like one, with its opening shots of oil workers moving through the machine clamor of a refinery, then the sweet strains of Tammy Wynette's "Stand by Your Man" leading us into a restless desert world of beers and bowling alleys. But not five minutes after I popped the DVD inside its player, I was transfixed: more so than I had ever been before by this movie; more than I had been by *any* movie in a long time. As I stared at the screen, oblivious to the afternoon traffic swishing along Sunset Boulevard outside, I was changed by it. Unlike its innumerable thematic cousins—those studies of American alienation that crowded the theaters between 1967 and 1971, films like *Husbands*, *Last Summer*, and *Zabriskie Point*; like *The Graduate* and *The Panic in Needle Park* and *Vanishing Point*—*Pieces* has what might be termed a kind of feral delicacy, a razor-sharp absurdism that ventilates its bleakness with dry wit and vice versa. If those movies, different as they all are, turn on the collapse of various social compacts, or present a near-total absence of such compacts altogether, *Five Easy Pieces* paints a picture of masculine self-isolation, a portrait of a complete prick that somehow, also, makes us feel for him. It is also the only film of the bunch that happens to have been scripted by a woman. Adrien Joyce was the name that appeared in the film's credits, a pseudonym that one can find (sometimes with a faint variation: Adrian Joyce) appended to a handful of films made in the late sixties and early seventies, used always in lieu of the writer's real name, Carole Eastman.

◎

Carole Eastman. Mention her around Hollywood today and get a knowing nod. "*Five Easy Pieces*, right?" (Eastman's script was nominated for an Oscar.) "Good writer." Ask after her with people who know a little history and they'll come up with *Man Trouble* (a flop, 1992's attempt to reteam her with Nicholson and *Pieces* director Bob Rafelson), *The Shooting* (excellent: her first produced feature, a stark and peculiar western directed by Monte Hellman and starring Warren Oates, Millie Perkins, and a younger Nicholson), and maybe possibly—with a little bit of digging—1970's *Puzzle of a Downfall Child*, a film that feels ripe for rediscovery, given that it's good and stars a young Faye Dunaway as a fashion model playing out the story of her own life of excess and subsequent collapse. It's a scenario that would appeal to anyone who likes, say, *Play It as It Lays* (although *Puzzle*, directed by Jerry Schatzberg, is likely the superior movie). Push really hard and you might find someone who's willing to stand up for *The Fortune*, a 1975 film directed by Mike Nichols and starring both Nicholson and Warren Beatty, although I'd never even heard of it until recently. A few years ago, I was commissioned to write a television pilot and my producer suggested that one of my minor characters, a screenwriter, be drawn as "a Carole Eastman type." By which she meant, I think, brilliant, but self-negating. Dazzling, but difficult; indeed—this was somehow implied, by the mysterious contrails of Eastman's name—downright impossible.

◎

Who was Carole Eastman? The myth of the "difficult" female screenwriter has come up before, but leaving aside that antique fallacy, in which a decisive man is just a cowboy defending his vision but a woman with an opinion is an unhireable night-mare, who *was* she? The bits of digging I did around the time I was writing that television pilot turned up not very much: a few brief obituaries (Eastman had died in 2004), an excel-lent online appreciation by the film historian Nick Pinkerton, a few scattered stories in Peter Biskind's *Easy Riders, Rag-ing Bulls*, and in his subsequent biography of Warren Beatty. But . . . that was it. A handful of blog posts seemed long on mythology, but short on information. There is a 1962 episode of *Alfred Hitchcock Presents* called "Bad Actor," which you can see on YouTube, that highlights Eastman as a young actress—brunette this time, sporting a Louise Brooks-ish bob—giving a stiff, inconsequential performance alongside a baby-faced Robert Duvall. Biskind describes her in both books, using almost identical phrases: "tall, blond, rail-thin, with a swan's long neck. In fact, she was very like a bird, high-strung, star-tled into flight by the rustle of a leaf." In *Easy Riders, Raging*

Bulls, Biskind adds that she was afraid to fly, afraid to have her photograph taken, agoraphobic, picky about food, reluctant to enter any restaurant she'd never eaten at before, and also an ardent chain-smoker. Pinkerton offers a description from the screenwriter Robert Towne that I would later track down to a biography of Jack Nicholson, Eastman's lifelong friend and artistic champion: "a head shaped like a gorgeous tulip on a long stalk." Nicholson, like Towne, had met Eastman early on in his career—early enough it was before any of them could really be said to have had much of a "career" even—in a class taught by the character actor Jeff Corey, who'd been black-listed by the House Un-American Activities Committee. The class met twice weekly at Corey's house, at the corner of Chula Vista Way and Cheremoya Avenue, and during 1957 and '58 in particular it included a staggering amount of talent. Besides Nicholson, Eastman, and Towne, there were Sally Kellerman, James Coburn, Richard Chamberlain, Robert Blake, Dean Stockwell. There were additional figures who hung around the class as well: an actor named Dean Stanton (he soon added Harry to that moniker), and his friend Warren Oates.[3] Patrick McGilligan's Nicholson biography describes it in some detail: the class was rooted in the Stanislavski method (everyone read *An Actor Prepares*) but was heavily weighted toward improvisation. Actors might be instructed to perform random menial tasks, or to restage a scene from *Oedipus Rex* in the

---

3. Across the street, at 1970 Cheremoya, lived a high school student who, one must imagine, watched the comings and goings with at least a little bit of interest, given what would become her vaunted eye for developing talent. Her name was Eve Babitz.

contemporary context of a drug deal. These people—the members of what would soon become the counterculture—would have found the course more appealing precisely because Corey had been blacklisted too. Whether they were there to act or (as future screenwriters Eastman and Towne would have been) to better understand the personalities and mechanics of actors, the class was, by several accounts, transformative.

Also in that class for a while? My father. As an aspiring agent, he, too, wanted to understand actors (although his additional reason for taking it, shared with many of the men in the class, was to meet attractive women). When my father told me recently he'd been in attendance, I was momentarily astonished, although I shouldn't have been. Hollywood is a tesseract, in which time and space are continually folding in upon themselves. One might frequently meet a person in one context—at a party, I recently encountered a woman named Jane Hallaren, a writer who'd been the casting director for Michael Cimino's film *Heaven's Gate*—only to have the same person pop up in another, as Hallaren appeared, three days later but also several decades earlier, as an actress in *Puzzle of a Downfall Child*. For my dad to have intersected with Eastman is no surprise. The industry is small. But though I wouldn't begin my serious inquiry into Eastman until later, long after my mother fell ill, I felt it even as I first sunk back into *Five Easy Pieces*: an oblique sense that in thinking about Eastman at all I was also, always, thinking about my mother. Or maybe I should say the reverse: that whenever I stopped to think about my mom, I was also, automatically, thinking about Eastman, whose brief flowering and protracted silence—seventeen years elapsed between

1975's *The Fortune* and 1992's *Man Trouble*, which was Eastman's next produced picture—seemed a kind of mirror. But
when I asked my dad about her, he gave a characteristically
evasive answer, one that reflects both my father's and Eastman's personal elusiveness and a wider truth about Hollywood.
"Sure, I knew her," my father said. "But I didn't really know
her." Typical, this was: fundamental somehow to a town that
runs on mythology. My father wasn't going to help me unravel
the mystery of Carole Eastman at all.

But Eastman wasn't in that class because she wanted to
pursue acting. She was there to expand her sensibility. Born
in Glendale, in 1934, she was already a natural for the motion
picture business; her parents were below-the-line people: her
father was a grip at Warner Bros., her uncle had been a camera-
man, and her mother worked for a time as Bing Crosby's secretary. This was the old Hollywood, the working-class Hollywood
of technicians whose roots grew deep into the economy of the
city, rather than the expensive, glamorous mirage. Glendale was
the back of beyond in those days: its primary industries were
agricultural—cotton picking, melon packing—and Eastman's
screenplays both produced and unproduced are full of cowboy
signifiers, things you can imagine are plucked directly from that
landscape rather than imported: Tammy Wynette, ranch slang,
Bob Wills and His Texas Playboys. The writer described herself as a "constant truant" through high school, given instead
to solitary and voracious reading. I imagine her as being much
like that other incandescent young intellect of the era, Jeff Corey's Cheremoya Avenue neighbor Eve Babitz: bored out of her
mind by an educational system that was still, in the 1940s and

'50s, organized to turn young women into secretaries. Eastman was first a model, then an actress—like my mother, she'd
skipped blithely across the surface of the Hollywood pond; she
was even, briefly, a dancer, appearing in Stanley Donen's 1957
musical *Funny Face* before a broken foot ended that portion of
her dream. But by the time she arrived in Corey's class, surrounded by people who were not just professionally but *intellectually* hungry, and fiercely so, she was dry kindling: ready, with
the striking of a match, to burn.

◎

Most of what I've discovered about Eastman comes from conversations with those who knew her, with friends, neighbors, and
professional colleagues, and, more so, from a trip I took to view
her papers, which are housed at the Harry Ransom Center in
Austin, Texas. With one or two exceptions, even the people who
knew her socially didn't seem to know her *that* well, and many
who did—Nicholson—seem slightly protective of her memory.
It can be inferred, from her camera shyness, from her evident
reluctance to go on record (aside from a few scattered remarks
to biographers of other people, and a pair of magazine articles
spaced twenty years apart, the writer granted only two interviews,
one of which remains unpublished),[4] that Eastman was what
used to be called—how quaint it seems now—a *private person.*

---

4. Even the published interview with Eastman, in the May 2, 1971, issue
of the *Los Angeles Times*, notes an absence of information so total that
before meeting Eastman, the interviewer, Estelle Changas, "could have
concluded that she did not exist."

No Facebook, no Instagram, no Twitter, were she alive today. One can imagine her trying, if she were here and if such a thing were possible, to implode the entire internet: to collapse it down upon her head to leave a Googlewhack, a blank avatar, a void.

◎

It is tempting, too, to succumb to this: to let that void stand in for brilliance. The narrative of the female genius (and it's evident on the basis of her papers that Eastman might deserve this epithet at least as richly as her male peers, those lions of seventies Hollywood, do)[5] often seems to rest upon this kind of withholding—a slim, aphoristic novel; a cool, affectless film like Barbara Loden's *Wanda*—just as the male-genius narrative often relies upon a torrential, Wallacian outpouring of pages, a filmography consisting of necessarily long, Tarkovsky-ish ass-numb-ers. Even if there are reasons for this, namely that women have not always had the opportunity to create as copiously as men, both notions are unfair, insofar as they run the risk of flattening the achievement, and also the difficulty, the human costs of creation, into caricature. But Eastman withholds more than most, and, while she was alive, withheld for reasons that were clearly deliberate. While she was no wilting flower (the screenwriter Barry Sandler, who lived next door to Eastman throughout the 1990s, noted repeatedly how

5. In his Beatty biography, Peter Biskind remarks that "*Five Easy Pieces* was the only decent script that Eastman ever wrote, or had produced at any rate." Even with that added disclaimer ("had produced"), this simply isn't true.

strong-minded she was, and that she "did not suffer fools"), she preferred to be left alone. She liked . . . silence. When she and Jack Nicholson sat down in January 1965, to hash out ideas for what would become *The Shooting*, the actor—who loved distraction—hung an affectionately mocking nickname on the pensive, plodding Eastman, one he would call her for the rest of her life: "Speed." The writer was not amused. "As one who reaches for her six-shooter if she hears a pin-drop on the next block," she said later, "it wasn't the most auspicious of circumstances that we started, at [Nicholson's] suggestion, to work in the same room."

◎

Do you hear it? That sound you hear in those words is the pin drop chime of Eastman's prickly, magnetic intelligence, which collides a frontierswoman's orneriness with a diction at once high-toned ("most auspicious of circumstances") and loopy (a "six-shooter"?). That's her in a nutshell. One hears this sound, this delicious mashing of the rococo and the ridiculous, running out of Eastman's writing everywhere: for instance, in *Five Easy Pieces*, when Partita Dupea gazes off at her father's male nurse and sighs, to her brother, "Do you think Spicer is attractive? Spicer was formerly a sailor." (A lush pause.) "Sailors are *sadistic*, I feel." One hears it in the same film when a hitchhiker spirals off into an increasingly forceful monologue about Alaska and mass production ("crap"), then begins splitting hairs to define a difference between dirt ("dirt isn't that bad") and "filth." One hears it in *The Fortune*, when Nicholson's Oscar Sullivan (with the actor here in full *Three Stooges* mode, hair teased into a Larry Fine–like nest) earnestly leans over and blurts out a bit of doggerel that feels as sweet and ungainly as a cheap magician's bouquet: "A mean man and a man of means often means the same." Critics commonly praised Eastman's dialogue for its fine attunement to the nuances of American speech, and its careful awareness of class (the *Los Angeles Times'* Charles Champlin referred to her dialogue as "the screen equivalent of the John O'Hara ear at its most precise"). But what sometimes feels left out of the equation is that Eastman was *funny*. Not necessarily in the make-an-audience-howl-with-laughter sense; Eastman was hardly a wild comedienne. But her writing is funny in an intimate way, like those untranslatable jokes you share with those persons who are closest to you. One gets the idea that she sat at her typewriter and, when she wasn't beating herself to ribbons, lavishly cracked herself up.

◎

We may as well get this out of the way. I am unabashedly in love with her. More than I am with any other figure in this book, all of whom have an ample corner of my heart, yet I do not quite know why. Is it—as I am coming to suspect—because she was not entirely visible, because Eastman's public outline consists predominantly of her *absence*? (It is not lost on me that this was my mother too: that she traced herself upon me as a ghost.) But it is also true I find Eastman's cool wit delicious. And when I say I am unabashedly in love with her, I mean, too, just a little bit. I am prepared to perform whatever acts of critical violence might prove necessary. Just as I am prepared, as every writer had better be, to cleave my own heart in two.

◎

Over the course of her adult life, Eastman lived at three different addresses. During the sixties, and into the early seventies, she lived at 551 ½ Westmount Drive (a house I parked in front of dozens of times, when V was a toddler and we went nearly every day to a café on that corner for breakfast). Later, she lived at 511 Huntley (a block and a half south of where V began preschool, around the time I moved into 1448 North Hayworth). Finally, she lived at 9035 Rosewood, an address I have both walked and driven by for years, as when I take my dog to the park. Occasionally—maybe when she was working, or else during periods when she merely felt like it—she stayed at the Chateau Marmont, in room 14. This was the case in 1975 and 1976, when she was doing research for a script that would have involved—the materials are a bit of a jumble—beached whales, quiz show prodigies, and a character based loosely on the feminist writer Kate Millett. It appears to have been the case too when she worked on an undated script called *Mumbling Jim* (subtitle, lower case: *post coitum triste*). At the head of one of her notepads she had once scrawled, in green ink: "I am Carole Eastman. I live at the Chateau Marmont Hotel. I have 3 cats. And I am a writer by choice. Tadum!"

I am Carole Eastman. I live at the Chateau Marmont Hotel. I have 3 cats. And I am a writer by choice. Tadum!

◎

Why should I care about proximity? If Eastman was, as Biskind claims, afraid to fly, if that's not merely the type of embellishment that gets hung on the legend of a woman the screenwriter Buck Henry once described as "born to be an eccentric old lady," then she spent almost every day of her adult life inside an isosceles triangle bound by Sunset and Crescent Heights on the northeast, Doheny Drive to the west, and Beverly Boulevard to the south. A geographic space I live inside myself, and have for more than a decade. But what difference does it make? Will it bring me any closer to Eastman, or to my mother (who lived inside the same triangle herself, once, before I was born), to pass each house with a paranoid lover's eye? To squint at every half-open window, gaze at every wind-stirred curtain and sunstruck lawn, inhale every lungful of exhaust-kissed air and think, *All this was hers too*?

Yes. Because geography might trump chronology, in this case, and because West Hollywood—which isn't the same neighborhood as Hollywood proper, and which doesn't hold any of the studios or major agencies inside it yet still contains half the things we think of when someone says the word "Hollywood" (the Chateau, the Whisky a Go Go, the Roxy, the Sunset Marquis)—might reflect her own longing for privacy. The streets on which Eastman lived, all three of them, are narrow, quiet, and anonymous, given still to smaller, Spanish-style houses tucked behind high hedges. They are exactly the kind of thoroughfares on which one practically *can* hear a pin drop a block and a half away; untrafficked, rarely disturbed except by the occasional drone of a mower, the odd barking dog. I can hear my own feet falling on them, when I walk, and I imagine hers—Converse-clad, casual—would have sounded exactly the same whenever she stood up to get away from her typewriter, to pace out the particular difficulties of a scene.

◎

Here are some projects Eastman worked on in the 1960s and '70s, things she finished—or at least roughed out substantially—but which were never produced.

1. *The Best You Can* (written while Eastman lived on Westmount Drive): a psychedelic musical intended to star the Byrds, along the lines of Bob Rafelson's surrealist 1968 film starring the Monkees, *Head*, only evidently written before *Head* since it contains a part for Gene Clark, who left the Byrds in early '66. Includes scenes set inside the Roman Colosseum, NASA/outer space footage, and some stylish descriptions of David Crosby inhabiting the alter ego of an English biker named "Teddy Torquewell."

2. *Tomorrow after Tomorrow* (a.k.a. *The Black and White Spiders*, written also at Westmount Drive): a fiery, apocalyptic western, even bleaker (and more violent) than *The Shooting*. Almost Cormac McCarthy–like in its brimstone and terror.

3. *Interval* (Westmount Drive): a paranoid thriller, written circa '67/'68, for Monte Hellman to direct. Story involved a folk-rock singer named Jo Partain, who falls under the sway of a San Francisco cult leader named Dr. Howard Coe-Raider, while at the same time being the subject of a D. A. Pennebaker–style documentary. In style and tone a bit like Antonioni's *Blow-Up*, with echoes of the JFK assassination to be found in its ending.

4. *A Loveless Crossing* (a.k.a. *Pauline in Aulis*, a.k.a. *The Eleusinian Mystery*, undated, but probably written at Huntley Avenue): another paranoid thriller, loosely based on Euripides's *Iphigenia at Aulis*, but with a contemporary setting. Roughly akin in mood and style to Don DeLillo's novel *The Names*.

5. *Feathers on the Wing* (Westmount Drive): another ferociously apocalyptic, McCarthy-like western,[6] with Eastman's hand-scrawled epigraphs taken from William Blake ("By degrees we beheld the infinite Abyss, fiery as the smoke of a burning city"), Auden ("Aloneness is man's real condition"), Ezra Pound ("O smoke and shadow of a darkling world"), and

---

6. Although McCarthy published his first novel, *The Orchard Keeper*, in 1965, and Eastman was writing these westerns only a year or two later, it would not be remotely surprising to discover she was aware of it. McCarthy's book may have received only faint attention, but Eastman's reading was—evidently—quite voracious.

Hart Crane ("The abating shadows of our conscript dust").

6. *The Last Roundup* (a.k.a. *News*, undated, probably Huntley Avenue): a story inspired by the twelfth-century Persian poem *The Conference of the Birds*, only transposed to ranch country and evidently intended to explore Eastman's hypothesis that "dereliction of any sort . . . primarily is the outcome of unrequited love."[7] Eastman's notes make reference to "the Hollywood stables period of my life," by which she presumably means her Glendale childhood.

I should not be alone in finding Eastman fascinating. Even if—*if*—these projects were all botch jobs on the page, notionally intriguing but lackadaisically executed (they are not), Eastman's was a weird, fierce, original intelligence, unlike any other I can think of in Hollywood. She is not like her generational peers, like Elaine May, Robert Towne, William Goldman, because she is knottier, both more pointedly intellectual and a little closer to the ground, and at its best her work is at least as good as theirs. So what happened, exactly? How did this weird talent of hers originate itself onscreen? And then—where did it go?

◎

---

7. This according to her handwritten notes at the Ransom Center.

In 1965, Monte Hellman wanted to direct a western. He and Jack Nicholson, both friends of Eastman's from Corey's acting class, buttonholed the legendary B-movie producer Roger Corman—Corman who'd swung from doing low-budget monster flicks like *The Brain Eaters* and *Night of the Blood Beast* in the fifties to, more recently, motorcycle pictures like *The Wild Angels*[8]—and told him what they had in mind.

"It'll be like *The African Queen* in the desert," Nicholson assured him over dinner, the three men tucked into some booth on Beverly Boulevard, picking at food that was, like Corman's movies themselves, inexpensive.

"Fine, fine." Corman nodded. He was used to this, to giving his directors permission. Nicholson was a nobody, but he'd done good work for Corman in things like *The Little Shop of Horrors*. Hellman could be counted on to bring things in under budget, as he had for Corman before. "Make two westerns if you like. Just give 'em lots of tomahawks and ketchup."

Tomahawks and ketchup. This meant blood and violence. The script they had, by their friend Carole Eastman, didn't have too much of either—it was Beckett-like, quiet, filled with existential dread—but they headed off to the desert to shoot, lighting out with a skeleton crew for Kanab, Utah, near Zion National Park. The end result was just as strange as

---

8. One of the strangest traces of Eastman's presence comes in the form of a song that appears thirty-one minutes into Corman's 1961 horror joint *Creature from the Haunted Sea*, directed by Hellman, in which a mysterious siren promises that her "full lips" will "make you forget the war." What war is not clear, but the tune's lyrics, so characteristically peculiar, are credited to Eastman.

Eastman's script. The story of a weary gunslinger (played by Warren Oates) contracted to pursue a mysterious figure across the plains, *The Shooting* is austere, elliptical, fraught with an odd American poetry. Oates's character is named Willett Gashade, while Nicholson plays a malign assassin named Billy Spear. The film's tiny budget is evident: there are no sets, no extras, only a scattering of secondary characters (one of them, a broken-legged man stranded without water, played by Eastman's brother Charles),[9] but it has a terrifying simplicity, a feeling of being pitched inside a yawning chasm that separates the incomprehensible from the inevitable. Written off as too weird for American release in 1966, the film screened a few times in France a year or two later. Eastman went on to write a pair of teleplays for a network drama called *Run for Your Life*,[10] and then hooked up to write *Puzzle of a Downfall Child* in 1968. But it was *Five Easy Pieces*, written, like *The Shooting*, with Nicholson in mind, based on certain things she'd seen the actor do (that famous coffee shop scene in the film was loosely predicated on something she'd witnessed between Nicholson and a waitress in a joint on the Sunset Strip), that

---

9. Of whom, more later. But it's worth noting that Charles Eastman, four years older than his sister, had his own worthy career as a screenwriter and script doctor, most notably writing the 1970 film *Little Fauss and Big Halsy*, and writing and directing 1973's *The All-American Boy*.

10. *Run for Your Life* is negligible—a bucket-list drama about a terminally ill man who hits the road to cram as much living into his remaining time as possible—but the titles of the two Eastman-scripted episodes are wonderful, like lost Bob Dylan songs circa 1966: "Hang Down Your Head and Laugh, Blues" and "Saro-Jane, You Never Whispered Again."

launched Eastman and the actor both to stardom, along with the film's director, the monstrously talented Bob Rafelson. It brought her an Academy Award nomination for Best Screenplay and, private person that she was, a whole lot of attention about which she almost certainly had mixed feelings.

◎

Making it. It must have been at least a little queasy for Eastman, this experience of being inundated with prize nominations (there was one for a Golden Globe as well), of being interviewed for the cover of *Time* magazine, of palling around with Nicholson—now the hottest actor in town, after more than a decade in which he could barely convince anyone other than Corman that he was a leading man—and their old friend Robert Towne, invited to an endless stream of parties in the Canyon and at the Chateau. In the 1972 *Time* article, headed "Behind the Lens," Eastman is interviewed alongside a bevy of women, strong writers and actresses all poised to direct: Eleanor Perry, Elaine May, Barbara Loden. The article kicks off with Eastman talking about her forthcoming directorial debut, which was destined never to materialize, alas, noting that one of her friends had asked her what she planned to wear on set ("a muumuu, a Gestapo uniform or a terry-cloth robe, mules and pin curls?"), to which Eastman had offered—naturally—the withering response that no one would ask such a question of a man. The woman who appears in a small photograph that accompanies the article is no tulip, anyway. She wears aviator shades and a T-shirt—allegedly, her daily uniform for much of her life was exactly this: jeans, worn tee, tattered sneakers—and she looks engagingly quizzical, her mouth half-open as if, could she be bothered, she would snap off something a lot more withering than she had. It is, I can't help but note, a wonderful face, drowsy and elegant, intelligent but relaxed, the face of a woman who might not actually give a fuck even enough to compose herself into the image of a Woman Who Does Not Give a Fuck. In other words: the terry-cloth robe, for sure.

◎

Which offers us the question: Did she actually want it? Did she actually—this is more the point—*need* it, the way those of us who are driven beyond all reason to write things, paint things, make things, film things, sing things, or perform things, driven beyond all reasonable hope anyone else should even notice, the way those of us who want to be fucking *stars*, need it? Did she? Or did she just like writing? Or—since not so many writers particularly seem to *like* writing, at least not the kind who are so high-strung they'll shoot up a saloon at the sound of a falling pin—did she just want to do it for its own sake? Maybe that is naive, since even the most private writing is a bid for somebody's attention, but . . . did she even want that? She took another name. She hid behind it like a pair of dark glasses (God knows where the "Adrien" came from,[11] but the "Joyce" was, naturally, a tribute to her favorite Irish writer), like someone who didn't like to be photographed, someone who didn't want—even—to be *seen*. The name was plausibly androgynous. *Who, or what, is*

---

11. She uses the variant "Adrian" on *Puzzle of a Downfall Child* only.

an Adrien Joyce? You'd think she lived in a concrete bunker. Even though lots of writers use pen names, Eastman seemed to work harder than most to disappear.

◎

Ah. Maybe I am conflating Eastman, again, with my mother. Whose own desire not to be seen, or heard, whose personal shame, I believe, drove her from Los Angeles; and whose later-life writings, and endless hours of piano music, were private. There are such people, you know. Even today, somewhere, the Instagram refusenik, the contemporary Robert Walser writing his coded messages not on Twitter but on the inside of a paper bag.

I was never going to be that person. During the time I lived at 1448, I was so hungry for attention it's a wonder I didn't stroll out onto Sunset Boulevard and spray-paint sentences in the middle of the street like an idiot Banksy. I admired the privacy of an Eastman, the person who didn't need to be loved, or—not "loved" but publicly admired; the person who didn't need to whip out her credit card and wait for the person who picked it up to exclaim, "Why, it's *you*! Love your work." Sad, I know. To crave that validation, but where else was I going to go? I wasn't going to look to the semi-estranged woman who'd once thrown bottles at my head, was I?

Watching *Five Easy Pieces* that fall, as I did several times while the season tilted from Indian summer toward the deeper coolness of late October, I found myself wishing I could do so with my mother. I made plans to go up and see her at

Christmas. I would bring V, who'd met her grandmother only briefly, twice before, but who gabbled brightly, even joyfully, about her "granma Katherine." Watching Eastman's film was thus, too, a type of rehearsal. It was a way of absorbing my mother's landscape, and her sense of humor, the person I had once, long ago, before her alcoholism more completely interceded, been able to love. And yet—I did, of course. I loved her still as I had all my life. I just didn't quite know where to find her, that human being I had misplaced—or who had misplaced me—like an unlucky set of keys.

Autumn in Los Angeles is a kind of shriveling, a contraction not just of time, the daylight hours, but of possibility. Everything grows more chromatic: the late sunshine, the shop windows, the cars. And then evening arrives like an orange rolling off a table, a struck match plunged into a bucket of water, that source of brightness just gone. There is that brief green moment between afternoon and night, and that is the space in which Eastman's film most lived for me. I sat on my couch with knees tugged to my chest as it flickered over and over on a screen. *Bobby Dupea.* It was all I knew of Eastman at the time. Her other films weren't available—not even through illicit channels—or if they were (*Man Trouble*), they seemed unimportant. My mother and her music: these things were on my mind. And my mother's brief career—"career"; it had barely been longer than that hour between daylight and dark—as a screenwriter, because as it happened the WGA was just then, as I sat there watching almost forty-year-old movies, about to go on strike. The Writers Guild hadn't struck since the eighties. In 1981 my mother, who was never a WGA member, had rewritten *Love Child*, a script that had been conceived by another writer, during a strike that had lasted several months. In other words, she became a scab. It wasn't her finest hour. Whether she'd been motivated by opportunism or by ignorance, whether she'd been solicited or even duped into doing it (the film's director was my father's client and her own friend; multiple people close to her had a vested interest in seeing the film green-lit), my mother crossed a picket line. Not good. This was the film that got made and the one that, once it went to the guild for arbitration, earned her a writing credit in 1982. Whatever she did or did not deserve—the other writer, the original one, decided to use a pseudonym, just like Carole Eastman did—my mother's one and only produced feature film both launched and ended her career. She found herself black-balled from the Writers Guild, and though she was occasionally hired over the next few years by a friend or an executive who took pity, that, effectively, was that. She never found meaningful employ in Hollywood again. All these years later I myself had no interest in crossing a picket line—I needed a break from screen-writing anyway, since I had just delivered a script I was actively embarrassed by in response to an assignment I would have been better off not taking to begin with—but I was soon to find some meditative solace in plodding around in circles before the gates of Paramount Studios, or Fox, waiting for other, better-heeled writers to show up with doughnuts or pizza for the improvement of morale. *On strike.* By the time it happened, my life was at an utter standstill. Living for six months now in a one-and-a-half-room apartment; watching my daughter, who was three, start preschool; watching my ex-wife, from whom I'd now officially filed for divorce, dive headlong into her relationship with

R; even hearing from my mom and realizing she was—let's face it—merely getting ready to complete a disappearance that had begun decades ago: I was painfully aware that everyone seemed to be moving forward but me.

This was a lie, of course. My stasis was the product of a fevered imagination, a dream—which could only ever be a dream—of sitting still. I had no hope of being "reborn" into something I might find better, but I did hope I'd box my way out of the maze. I made lists of possible opportunities, made lists of things—which weren't "things" at all—that might serve as purposes, if not advantages. I loved my daughter with everything I had. I loved her with an intensity that shocked me, insofar as no actual presence in my life had ever fully prepared me for it. I loved my mother with a pallid *lack* of intensity—it felt like cave diving, a murky, deep-sea searching for the faded intuitions of former feeling—that also shocked me, as I wondered if this was something any other person would possibly understand. And I loved my future, to the extent that I hoped it would eventually present me with another human being to love as I had once upon a time loved N. But together these things offered up a taste of failure. I woke up sweating, terrified my daughter might someday, for some unknown reason, feel that far away from me. My life seemed rancid, even if, too, I could feel somewhere, buried deep inside me, the existence of green shoots. At the end of *Five Easy Pieces*, Bobby Dupea walks away from everything, hitchhiking his way into the tundra of Alaska. It is an ending that still shocks: one can feel the coldness, the terror that courses through him as he talks his way into a trucker's cab at a gas station and then pulls off without so much as a jacket on his back. I didn't want that to be me. Because I had a sense, indeed, that it had been my mother: that when she left LA, she wasn't moving toward anything specific, but rather, simply, *away*.

◎

What about Eastman? Had she ever loved? Lying awake at night, I wondered that the only potential failure that mattered was this. "All time is truly lost and gone/which is not spent in serving love." A woman I had lost long ago had told me that decades earlier—shortly before I met N, in fact—and it came back to me now, this line from an Italian poet that I had found too easy to forget. Sifting through Eastman's papers, years later, I came upon a loose page, not attached to any script, that laid out a familiar dilemma.

> *Sylvia Ashton-Warner wrote that everything she did was "for" the love that might be received, every thought she had . . . was that someone might love her. I have been so long discouraged in love, that I wonder if I am insensible to it. I am often with someone who loves me, but whom I don't love except in an affectionate companionable way . . . I become tired, and my thoughts drift . . . I become bored with them as I become bored with myself.*

I know that feeling. So do you, perhaps. As for Eastman, it's difficult to know when these words were written, or in what context. I found them tucked back among the research materials for a film that would have been called *Kitty and Georgia* (this was the Kate Millett/beached whales/quiz show prodigies folder), and they may just be character notes for that project or some other. But I doubt it. They sound—they *are*—too purely confessional, too full of despair. She goes on to tie this problem explicitly to her work ("I find here again, as with my writing, I don't want to do the work that reveals me to myself"), and then lays it all down to her own flaws, real or perceived: laziness, timidity.

> *I have seen that it is because of my lack of courage to go where the feather flies, in love, to embrace it, and to brave what ever comes, that is in great part the cause of this disappointment . . . I did not even give the chance to be disappointed in the other . . . I did not venture far enough to even experience that.*

She alludes in passing to a success she'd already experienced ("If I had worked only for . . . the celebrity of the world at large, if for money, if for [security] I have received in some degree all of these things"), and notes that this had never made her particularly happy. If I had to guess, I'd say she wrote this page sometime in 1976 or '77, an era in which her star had dimmed, after *The Fortune* came out and flopped. It's possible Eastman wasn't set up to handle failure, any more than she had been, really, to handle success. Public derision tends to kneecap people (although, honestly? So does public acclaim), but maybe Eastman was feeling the way she did because she'd already experienced all the other forms of success, and these things had left her cold.

◎

The Fortune isn't nearly as bad as its reputation. Look at the record and see, on the one hand, a 20 percent rating on Rotten Tomatoes (oof!), but also an enthusiastic—indeed, a rave—review from Vincent Canby in the *New York Times*, and a belated championing from the Coen brothers, who consider it one of their favorite films of all time. The galumphing story of a 1920s ne'er-do-well (Beatty) who marries his sweetheart (Stockard Channing) off to his own clumsy chum (Nicholson) in order to circumvent the Mann Act (Beatty's character is himself married, and so could otherwise be charged with "transporting a woman across state lines for immoral purposes"), *The Fortune*'s chaotic narrative turns on the friend's discovery said sweetheart is actually a wealthy tampon heiress. Each therefore decides he wants her for himself. *The Fortune* is no masterpiece. It sags in spots, is mis-pitched in others (as if Nichols's screwball direction and Eastman's screwball writing themselves can't agree), and as every account of the film's making is quick to point out, it went through dozens of alternate endings before arriving at one that doesn't work either. But it's also, at least in places, funny as hell. One suspects the film's crummy reputation hangs largely on the immense expectations that preceded it. Nichols, Beatty, *and* Nicholson? A guaranteed hit if ever there was,[12] and since, ultimately, the film wasn't a commercial success, well, the blame had to lay itself somewhere.

---

12. In fact, according to Biskind's *Easy Riders, Raging Bulls*, *The Fortune* was such a guaranteed hit that the green-lighting of Hal Ashby's enormously superior (and more successful) *Shampoo* was essentially just a chess move, a favor that would ensure Beatty stayed committed to *The Fortune*.

Unsurprisingly, it wouldn't be on the expensive male stars and/or the renowned director with a successful track record, not when there was somewhere else to put it. Production on the film had been embattled from the beginning. According to the production designer, Polly Platt, Nichols had gone so far over budget on previous films that he wanted to be a good boy this time, and "kept cutting all the good stuff out of the [script]." Eastman apparently wasn't thrilled, but—in the end, so what? The movie tanked. It may even have tanked egregiously, but was that so unusual, to a writer who'd already ridden the Ferris wheel for a while? Was it worth outright despair, or seventeen years of silence? Particularly for someone who didn't necessarily seem to care all that much how things were received? Of course she cared, because every writer does, but Eastman had never been wrapped up in questions of reputation. ("I have received in some degree all of these things, and found little happiness residing in them.") So what was it about this experience that rattled Eastman's cage so badly?

◎

I keep returning to that period, those years between 1975 and 1981, when Eastman was MIA, bouncing between Westmount Drive (later, Huntley Avenue) and the Chateau, working but not necessarily *working*. This was the period in which David Geffen had given her $100,000 to write a script, betting on her blind, the way he had as a record executive on Laura Nyro and Bob Dylan and Joni Mitchell, just because he believed she was brilliant. The script she would arrive at, in the end, was *Man Trouble*, which took another decade to be made, by which time Geffen had long since bowed out of the project, but the point is: she did what she wanted. She could have lived off that money for a while, even if the Chateau was never cheap, but she must have also been working on other things. Five years is a long time, for a screenwriter. In 1991, a brief column in the Calendar section of the Sunday *Los Angeles Times* refers to the pending production of *Man Trouble*, and quotes Eastman as saying she'd gone through a "self-imposed hiatus" of five years. "Maybe longer," she says. "I don't keep track of time." She notes that this hiatus was "enriching. I explored other forms of writing." That's all we get, but it's something. *I don't keep track of time.* Much as I love the wryness of this remark, it's almost certainly not true. There isn't a writer alive who isn't acutely aware of the time, who isn't losing it—and finding it—constantly.

I like to think our paths may have crossed during that period, that even as I was a teenager on the verge of discovering *Five Easy Pieces*, she brushed by one afternoon in the Chateau lobby, or sat at a neighboring table at Chasen's or Scandia. I squint now at the only other photograph of Eastman I've been able to find, one included in the program for a 1998 Women in Film luncheon, but clearly taken years earlier, since it depicts a person most likely in her forties. No aviator glasses this time, but a shrewd, owlish expression, and a hint of irony in the presence of an enormous dog, a shepherd of some kind, who crowds her to the side of the frame. Carole Eastman. Adrien Joyce. A.L. Appling, even. Which of these people, I wonder, am I looking at?

◎

A word about Eastman and names, since she never quite anchored herself too firmly to any one of them professionally,
and since her notebooks are filled with lists of them, names
she must have used in order to generate characters. I see her
films, too, and marvel at her ear's delicious oddity. Catherine
Van Oost. Robert Eroica Dupea. Partita Dupea. Palm Apo-
daca. Rayette Dipesto. Harry Bliss. Nicky Stumpo. Frederica
Quintessa Biggard. ("Bee-GARD.") Willet and Coigne Gashade. This reads like a list from a Proustian ball, one that has
been gate-crashed by miscellaneous Muppets, bowling alley
employees, and characters from an English spy novel, but it
also suggests that Eastman found inordinate power in what
human beings are called. In the absence of endearments, one
imagines her rolling these monikers around on her tongue,
speaking them into the privacy of her own cupped hands. But
maybe she was just messing around. Or maybe—she was trying to name the world, the way we do, we always do, when we
are, however secretly, in love.

◎

This is where Eastman's story could end. With a little money
in her pocket and a room at the Chateau, a headful of ideas
and a proliferation of aliases. Isn't this how we all want to live?
The future has yet to arrive. Some validation has been conferred,
but we are still turning over the cards, laying out the configu-
ration of our fate. There is no spouse or partner (for now), and
no children—that ship has likely sailed—but there is the joy of
a mind at play. Isn't that enough? I like to think, for Eastman,

it was. As my mother entered her descent in the Pacific Northwest, as her illness began to consume her body, I cast my mind back to a time when she was fully alive, that mighty prime of the late 1970s in which alcohol had not yet wrecked her life. Sentimental, I suppose. But we do our best to preserve our loves. My mother's marriage to my father was soon to fail. A previous marriage had also long ago collapsed, as would her brief rebound marriage in the mid-1980s. But just then, nothing was wrong—not yet. Katherine Specktor. Katherine Korey. Katherine McGaffey. Katherine McKenna (this being the pseudonym she adopted, briefly, when she was a model in the late 1950s). My mother had never quite settled down inside her own name either. It's as if she had put them on and taken them off, rotating them almost like scarves. For a while she had been a beautiful, luminous guest inside them. Love might come, and love might go. The unknown self, only, remains.

◎

Hi Jeanne, dear Jeanne:

As I said, things are difficult, and remain. Even the moon is saturnine, so I've been told. I think too much and I take too long.

In 1971, Eastman was supposed to direct a movie. There is no mention of it in any of the formal records, not in Peter Biskind's book or in any of the biographies of Jack Nicholson. It is alluded to without a title or details in the 1972 *Time* magazine that interviews her alongside Eleanor Perry and Elaine May, but the most precise description I've found occurs in the introduction to an unpublished interview Eastman gave to screenwriter Betty Ulius around the same time.

> *She will be writing and directing a script whose working title is "The Second Interval." It will star Jeanne Moreau as a lady entymologist [sic], and Jack Nicholson as a trainer of attack dogs. The story sprang out of a chance meeting that Carol [sic] had with a Frenchwoman in the Hollywood Hills. It was a short, casual encounter, but the writer was very struck with the woman. When, shortly thereafter, she met Jeanne Moreau, and Moreau expressed an interest in working with her, a story began to evolve based on the Frenchwoman. Then a dog trainer story for Nicholson she'd been thinking about meshed with this one—the male dog trainer and the Frenchwoman together—voila! (Or "heel!")—"The Second Interval"!*

The Second Interval. Not to be confused, evidently, with *Interval*, the aborted folk singer thriller she'd sketched out for Monte Hellman a few years earlier. (Nor with *Man Trouble*, the muddled 1992 re-teaming of Eastman, Nicholson, and Bob Rafelson—Eastman's nominal "comeback"—in which Nicholson plays an attack dog trainer.) This was something else, something that, I dare to imagine, she might have tagged with her own name. The title surfaced, the intention to write the movie, the announcement—in *Time* magazine, even—that she would direct. And then nothing. Where did the project go?

Dear Jeanne:

This year I've come again to grief upon the experienced facts of the external world and found them indistinguishable from the dark play within the mind. Matched the inward with the mirrored outward, chemically married thrice within the year, without rejoice.

The letters Eastman wrote to Moreau are undated. They are the only personal correspondence that remains among her papers, aside from the stray note from Nicholson, and she appears to have kept both halves of it. Her own half, the letters she wrote, appear to have been labored over; there are often multiple drafts, with finely tuned revisions, and one can feel in them, as with much of Eastman's writing, the pressure of sentiments that have been overthought, if not necessarily overwritten. In Moreau, she'd found something, for sure. The lady in the Hollywood Hills wasn't the only Frenchwoman who'd impressed her.

Dear Jeanne:

I think of you. See you unbidden, see you at will, and sometimes against the same. You are made so well. Just so high as my hand held above the ground . . . I think I see you divide the falling light into varied shades of brown, and I think I see what moves and sounds shape beyond the rectangular theater framed by your window, and think I catch a few colors of the turning year from your eye.

These are not the words of an anxious young writer/director trying to woo an actress into making her picture. They are the words—how else can one possibly interpret them?—of an anxious human being trying to navigate some complicated feelings. There's only so much one can infer from a letter, but Eastman felt something, something that may not have been merely companionable. (I suspect anyone who has ever watched Moreau in *Jules et Jim*, or in Louis Malle's *Ascenseur pour l'échafaud* or in Antonioni's *La Notte*, or in anything, at all really, can relate. Moreau's presence was incandescent.) There don't appear to have been many letters between them: Eastman wrote five, and of Moreau's responses (which *are* dated, between October 1971 and January 1972), only two survive in the folder housed at the Ransom Center. There are later pieces—notes from Moreau dated from 1987 and 1994—but the bulk of their correspondence took place as the year turned from '71 to '72. Eastman's writing here is tremulous, full of doubt ("I've finally begun to work: I can't tell you how very hard it goes"), and loaded— overloaded, really—with feeling.

> *Does it bear repeating that I loved receiving your letter? I'm newly conscious, and from another quarter have been told that my responses are often in a code so private that they seem not to exist at all. Maybe. But I consider that quarter too deeply suspect with demand to be completely regarded. You would understand.*

Too deeply suspect with demand. Even as Eastman was brushing off some other, too-importunate, lover—someone who must have complained that her feelings were incomprehensible, that her demeanor was too cool—she was losing it over Moreau, begging her for the smallest of scraps, the most intimate ones, of her experience. "Tell me about nothing . . . about what is dull and repetitive, and if boredom ever sedated you for a brace of days . . . it is probably the intensity of your inner life which created it." She writes, "I would not find your humanity boring in any wise nor any part of it uninteresting." She dreams of being shipwrecked, of spelling out messages to her airborne rescuer— Moreau—with stones. And when she laments, again, that her work is going poorly—one might safely assume this work was on the script for *The Second Interval*—she writes, "I should be frightened at the thought of letting you down . . . I am, a little. But the sun is westerly towards the sea and its slant light accompanies a breeze moving my curtain inward to the room."

◎

How intimate is that billowing curtain! Like any frustrated admirer, Eastman was reduced to communicating in signals; to the semaphore of a diaphanous curtain saying, *See me! See me! Come inside!* (Have you ever been reduced to powder by the force of your feelings for another? I had. I would be, soon, again.) Moreau's responses are evasive. They are handwritten, in a looping script, vigorously dashed off where Eastman's are typewritten, *re*written, meticulously phrased even to the point of being inscrutable. They are flecked with endearment (there is liberal application of the phrase "my darling"), but they are, also, edged with warning, as Moreau urges Eastman to protect her film, protect her feelings, as she worries that Eastman might be lonely or unhappy, then notes that they are—no matter how simpatico in their friendship—different, in their respective temperaments. When one reads them today, it's clear that Moreau was above all hoping to give Eastman what she felt was most important: a strong performance in the film they were plotting to do together. In one of the letters—one assumes the last of the batch, though they are not ordered in their folder—Eastman's tone pivots. She drops for a moment into doggerel—"I said, everything's known that is unsaid. Your face turned counter and your eyes went miles instead"—and then accuses Moreau of leading her on: "You desired me to follow you 'in order' that you could move away . . . and so I did." She writes, "If I live in a one-sided world, then the burden of all mistakes is on me." We've all made those mistakes, at one time or another. We've all tried to articulate our impossible po- sition, the position of the lover who is not fully loved back, and so we know how it goes, and how it feels. It is one of the few spaces on the spectrum of human experience where language feels infinitely renewable—*Let me just tell you one more time how it is; let me finally make myself, again, clear*—and also entirely, inescapably useless.

◎

It doesn't matter what happened between Eastman and Moreau, what their friendship was or was not. It matters, rather, what Eastman felt. It matters the way the pulse of a distant star matters—the way your own experience of such unrequited desire does too—it matters that the fiercely imag- inative, galactically strange container of "Carole Eastman"

("Adrien Joyce") was blown so powerfully by human feeling, because it remains the only meaningful evidence (by which I mean evidence presented in the court of record: the court of Eastman's private personality) that she was even here. The 1971 *Los Angeles Times* interview, which begins with the interviewer musing that she "could have concluded that [Eastman] did not exist," reels off the various proofs of Eastman's absence (no biography, no filmography, no appearance in film history or textbooks), and while the writer may have gone on to accumulate a few of those things in the years that followed, there still isn't much beyond a handful of anecdotes, and the memories of those who survived her. And the films, of course. But of the *person*, whose intimate life is otherwise unrecorded? Not much. And when I think of Eastman, that conspicuously guarded, deliberate, publicity-shy individual—dead now for more than fifteen years, without any heirs—feeling inflamed, well, it warms me, to picture her ablaze. Perhaps this is perverse of me. The tonic note, in all her early letters to Moreau (a handful of later ones are cordial, and suggest a friendship survived), is pain. But it's gladdening to know that someone of such magnetism and talent, such playfulness and decency, and such vulnerability ("despair" is where she keeps arriving in that note to herself about her failure to love: "If it is that I have worked for love and acceptance, to be important and therefor [*sic*] worthy of love . . . Despair"), it is gladdening to know that such a person was, in her innermost heart, alive.

Maybe I am just sentimentalizing. To reduce another person's heartbreak to an idea of "aliveness" is unkind. We'll never know what Eastman felt, but we do know that the film, *The Second Interval*, was lost. Given the paucity of Hollywood films of that era—of any era—directed by women, that seems a meaningful loss. Even if the film had been executed with checkered results, if the direction had faltered, if the performances didn't jell, or if the script itself wasn't up to snuff, it would have been interesting, further record of an artist whose singular intelligence was at least the equal of her celebrated masculine peers. But it wasn't. Because it never happened.

◎

The year was hurtling to a close. The WGA remained on strike, which left me plenty of time, when I wasn't marching, to fill my own notebooks, and to write a short novel: a lyric parody of a rock 'n' roll story other people seemed to read seriously, and which I would eventually publish to dead silence. I made my plans to go up and see my mom at Christmastime, and to bring V. All these things happened, and in my mind, it is always twilight: the peach glow in the room at 1448 expelling itself like oxygen from a lung, my lycanthropic urges—sexual hunger, a general restlessness, an impulse, on those nights I was not with V, to get alarmingly drunk—beginning to stir as I stared at my laptop in despair. In my imagination's eye, I am like a diver navigating a shipwreck. I am also the shipwreck itself.

Carole Eastman had died in 2004. The cause, one obit claimed, was the Epstein-Barr virus, although others asserted it was, instead, cancer. In December 2007, I flew up to visit my mother. The landscape was exactly as sodden as I remembered: western hemlocks and Douglas fir trees reaching up into a cloud-bound sky, my mother's house confining and chilly, its windows fronting the gray of the lake. We went to the movies a few times, played listless games with V. But we didn't talk about her illness. I couldn't get it out of her.

"What does Blau say?" This was the name of her oncologist. "What does she expect?"

My mother shook her head. Her face was drawn, and her hair was gunmetal silver, thin from the chemo she'd undergone in the fall, but she was still herself, the avid reader, the crossword puzzle doer, the coffee drinker: the person I'd known my entire life.

"It's not clear." This meant, *I haven't pressed for answers*, or, *I don't want to tell you.* "She doesn't know."

During that visit, I sat one afternoon in her study and pulled a box of papers from her closet: all she had kept from her prior life in Los Angeles. There were pages torn from her high school yearbook, and clippings from the UCLA newspaper; there was a folder of unpublished short stories, and there were drafts of her various screenplays, both *Love Child* and a handful of unproduced others, along with reviews and clippings from the *Los Angeles Times* and *Daily Variety*, articles about the movie and about her subsequent blackballing from the Writers Guild. It wasn't much. Sitting there cross-legged on her office floor, with my head resting a moment in my hands, an old Bogner ski jacket—I remembered that too, with a Mammoth Mountain ski lift ticket still hanging from its zipper, even—draped on its hanger above me, I wondered that this one rectangular box could in essence contain all the evidence of my mother's life from cradle to grave. The air reeked of cigarette smoke—Merit Ultra Lights—and her piano sat, immutable, in the corner. No amount of staring at it would produce any music. Was this all she would leave? This thousand-pound instrument, and this cardboard box that I was one day soon going to tuck under one arm and carry back to Los Angeles without breaking stride? I wasn't fair to her, I know. Life is *lived* in the intervals between these peaks, large or small, between the graduations and weddings and Academy Awards, the highlights that, no matter how lauded you are, how celebrated and famous and lavishly hailed, amount to nothing in the face of the rest of it: the toothbrushing, the nodding, the traffic jams, the conference rooms, the airport gates, the hours of glamourless boredom that make up every last life on earth.

◎

I keep going back, then, to Eastman's most private writings: to a small folder I found tucked at the very back of her archive that is titled, simply, "Poems." Given how often Eastman spoke in her notes of an impetus to "play," how frequently even her hand-scrawled explorations of character and scenario are punctuated by little marginal exhortations to just "let yourself go," it would have been here that she was most fully herself, most willing to lose track of time and let her mind go where it wanted. Or maybe I just like these pages, which are not "poems," for the most part: they are aphorisms, images, sharp-eyed fragments of such startling particularity they are as exhilarating as a stroll through the notebooks of a Theodore Roethke, a Wallace Stevens, or a Hart Crane. "Stranded beanless on the boulevard"; "My windows, clouded as the fly's segmented wing"; "A Falstaffian faker, parading his lordly pork, proud as a turd, and on feet too little for his listing bulk, trying to dance"; "Hail to the over-filled ever empty." Who knows what lines like these, so endearing in their weird musicality, wanted to be, what purpose they served except to amuse Eastman on her own. In places she is theosophical ("Their God, stern as a stick, kept book, was hardly to be pleased"), others, aphoristic ("Learn to pass between the horns of the bull and the baloney"), and everywhere she is patiently attentive. Writing about dropping a water glass on the kitchen floor—"After sweeping up the silver shards and diamond glisters, I went in to stare at the couch, the rug, the room, wondering if there was anything inimical to me in the worn fabric of the couch. . . . For now the eyes must find beauty in the blue color of the gas flame and the sun's dashing dance on the pan I wash at the kitchen window"—she notes: "Beauty is pandemic, though I'd prefer the whole landscape to proclaim it. For now let me find it in the cathedral shape of my thumbnail."

◎

Let me stay here, I think, whenever I read these pages. I carry them on my phone—there are only a dozen or so—and sometimes, when I'm feeling pensive and alone, I pull them open. *Let me crawl within the Attic mind of Carole Eastman*, I think. Naturally,

I can't. And naturally, I miss my mother, who was Eastman's contemporary if not quite her peer, who shared with Eastman a vocation, and a geography, if not a level of talent and capability, and who, like Eastman, was mostly invisible even while she was alive.

I close those pages and feel both of them tumbling away, vanishing into the distances of history. The older I get, the more I miss her, that woman I couldn't love when I was younger—who did everything she could to keep me from doing so—and now, now that time has revealed her energetic cruelties as misdemeanors (she threw a bottle at my head; she abandoned me one night at the Directors Guild; she also imbued me with whatever tenderness of spirit I may now possess), she stands revealed to me as my unacknowledged twin. I cannot bring her back, and I cannot understand what happened in those hundreds of thousands of hours she lived outside my sight. But I can forgive her. I think.

◎

"Hello?"

It was my cousin who called, a favorite cousin: my mother's brother's daughter Deb.

"Hi." Her long exhalation told me what I needed to know. This was a few months later, in the spring. "Your mother's back in the hospital."

"Ah."

"Apparently, she fell last night. It's not looking good."

I hesitated. My eyes swept around the apartment to which I'd just moved—I'd needed to borrow a little money to do it— in order to have more room for V to sleep over.

"Should I come up?"

Deb took another deep breath. It was, evidently, a bad fall: my mother had suffered a concussion, and two of the bones in her face had shattered.

"You don't want to see her like this," she said.

Again, my eyes swept this room, a place I have not yet described to you, although all rooms are the same in moments like that; an illegible cluster of *things*, no more decodable than a maternity ward is to a newborn. I shut my eyes and pictured my mother, pummeled and swollen and bruised purple like a boxer, her face veiny and contused; pictured her rabid and snarling at me like Medusa, her once-drunken furies.

"No," I said. (*Yes*, I meant, my heart halved to the end. *Yes, I do, yes, I do, YES.*) "I suppose not."

IV
the slowest moment of your life
thomas mcguane

Nobody knows, from sea to shining sea, why
we are having all this trouble with our republic . . .

—THOMAS MCGUANE, *Ninety-Two in the Shade*

I **WANTED SO** badly to be him. From the depths of my
screaming adolescent soul, I wanted nothing more, as I stared
at the dust jacket of a book plucked from my parents' shelves.
A man stands at the helm of a fishing boat, bronzed and
brooding—a real centurion—with his eyes fixed on the horizon, his gold watch flashing in the sun. This image was so vivid!
It represented liberty, represented license, represented, I suppose, success. Success! I was fifteen years old, and all I wanted
was a blow job, a little cannabis, and, in the more rancid cor-
ners of my jilted little heart, world domination, but even then
I knew what it looked like, more importantly what it *sounded*
like: real genius on the page. And if, like most adolescents, I
conflated the image of genius with the expression of it—if I
thought writing a great book meant living an expensive dream,
thought writing sentences that made a teenage brain fizz like
THC, like MDMA, like *cocáina* did could somehow guarantee
a person the loud life of a rum runner—well, I was still a kid.
There would be time to sort out whatever minor discrepancies
may have existed between my idea of a writer's existence and
the reality of one.

Not long after I'd cracked the spine on *This Side of Para-dise* and had my little epiphany on the terrace of my father's house in Malibu, I found myself browsing the shelves at my mother's place in Santa Monica. This house had belonged to my parents together—I'd lived here, with my sister too, since I was eight years old—but only now was it borne home that my parents, my mother especially, were readers, and that their shelves in the living room were a bounty for me to explore. Another bounty, for that house, on Georgina Avenue, seemed to hold everything I needed. There was the cabana out back, where my mother rattled the keys of her Selectric and paced the brick floor barefoot, smoking, taking thoughtful tugs from her glass of what I mistakenly took to be ice water; there was the high hedge that ran along the western edge of the property, through which the twilight sun filtered just so (an ideal place to stash my drugs, whenever my mom, in one of her rare para-noid moods, decided to toss my cell); there was the kitchen, in which my parents had railed and screamed during the waning days of their marriage, with its cupboards now filled with un-attended Henry Weinhard's beer and matches for contraband cigarettes; and there was the living room: the white couch and the cream-colored alpaca rug; the artwork, by Laddie John Dill, Bernie Casey, and others; the glass-and-chrome table, so perfect for carving out lines of cocaine. And there were my mother's bookshelves, her copies of Joyce and Nabokov, of John Dos Passos's *U.S.A.*; there was her Cheever, and there was her Sontag, there, her Didion and Philip Roth, her Baldwin and her Richard Wright. There, too, the books that seemed to be on every American middlebrow, middle-class, middle-everything shelf in those years: Updike's *Couples* and Judy Blume's *Wifey*, Oriana Fallaci and Gay Talese, Stephen King, Peter Straub, and Leonard Michaels. I might never have run out of things to read or jerk off to, could have spent my entire adolescent life in this room, watching the rosy fingers of dawn pierce through those street-facing blinds, hallucinating helicopters, bending down to do—and to read—another line while my warden slumbered drunk upstairs, like some Scorsese mug reborn as a teenage scholar. But the one that grabbed my attention hardest and shook me to my core—shook me so deeply that all the drugs in the world wouldn't derail my concentration upon it—was *Panama*, a novel. By one Thomas McGuane.

◎

Panama. It came as a surprise to me later to discover that book was considered a failure in its time, that it derailed, at least briefly, the career of its creator. To me, it was electrifying. The story of a worn-out rock star who comes home to Key West hoping to win back—or win forth—the woman he loves, *Panama* is, like all McGuane's novels to that point, *about* failure. It is a chronicle of anomie, of excess and collapse, except that—like those other novels, too—its telling is so galvanic that the very narrative structures seem to seize and bend. There are sentences in McGuane that pull the weight of an entire novel by themselves; there are passages that fracture into prismatic units of meaning, neo-cubism, dazzling rays approaching gobbledy-gook before they bend back to reality again. They are poems, these books, as well as novels, manifestos as clearly as they are coded confessions, and I loved them with all my heart. I do not know why my mother owned them, given that her personal tastes were more Nordic, cool, and McGuane's Floridian chaos would have been a little outside her wheelhouse. Maybe it was the fact that McGuane's first novel, *The Sporting Club*, had been adapted, poorly, into a movie in 1972 by the same man who'd directed her film, Larry Peerce. Whatever it was, the books were there, and no one prevented me from reading them. (Much as I occasionally wish—just as anyone confronted with the harbinger of his eventual ruin might wish—someone had.) They cemented in place what had begun with Fitzgerald: my wish to strike sentences into being. Maybe I was never as hapless as any of McGuane's lurching and miserable heroes—as Tom Skelton, Chester Pomeroy, Nicholas Payne, or, alas, poor James Quinn—or his imperious and deranged antagonists (they tend to come in pairs, these McGuanian ne'er-do-wells), but I was hapless enough. To what degree I still am, I pin a little of the blame for that on Mr. T. Francis McGuane, lately of McLeod, Montana, born December 11, 1939, in Wyandotte, Michigan. He is the man who lit the fuse that ultimately exploded my very own crate of Acme dynamite, and for that, like any blessed loser, I will love—and curse—him to my final breath.

◎

After my mother died, I trained my eyes upon my father. How could I have done otherwise? If our relationship was nowhere near as tormented as hers and mine had been, thank God, it was hardly less complicated. He represented the other path, the successful path: where my mother had been ambivalent, uncertain, and swept along on the current of her own passivity, my dad was forceful, driven, and decisive. He was, as they say, a kind man, a decent man—he still is, very little like the ste- reotypes evoked within most portraits of his profession—but every morning he woke up and drove his Mercedes to the of- fice. Approaching eighty, he was the picture of health, and as he walked through the halls of a talent agency he'd long ago helped build, people practically stood up and saluted him in his Brioni suit, his Hermès tie. They wanted to be like him, perhaps even more than I ever had. But . . . what spun me away from that life? What made me decide, instead, to be a writer? *Panama.* The answer is always *Panama.* Which was McGuane's own answer, as it happens, to a similar question: a turning away from Hollywood of his own.

◎

Cayo Hueso. The Island of Bones. If you watch the 1975 film adaptation of *92 in the Shade*[13], written and directed by Mc- Guane himself, you can see it, in Margot Kidder striking bal- letic poses against a backdrop of palms and sunlight; Peter Fonda languidly walking his bicycle down sand-strewn streets, past the minarets and cupolas of a building marked "Sociedad Cuba": Key West, pictured exactly as it was. This was the cru- cible in which McGuane the novelist attained his maturity—if

---

13. The film adaptation, which McGuane would direct two years after the novel's publication in 1973, uses the numerical-variant title, *92 in the Shade.*

"maturity" is the right word—and the one to which his surrogate, *Panama*'s Chester Pomeroy, would return after his own brush with stardom. It would be idiotic, of course, to fully conflate McGuane with his creation—more idiotic even than usual, because those punch bags you see in the man's novels, those antic, demi-heroic vessels of defeat, seem fundamentally parahuman, a little expressionist in the way Greek gods and cartoons are—but nevertheless. McGuane, like Pomeroy, had flown a little close to the sun. He'd become something of a myth himself. *Panama* was published in 1978, and by the time I reacquired a copy nearly thirty years later, in the same edition that had lived on my mother's shelves, I knew the story in its broader strokes: how McGuane had come to Hollywood after a severe car crash had left him disenchanted with the monasticism of a writer's life, how after three novels and critical success he strode out of the wreckage and into sheer California chaos. Money. Showbiz. Actresses. Models. Cocaine, naturally. There were three films and two divorces, one quick-burn marriage and an extracurricular affair, wild encounters with various movie stars and a love rhombus, a polycule of sorts that involved McGuane's wife and two of his own leading men, all in the span of about eighteen months. And then the man walked away from the movies (so the story went) back into a novelist's life, a calmer—and lasting—remarriage, and then into sobriety, the life of a rancher and fly fisherman in Montana. At least, that's how I heard it. Hollywood passed through him—and he through it—as cleanly as a bullet, leaving a small but permanent alteration. He survived. That alone ought to have earned him a medal.

◎

Here is the origin story: McGuane was behind the wheel. I've
heard versions where the crash happens in the Keys, but according to the writer himself it was outside Dalhart, Texas:
"I was driving fast, one hundred and forty miles an hour, and
there was this freezing rain on the road that you couldn't see,
so when I pulled out to pass, suddenly life was either over or it
wasn't. I thought it was over. The guy I was driving with said,
'This is it,' and all of a sudden it did appear that it was the end:
there were collisions and fence posts flying and *pieces* of car
body going by my ears."

Picture that: the writer opening up the throttle on the
highway when *boom*—the swerve, the brakes, and then the moment of silence, the eye of the glass-and-metal storm. The car
was a Porsche 911. He'd bought it off the literary success of
Ninety-Two in the Shade, which earned him a 1973 National
Book Award nomination. If he really was traveling 140 miles
an hour, there wouldn't have been anything left of him. But the
crash left him mute for a week, unwilling or unable (according
to the legend) to speak while he was laid up recovering in the
hospital. "Suddenly you're standing in the middle of it with the
chance to choose and it seems like a miracle or a warning that
you've been spared this time but you'd better get your life together." Given that chance—the chance to choose, to pull it all
together—he decided to go to Hollywood. He'd had just about
enough of his solitary life of the mind, the one in which he sat
in his house on Ann Street all day and wrote, while his buddies
were fishing and drinking and carrying on. He'd been living like

a monk now for years. Some say he saw a girl on a bicycle ride past him one morning and then—for a certain type of man in the mid-1970s, a woman's ass could be a burning bush, one of God's own signs and wonders—just followed her down to Duval Street. It wasn't the movies he wanted; it was the life. He had a wife, and he had a baby girl, but fuck it. It was time to get born.

◎

All of this is just a story, the tale of how Tom McGuane, American novelist, became Captain Berserko, Hollywood hell-raiser. Like all such stories, it leaves me skeptical. It's not the facts I would dispute (or even the subject's possibly inflamed recollection of them) but rather the arrangement of them, the way they seem almost to embellish *themselves* into myth. A Porsche—a *silver* Porsche, for God's sake—a freezing road, a National Book Award nomination, a girl on a bicycle, 140 miles per hour. You see what I'm getting at here? Even if these details are true—and why wouldn't they be, more or less?—they tell a story that is probably the wrong story: a story in which success is not just a product of luck or accident or hard work or, as is usually the case, all three, but rather one of fate. It seems an insult to my intelligence, and also to McGuane's own excellence, to read this story in quite the way it proposes to be read, as if a car wreck, that quintessential American crisis, was all you really needed to build yourself a launching pad to fortune and fame.

◎

Then again, maybe it is. The list of figures who've been anni-
hilated in this way—James Dean, Jayne Mansfield, Jackson
Pollock—is certainly—Grace Kelly, Isadora Duncan, Bessie
Smith—formidable (and—Marc Bolan, Roland Barthes, Lady
Di—not inescapably American), but it's a funny thing to fe-
tishize. McGuane's actual decision was probably predicated on
other things (for instance, being offered whatever quantity of
money he had been for the film rights of previous books), and
the car crash was incidental. But let's take this story at face value
for a moment. Or rather, let's let McGuane's metamorphosis
from celebrated, but solitary, American novelist to full-blown
monomaniacal success monkey happen in just this way. One
day, he's sitting in his book-lined study in Key West trying to
ignore the drinking and screwing that's happening outside—
his buddies, Jim Harrison, Russell Chatham, Tom Corcoran,
and Guy de la Valdène all conspiring to lure him down to the
Chart Room or the Snake Pit for a snort and a toot—the next,
he's wearing a brand-new nickname, palling around with said
buddies in a gonzo fraternity they've christened "Club Mandible." He's writing scripts and making handshake directing
deals, banging his leading ladies, and other ladies, in barroom
closets at midnight and movie theaters at high noon, bombed
on psychotropic chemicals as he captains his fishing boat over
shallow waters. It's a better story that way. And, far more the
point, the details remain a little murky, no matter which way
you turn in pursuit of them. The stark biographical facts, and a
goodly number of reckless anecdotes, are engagingly recorded
in William McKeen's book *Mile Marker Zero*, which recounts
the tale of Key West's rise to literary prominence through the

twentieth century, a story that encompasses not just McGuane's but also that of his best friend, the novelist Jim Harrison, alongside Hunter S. Thompson's, Ernest Hemingway's, Tennessee Williams's. But as always, when there are so many storytellers in one room, a sense of embellishment, of one-upmanship, can creep in. It's not that McKeen's book feels inaccurate—not at all: it's scrupulously reported—it's just that I know bullshit when I hear it. Or rather, there's a certain kind of mythmaking, the mythmaking of young, ambitious, boisterous drunks; and also, of older, less ambitious, still boisterous drunks, I've listened to all my life, and which I've learned to recognize as somewhat false even when it's mostly true and vice versa. All these years in Hollywood haven't trained me *only* in the fine art of screwing up. I've learned, also, to follow my nose.

◎

McGuane grew up in Michigan, the town of Grosse Ile. He was a III—his father, Thomas McGuane II, owned an auto parts company—which is always a tough row to hoe. Once they start jabbing picket fences up next to your name, you're dealing with certain weights of expectation. McGuane describes his dad as hardworking, alcoholic, and angry, a guy who'd worked his way up from nothing and might have been ill-disposed toward his son's hedonistic approach to life and education. From both parents, particularly his mother, he inherited a love of language, and of books. He went to Michigan State, as did his future friend Jim Harrison, and after graduating with honors, was accepted to Yale's School of Drama in 1962. There, he wrote his first draft of a novel, *Fire Season*, which would eventually be revised and published under a different title: *The Bushwhacked Piano*. He struck up an epistolary friendship with Harrison, after the latter published a book of poems McGuane admired; he traveled with his wife, Becky (née Portia Crockett, a direct descendant of the legendary American frontiersman), to Ireland and Spain, then came back to the States to accept a Wallace Stegner Fellowship at Stanford. So far, so good, a typical profile for an aspiring novelist, back when "aspiring novelists" were all the things—white, male, middle-class or greater—they tended to be in those days. Still, he made a better one than most: McGuane's sentences were explosive even before he knew quite how to arrange them. Unable to get anywhere with *Fire Season*, he wrote a second book, *The Sporting Club*, and then, thanks to the intercession of Harrison, sold it to Simon & Schuster. When Embassy Pictures came calling and optioned the film rights, McGuane was able to buy himself two things: some land in Montana, and a house in Key West.

◎

How quaint it all sounds now, really. ("Quaint," at least, is one word for it.) McGuane and Harrison, a couple of high-rolling Michigan boys who wanted to drink and fight and fish and fuck, who wanted to write the Great American Novel, back when that idea didn't even seem ridiculous, when *none* of those ideas—the "next Hemingway," the idea of literary stardom being forged out of masculine identity—seemed ridiculous just yet. Hollywood enabled it, is all. *The Sporting Club* is not a great novel, but it is an energetic one, filled with excellent *writing*. Joyce Carol Oates, reviewing the book for the *New York Times*, compared it to Saul Bellow's *Henderson the Rain King*, which seems about right, in terms of its linguistic vitality, and about wrong in other ways. Where *Henderson* is a brilliant—if politically iffy, certainly in contemporary terms—internationalist parable about an American millionaire who lights out blind for Africa in the throes of a spiritual crisis, *The Sporting Club* is narrower and more domestic, the story of two old chums who convene upon a sporting lodge in Michigan's Upper Peninsula and then proceed to shoot each other with dueling pistols, drink themselves silly, blow up a lake, and generally raise such a ruckus that the entire establishment (precisely the types of people you'd expect to belong to a "sporting club" in the UP, in 1968) is aghast. The story has the linguistic zaniness of a Richard Brautigan novel, the expressionist violence of a Tex Avery cartoon, and the whole thing ends in a cloud of insanity and dust. However much I loved it when I was a teenager, the result is . . . faintly exhausting to me now. In fact, had I not recently set out on a mission to reconstruct the mindset and the geography that formed the later, far greater McGuane, a mission that would take me to Key West and back again, I might have marked the book as almost incomprehensible, the kind of slapsticky, ur-psychedelic performance best left on one's adolescent shelves.

◎

Thankfully, I did not. McGuane may be under-celebrated these days, but his subsequent work brings the thunder. As I discovered when I decided to reread everything of the man's I could get my hands on, and then to sit up at night and watch *Rancho Deluxe*, the 1975 western that launched him on his hot streak as a screenwriter, three times running, drinking beer and willing myself into a you-are-there trance at two o'clock in the morning, staring at Elizabeth Ashley and dreaming my way toward a Livingston Saturday night; after that extending the same hypnotized attention to his self-directed adaptation of *92 in the Shade*, a movie that feels a little rudderless, like it might have been directed by someone who didn't entirely know what he was doing behind the camera, but which retains a deliciously languid feel, a sleepy, heat-dazed charm that is like that of Key West itself. McGuane might not *need* our attention—his later books seem less avid for it, and I mean that in the best possible way—but he rewards it amply. The early books do so with their bucking, deranged vitality—a vitality that can be taxing, even at its best, but which can also make other writers seem somnolent by default—and the later ones do it with a creeping, almost Buddhistic calm, a patience and elegance that makes them, also, funnier than the antic, reckless, machine-gun craziness of things like *The Bushwhacked Piano*. *Panama* is the hinge between them. It may have been, for McGuane, an encounter with failure both critical and commercial, but it has a lot to say on that topic, and about what it meant to be a twentieth-century American.

◎

When I was sixteen, not long after my birthday, I bought a car. I was young and stupid, and as for most Angelenos, and as for teenagers everywhere, that automobile represented to me an ideal of freedom: the freedom to come and go as I liked. Finally, I wouldn't have to ask my parents for a ride, to climb into the passenger seat and sit, sullen, while one of them hauled me across town to a friend's house, or to the movies; I wouldn't have to take the bus to school or borrow, as my young friends and I now and again had before we had licenses, a vehicle that had been left in someone's driveway, some parent's Porsche or BMW that stood neglected long enough for us to go on a midnight joyride, white-knuckling our way through Westwood and Beverly Hills before returning the car (well, most of the time) unscathed. We didn't have anywhere to go—the risk of being pulled over for driving underage was itself the point—but these meaningless excursions were exercises in the sort of nihilistic delight that is common to teenage experience. We wanted, I think, to get caught; or else we wanted to get away with something; or else— more than anything—we wanted to have a story to tell.

The car I got, when I was sixteen, was no silver Porsche. It was, to my snotty, haughty, adolescent eye, a real piece of junk: a Toyota Corolla I would loathe for as long as I drove it, and which happened to be all the car I could afford. (I'd scrimped and I'd saved for several years running, storing up all the money I could from summer and after-school jobs, because my father, in a rare burst of parental wisdom, wasn't going to do what a lot of his Hollywood peers did and buy his spoiled child a car. No way.) Irrespective of my feelings, I *lived* in that thing, turning it into a mobile wastebasket of cigarette ash, fast-food wrappers, marijuana smoke, clothing, cassette tapes, books, pencils, undelivered homework assignments, draft pages of a one-act play

I was writing: a landfill, essentially, in miniature. I may have hated that car, but I—also—loved it for all it was worth. Every Angeleno, and every teenager who is privileged enough to lay his or her sweaty paws upon a very personal set of keys, knows exactly what I mean.

One neighborhood over from where I lived in Santa Monica was the Pacific Palisades, a sleepy suburb that just happened to contain most of my friends. Sunset Boulevard splits the Palisades for its final leg, running between Santa Monica Canyon and the Highlands, all the way to where it meets the sea. At night those roads, Sunset and all the residential streets that branch off it, are so quiet you can hear for miles: the whisper of stray cars; the wind and its faint rattle through the palms and eucalyptus; the surf, it even seems, when you close your eyes to listen. The air is heavy and damp. As you pass Will Rogers State Park, on your right, Sunset Boulevard widens and bends, flaring momentarily into five lanes as it executes a hairpin turn. This particular spot, which is popularly known as "Dead Man's Curve"—not the same one popularized by the Jan and Dean song, which is in Beverly Hills—enticed us endlessly. Naturally, it did. Coming back from the beach late at night, our skulls full of weed, beer, MDMA, psychedelic mushrooms—whatever, exactly, we'd ingested on any given evening, us troglodyte teenagers of the Hollywood eighties—we'd pull over sometimes to the side of the road and take the measure of the situation: the streetlights flashing yellow, the sycamores and Italian cypresses stretching up to either side, the Pacific air salty and cold. How tempting it was, under such dubious conditions, to do something stupid, as we stepped out onto the street with noses twitching and eyes ablaze, our catcalls rupturing the silence. One of us would walk out into the middle of the street—we'd take turns doing this—to find the place where the bend was most acute, where both sides of it were visible, and then signal to the rest of us, the drivers, like a switchman. We'd climb back into our cars and then hit the accelerator, each of us in sequence, fantailing across the avenue and using all five lanes, so we could take the curve at maximum speed: eighty, ninety, one hundred miles per hour. *Idiots.* Like teenagers around the world, we thought we were immortal. Oncoming traffic, had there been any, would have liquefied us before we even saw them coming, as we screamed beneath the halogen streetlamps, baying our idiocies to the moon. Instead—we were lucky. Somehow, against the common-sense odds (and against the statistical ones too: there were, according to the *Los Angeles Times*, 232 accidents on the westernmost portion of Sunset Boulevard in 1983, and four fatalities in the Palisades alone), not one of us was hurt. We lived to pursue our feckless and irresponsible dreams another day. Which raises the question—why, then, even mention it? Who cares about the things a bunch of dumb California rich kids did forty years ago, when they didn't even get what they deserved?

◎

Because of the lesson that inheres inside the gamble. Because the evident pointlessness of this pursuit *was* the point, and—the fact that we were a bunch of callow children who lacked even the basic empathy to consider that we were also putting other people in danger notwithstanding—we knew this much: that life is, to some extent, for the wasting, and that its value depends, also to some extent, on its very cheapness. *Panama* puts it this way: "I saw an old drunk fall in front of the laundromat at Elizabeth and Fleming. He cracked his head open and made a terrible pool of blood. . . . I looked down through spinning air filled with frangipani and rock and roll and saw how quickly you are alone, how that can be shown to you in an instant." Later, McGuane writes, "There is a trigger that makes the day begin and all life end and it breaks like a glass rod. It lies at the middle of everything that breathes or dreams. It will bend and break, and when it breaks it is night." The entire book, in some sense, occupies this frail space: the narrator seems to have heaved, shuddering, out of a blackout, and to be trembling for the novel's duration on the verge of another. There are gaps, little seizures, between one sentence and the next, and you can practically feel the synapses frying, whatever drugs the writer had taken—or whatever he simply lived through, in the prefatory years before writing this book—creating short circuits of perception. All this, and still—

Panama is trying to show us something (maybe it is this, too, that confounded reviewers at the time, who might have preferred lucidity and remorse): that we are all sad clowns, hapless figures at the mercy of a cosmos that doesn't want us and in pursuit of a redemption we can't have. Not that I knew any of this, when I was sixteen. But I knew the roulette of driving ninety miles an hour on the wrong side of the road was fun, and, when I came to a complete stop, my hands shaking as I braked to a halt, having swerved back across the yellow line, I felt present. Adrenaline had punched a hole in my high, and as I snapped back to regular life—David Bowie blaring on the car stereo, a cigarette burning between my fingers that could as well have been there for years, the smell of Jack in the Box tacos, that stoner's delight, reeking beneath the streetlight—I was *restored*. Ask any writer. Ask any marathon runner, any surfer, any extreme skier, any war correspondent, any gambling addict: ask anyone who takes any kind of risk, or does anything that might be (really, when you think on it) fundamentally pointless, but still feels, in some way, necessary. *Would you still do it, if you stood to lose nothing?* The answer is obvious. The answer is *No*.

◎

What kinds of risk was I taking? What did I stand to lose, now that my mother was dead and my marriage—signed-and-executed divorce papers arrived at last one afternoon in the mail—was over? Everything, of course: my remaining family, my child, my health. Failure is rarely terminal, not until the very end. But now that the WGA strike had been resolved, and I was able to go back to work in the industry salt mines, I found myself reluctant to do so. I had other ways to earn money, thankfully—teaching, editing, both in person and online; I had the minimal advance from the novel I'd just sold—and my lifestyle was spartan enough that I was able to take a short breather. But I couldn't help but question the very premise of Hollywood itself. I'd never quite felt comfortable screenwriting, never enjoyed it the way I did teaching and other forms of writing, and while the freedom to "enjoy" one's work may be an obscene privilege . . . I wondered whether even succeeding at it would ever bring me pleasure. I'd known people over the years who loved it, who derived from it not just money but delight. And now that I'd outgrown my adolescent snobbishness—at least, I thought I had—I wondered whether this, too, wasn't just another shortcoming: a failure to take joy in opportunities other people, sensibly, would have killed for.

Had McGuane enjoyed it? In that span of about a year and a half from 1974 to 1976 he wrote *Rancho Deluxe*, his gently rolling buddy picture starring Jeff Bridges and Sam Waterston, then *92 in the Shade*, and then a fucked-up, fascinating western called *The Missouri Breaks*. Anyone who's ever worked in Hollywood, any writer especially, will tell you that three movies in eighteen months represents a jackpot, a run of success that, however temporal, is enormous. So, did he like it? As he sat down to work those nights at the Chateau (naturally, his port of call when he came out to LA), his sinuses feeling like they'd been stuffed with ice cubes, was he having fun? Or was he just, as I had been, grubbing for money, trying with all his might to pay the bills?

◎

Let's say it began with a restlessness. The movie of *The Sporting Club* had sucked; *The Bushwhacked Piano* was published that same year, 1971, to wild acclaim, but did that fix anything? Even without that car crash epiphany, I suspect, McGuane would have been on the move. Rave reviews from Saul Bellow and Jonathan Yardley were great, but what's the old saw? "Poetry makes nothing happen"? Almost anyone who's ever published a book knows what this is like. "Congratulations! You must be so proud!" "Uh, yeah." (Says the writer. The one who feels, not

infrequently, like they forgot to put their pants on in public.)
"It's fantastic. Thank you." Even when the attention comes, the
honest writer knows that it's fraudulent, that the book that was
written and the one being discussed are not entirely the same.
And there remains, almost always, that question of money. Not
for everyone: sometimes the skies open up and it just . . . *rains*.
But much of the time—most of it—the deluge is described,
and the writer walks outside hoping to be drenched, only to
feel something more like being shat on by a bird.

Say McGuane felt these things. For all that crazy praise, the
rent remained due. And in his heart, his secret heart, the man
was a screwup too. You can feel it in *The Bushwhacked Piano*,
which tells the story of a young man's hungry pursuit of a woman
from an establishment family and their shared flight, first from
her parents and then from a man named C. J. Clovis, a Melvillean con artist intent on building a high-rise tower for bats. The
narrative careens from Michigan to Montana to Key West—it's
not a million miles from *Lolita*, in this respect, a bent catalogue
of the American highway, buzzing with motel signs and dense
with humidity—but it's the language, the *language* that makes
it live. The book earned McGuane innumerable comparisons to
Hemingway, and I get it—the locations (Michigan, Key West),
and the preoccupations (huntin', fishin'), are similar—but the
writing is nothing like Hem's.

*A dark brown elevator cable suspending a conventload of
aging nuns in front of the fortieth-floor office of a Knights
of Columbus dentist, popped one more microscopic strand in
a thousand-foot shaft of blue dust light.*

Certain soldiers took up their positions.

An engineer in Menlo Park pondered possible mailboxes of the future. . . .

Millions of sonorous, invisible piano wires caused the country to swing in stately, dolorous circles around the telephone booth. Payne felt it hum through the worn black handle of the folding door. The directory, with its thousandfold exponential referents, tapped with the secret life of the nation.

Does this sound like Ernest Hemingway to you? Maybe it sounds a bit like period zaniness, like the slapstick absurdities of the sixties and seventies writ a little too loudly and a little too large, but I don't think so. Those "thousandfold exponential referents" (to say nothing of the "secret life of the nation") are McGuane's real concern, always: the way "reality" is forever constructed of disjunctive particles, particles that are neither quite connected nor disconnected, and how we move among them like mountain goats leaping from one rock to another. The passage might simply be describing a man making a call from a phone booth, but it's also an act of ESP.

◎

That's where McGuane was at, when he decided to "go Hollywood." *Ninety-Two in the Shade* would offer more of the same— critically lauded, with that National Book Award nomination, even—but the itch persisted, a hunger that went even beyond money, and so he went for it. There's a sense in which "go Hollywood" is always a misnomer. A certain sort of ego trip requires no relocation to achieve. But McGuane would never leave Key West. In a 1985 interview, McGuane was to claim that he'd barely spent time in Los Angeles at all. "According to reviewers, I've spent the last ten years of my life in Hollywood, but to tell the truth I have logged less than thirty days in Los Angeles. Total." That estimation seems a little light, knowing what I know about the film-development process—the meetings, the studio sit downs, the number of times he would have needed to appear—but the point stands. The three films that were made in 1975 and 1976 were shot entirely in Florida and Montana. He didn't even have to leave home to "go Hollywood."[14] Hollywood, it turned out? Was really just a state of mind.

◎

Unlike my mother, and unlike myself, McGuane was built for it. He'd studied playwriting at Yale, and never saw screenwriting as any real down-market disaster. In 1988 he would tell Jean W. Ross that "I don't think screenwriting ever destroyed the talent of anybody who was meant to survive." Which flies in the face of a long-standing mythology: Hollywood as destroyer of artistic talent, corrupter of souls. My mother saw it that way—all her life she wished she'd been writing fiction, spent portions of her time writing stories she never quite felt were finished—but did I? I found myself thinking of my last visit with her, of a drive we'd taken one afternoon in which we'd passed out of Edgewood and

---

14. Nor was it even McGuane's first rodeo, quite. In 1971, he'd written an adaptation of *The Bushwhacked Piano* for a relatively unknown actor—one Robert De Niro—but the script was never produced.

down a winding hill that let us out to what seemed a lattice of orchards, grass, and damp trees shimmering in the cloud-filtered light, a break in the rain that made everything suddenly silvery and radiant. Against that backdrop especially it was difficult to square the image of my mother—stooped, shrunken, and shy in her amber-tinted glasses and threadbare sweats—with the woman I grew up with, often raucous and funny and endlessly elegant, even if she was just walking around in the clothes she'd worn to a dance class, leotard and pink tights, with a sweater knotted carelessly around her shoulders. In midlife, she'd looked like her peers: a more robust, blond Joan Didion, less birdlike but similarly sleek; a Carole Eastman built largely of apologies instead of opinions. Even beyond the ravages of age, alcohol, and illness, something had gone missing. Was it Hollywood that had done this to her, that had welded her into a sculpture of misgivings, a sort of remnant, like a Giacometti rendering of a stork? Looking around that orchard, I saw the possibility of another life, the way the confinements of ambition might blind us, too, to the real.

For McGuane, though, Hollywood included the real. He might rather have been writing novels—over and over, he told interviewers that fiction was his preference, that it was what he was built to do—but screenwriting was a viable means to an end. It was better than flipping burgers, better than selling auto parts, better, much better, than teaching in the academy, which for Mc-Guane and his buddy Jim Harrison seemed disconnected from what they saw as the genuine. And while that binary, now, seems false—*Hollywood* is where you'd go looking for the "genuine," besides?—screenwriting wasn't anything that could destroy him.

Indeed, he didn't even find it a departure from anything he'd already done. "I don't feel the profound difference [between a book and a movie]," he told an interviewer, later. "Ten or twelve years of moving back and forth between the two has perhaps evaporated the boundaries for me. They seem to be directed on very similar missions." Fair enough. But what was that mission, exactly?

◎

What do people want from the movies? What do they want from their lives? In our secret hearts, I think—perhaps this is not true for everyone, but I'll assume to speak for a plurality here—we want to fuck things up. We do not seek structural perfection. Even when we have the things we want (tell me you've never felt this, not even once), we gamble with them, start playing with the lighter or the bottle or the handgun on the table. *This thing isn't loaded, right? It is? Yes? No?* We don't want to destroy ourselves—or, God forbid, anyone we love—but we don't quite *not* want to, either. This isn't just a question of privilege: it happens all along the socioeconomic spectrum. The risk, the threat, the muddle, the crisis: *this* is the thing we're looking for, if only because it shakes us out of our torpor. The movies show this to us, again and again, with their kidnappings and bomb-strapped buildings, domestic calamities and spiraling planes. There is a moment at the center of every disaster—maybe it is the one in which the addict finds rock bottom, or the one McGuane describes: the car, fishtailing on the highway, auto parts and fence posts whistling past his ears—when it all comes clear, and when you remember what the true stakes are. It passes in a chronological flash, ends in collapse or in the sudden apprehension of an incredibly good fortune. And yet this moment? This moment is the slowest moment of your life.

◎

In 1974, the producer Elliott Kastner came knocking. He optioned the film rights to *Ninety-Two in the Shade*. Kastner was a heavy hitter—he'd recently produced the Altman adaptation of *The Long Goodbye* (the same adaptation he had, once upon a time, approached Eleanor Perry to tackle)—and if there was anything he understood, it was writers. He knew McGuane was mercurial, and that he might have needs. When Kastner discovered it might take a moment to get *Ninety-Two in the Shade* made, as movies about warring fishing guides in the Florida Keys weren't an automatic sell,[15] he hired McGuane to write another screenplay on the quick. The result was *Rancho Deluxe*.

Rancho Deluxe may have been a laid-back affair—the story of two cattle rustlers who run afoul of a wealthy rancher, the movie never quite gets going—but it was on this set the long-married McGuane had his first volcanic encounter with Elizabeth Ashley. Dark-haired and sultry, with a voice that sounded like it had been aged at the bottom of a barrel, the actress had just signed on to do *Cat on a Hot Tin Roof* at the American Shakespeare Festival, the break of a lifetime after kicking around for the past decade doing small parts on television. Still, when her agent sent

---

15. Albeit, McGuane and his pals had already made one. In 1973, the novelist, Harrison, Guy de la Valdène, and Dink Bruce, Club Mandible members all, had grabbed their cameras and headed out on the water to shoot a documentary called *Tarpon*.

her the script for *Rancho Deluxe*, Ashley, a fan of McGuane's novels, accepted. She'd fit it into her break before rehearsals began on *Cat*. In her 1978 memoir, Ashley describes arriving in Livingston in time to wander into a storefront where director Frank Perry was showing some dailies.

> *I looked around and spotted this wild man in cowboy boots and jeans talking intensely to a young girl over in the corner. He was well over six feet tall with thick black hair hanging all the way down to his waist. There was something hard and mean about his face, but he also had huge, round, hound-dog eyes and a lovely warm grin. He wasn't a pretty man . . . but he definitely got my visceral attention.*

Ah, lust. McGuane may have been married—happily so—but this "visceral attention" ran both ways. There he was on the set of his first movie, feeling, like most every writer under such conditions, like king of the world, watching the machinery get ready to make those words *real*, crunching through the Livingston dust, elbowing his way through the gaffers and grips when—*boom*, there she was! His star, making eyes at him like that, even while he'd stopped to chat up someone else. ("Don't go away, honey, I'll be right back.") McGuane was smitten too. Still, the actress wasn't gonna just give it up. When Ashley met Becky McGuane the next day ("funny and warm and bright . . . almost enough to make me forget about her husband"), she was determined to keep her hands off the man and vice versa. A resolution that was put to the test immediately when McGuane dragged her out of a bar a day later and hit her with the full force of his eloquence: "Let's fuck."

Picture this too, the two of them standing outside some Montana watering hole at twilight. It's 1974, and sex is everywhere. Why be nice about this stuff, now that the sixties have loosened the screws around such old-fashioned ideas as monogamy?

"I don't fuck married men," Ashley said. "I adore your wife."

"So do I." He flashed that hound-dog smile again. *Goddamn.* "But she doesn't mind. I screw everybody. Becky and I have an arrangement. Besides." He mopped his brow now, casually, just for effect. "Becky's crazy about you. As am I. It's fine."

"Bullshit."

Gnats fluttering in the twilight, in that pink mountain air. McGuane didn't have to say a word, and he surely knew it. When Ashley saw Becky the next day, she asked if she knew her husband was catting around, hitting on available women.

"Oh, we've been married a long time," Becky said. "We don't have those kinds of jealousies, honey. I approve."

Game on, then. *Game on.*

All of that, at least, according to Ashley. There are reasons to question the precision of her account (as there would be to question anyone's postmortem of a relationship, particularly in a performer's memoir that might bend a little toward the dramatic). But whether or not it happened in quite such blunt terms, McGuane wasn't the first Hollywood hotshot to have it off with an actress on the set of his own movie, and there was no predation involved, just good old-fashioned open-practice non-monogamy. So while Ashley rhapsodizes, in *Actress*, about sex with McGuane as "blood sport," about boning in dressing rooms and restaurant bathrooms and in the middle of a movie theater during a matinee showing of *The Sting*, I can't help but think—if it were 1974, and I was a happily open-married guy who looked like Tom McGuane, stoned out of my mind and free to hedonize to my heart's lascivious content—wouldn't I have done the same? McGuane was living high, but he had every right to. He was going to *direct* his next movie. Not only was he gonna have his cake and eat it; he was going to tell everyone else how to eat theirs as well.

For a moment, though, there was doubt. *92 in the Shade* was ready to go, but Kastner had initially wanted Robert Altman, whose vinegary, countercultural snottiness would've been perfect, to direct the film. When he, and then Nicolas Roeg, proved unavailable, the job had fallen to McGuane.

"Any asshole can direct a movie," the producer said, when McGuane hesitated. You can picture it, can't you? The writer and his producer out to lunch at Louie's Backyard, let's say, when the moment of sobriety, the pinprick of self-doubt, arrived.

"You think?" McGuane stared out across the water. It was hard enough to write a novel, but here you were supposed to stay on top of your own shit and everyone else's too? You were on the clock? "I mean, why not, right? Why not?"

"Look." Kastner leaned forward. "We have a start date, but no director. If we don't have a director in two weeks, it's back to the drawing board."

McGuane nodded. "So that's it? If I don't direct the picture, it doesn't go at all?"

"Bingo."

Ah. Whatever doubts McGuane had evaporated under the weight of necessity. He had a family to support, after all. Full steam ahead.

◎

Ninety-Two in the Shade is a great book. There are those, and I wouldn't argue against them, who say *this* is McGuane's early masterpiece. The story, like that of its two predecessors, is one of screwups at war, in this case a man named Tom Skelton (played, in the film, by Peter Fonda), who comes home to Key West to confront his mysteriously bedridden father (nothing's really wrong with him except a sort of . . . Southern neurasthenia), his imperious grandfather, and a fellow named Nichol Dance (Warren Oates, in the adaptation), a local fishing guide who resents Skelton's decision to take up the same profession. Mayhem ensues: Skelton blows up Dance's boat, Dance comes after Skelton with a pistol, but Skelton remains stoically—enigmatically—devoted to his mission. Is it worth getting killed over, the freedom to guide a few assholes from Connecticut over the water in search of game fish? Evidently, to Skelton, it is.

The summary is as casually antic as the book's two predecessors, only *Ninety-Two in the Shade* isn't about boating guides at all; it's about American malfeasance, American sociopathy, about the blend of incompetence, quietism, adventurism, and nativist violence that had led us into Vietnam (not for nothing does Skelton live in the abandoned fuselage of a crashed navy plane) and the subsequent morass of the 1970s. Read the novel now and swoon over its language ("Duval Street, crowded and Latin all day, now seems filled with space and breeze, serenely modified by a taxicab spinning along in golden light"), realizing there's a reason people—like me, or like Elizabeth Ashley—went ape over the guy. But how do you turn all that into a movie? Particularly when you've never directed one before, and there just might, let's say, be a few further complications on the horizon?

To wit: Warren Oates. You've probably seen him as Lyle Gorch in *The Wild Bunch*, or Willett Gashade in *The Shooting*; you've seen him in *Two-Lane Blacktop* and *Bring Me the Head of Alfredo Garcia*, or in Terrence Malick's *Badlands*; if nothing else you've seen him—please tell me you have—as the bullying Sergeant Hulka in *Stripes*. Oates is delicious in everything: putty-jawed, craggy, with a face so radically expressive a simple raised eyebrow seems to contain a novel's worth of information. In the mid-1970s he, too, was having his moment. And, like his good friend Peter Fonda, Oates was also a part-time resident of Montana: Tom and Becky McGuane's neighbor. It was a hot time to be there. That "Livingston Saturday night" Jimmy Buffett sang about in *Rancho Deluxe* attracted a lot of gonzo cowboys and Hollywood hustlers chasing that High Plains mystique, that mountain poontang and alpine—*wink*—snow. So, while McGuane was jetting off to Connecticut to slip it to Elizabeth Ashley, as their relationship remained hot and heavy, Oates and Becky McGuane had become . . . friendly, so to speak. They were spending a lot of time together. They were—

Fuck it. All of a sudden, they were in love too. (Can you blame her? Not even a little bit: Oates was a charismatic guy, and a decent one, by most accounts.) But when they broke the news to McGuane, he didn't take it well. A little something on the side was one thing, but—was he ready to lose his family? While he was out in Connecticut with Ashley and Becky was visiting Oates in LA, McGuane got the actor on the phone and listened to Oates's proposal that they shuffle the deck, real civilized like.

"Now, come on, Tom, we're all adults here." (This, too, according to Ashley. And while there are reasons to wonder if this was precisely how it went down, you can imagine it: McGuane prowling the room with the telephone in his hand, its long cord snaking along while Ashley looked on—"For God's sake, stop"—and Oates spoke with a calm voice on the other end.) "Shouldn't we be with the people who make us happy? *All* of us?"

"Goddamnit, put Becky on."

"Tom, come on. Man to man. Let's do the sane thing. The grown-up thing."

"Put Becky on."

No soap. Becky felt guilty, McGuane was raveningly jealous—for all the fun he'd been having with Ashley (jeez, just a few weeks ago they'd staggered around Midtown high on psilocybin, wandered into the Russian Tea Room bombed out of their gourds), he just couldn't deal.

"GODDAMNIT!"

No one budged. But in any case, McGuane still had a movie to direct. He couldn't just run around making scenes because his wife had decided to cuckold him back. Peter Fonda had been agitating to play the lead in *92 in the Shade* for a while, and after he'd beat out the other suitors for the role (among them Oates, who'd wanted it so badly he initially came calling on the *Rancho Deluxe* set to hustle for it), he proposed his best friend for the part of the antagonist, Nichol Dance, an actor with whom he could work better than any other—Oates again. It must've been an interesting conversation.

"Jesus, Peter. Do you not know this? The guy's screwing my wife!"

"Yeah, but"—the actor would have taken this matter in stride. Born into a Hollywood family, the son of a star himself who'd been deep in a hedonistic rock 'n' roll scene for almost a decade, he wasn't gonna let a little foursome freak him out. "So what? It could put a charge into the movie."

What the hell. Art was art and life was life, right? Besides, Ashley was committed to be in the picture too. Why not bring everybody onto the set and just—see what happens? *Ah, the 1970s.*

There was one more part in the movie, a role for an actress that happened also to be coveted around town. One woman came in to audition, spread her legs, and just started masturbating in front of McGuane, apparently hoping this would snag her the part. Fortunately, McGuane took the more conventional approach: he went with the one who'd read best. It may have helped that this person, a relative unknown at the time, was also a fan of the novelist. When she left her reading, to bolster her case, she left a message with McGuane's secretary, written on a cocktail napkin. "I think you're a genius. I love your book. . . . Call me."

Her name was Margot Kidder.

◎

92 in the Shade started shooting at the end of 1974. From the vantage of nearly half a century, it becomes difficult to assess the blame for—or even to separate the vectors of—an accumulated chaos, but the shoot itself was a mess. Whether it was Fonda's drug problem, as McGuane later claimed, or the fledgling director's decision (maybe not the wisest, in retrospect) to start sleeping with Kidder even before his relationship with Ashley had quite come to an end,[16] McGuane was left to make—as he put it to me himself, later on—"chicken salad of chicken shit." Oates was good, but Fonda's performance was unfathomably wooden, and apparently the best parts of the movie, scenes between William Hickey and Sylvia Miles (who played Skelton's grandfather and the grandfather's mistress, respectively) were left on the cutting room floor. It's not an atypical story: the man who appears to sit in the catbird seat—the director—has the film taken away and massacred by an unhappy producer. But it leads me to wonder whether success, that dream of ultimate license and irresponsibility, doesn't ultimately fold in upon itself. One winds up indentured to forces one hasn't anticipated; one winds up, instead, the very opposite of free.

One night, when I was ten years old, my father brought a record album home from the office. He often did that with things he thought I'd like, brand-new releases, and looking it up, I see it would have been two years to the day after *92 in the Shade* was released. I—being as pig-ignorant of music at that

---

16. Ashley wasn't thrilled. During a fight, she broke a lamp over McGuane's head, a detail that would find its way into *Panama*.

age as I was still about cinema—glanced at the dopey-looking nerd on the album cover, with his ridiculous grin hovering under the semi-promising title of *Lust for Life*, squinted at the credits (who on earth was "David Bowie"? What the hell was an "Iggy Pop"?), and binned it, wondering why my dad didn't just bring home a Kiss record like a cool person would have. I didn't get around to listening until a couple of years later, when I retrieved the album from a cabinet in my parents' den, and when I did, one song stood out to me especially. "Here comes success," the lyrics go. "Here comes my car . . . here comes my Chinese rug." The fruits of that success stack up, until eventually the singer decides he's going to "go out in the street and do anything," as if this, really, is the point. As if the whole entelechy of success is this nebulous freedom to do—"anything." Once you have that—and God knows, there's not a prison on earth like a limitless, but undefined, freedom—but once you have it, what then? What exactly is the point?

In his beguilingly shaggy 1972 novel *All My Friends Are Going to Be Strangers*, Larry McMurtry describes the moment at which his hero is struck by lightning, in the form of a telegram from Random House offering a fat advance for his novel.

> *Things were swirling. I never expect most of my dreams to come true, even though I keep dreaming them, and when one does come true I don't know how to handle the feelings I have. I felt very odd—I was glad and excited and curious and a lot of things. I became instantly giddy, and within the giddiness was a kind of fear. I had got one dream but something felt wrong in the pit of my stomach. Maybe some*

other dream was being taken away from me forever. Maybe
I wanted that one more. I didn't know, and at the same
time I felt dizzy with relief.

In the novel *Turnaround*, one of several the perennially underrated writer Don Carpenter drew out of his own experiences
in Hollywood, a long-aspiring screenwriter who has finally—
finally!—made good in Tinseltown sits down in his newfound
wealth to write a novel, that thing he has always most wanted
to do.

Jerry now knew with terrible contempt for himself that he
would never write any books. Something immense within
him died. He looked at the blank piece of paper in his type-
writer and saw his fate written there. The fate of nothing. To
have been nothing, and to be nothing. And nothing to become.

Both of these men, poor bastards, are learning the same thing,
the one at the beginning of his success and the other who has
lately been used up by it. Each has been robbed, not just of his
dream but of a capacity to dream at all: of that freedom that
comes from wanting something desperately and not being able
to have it. The loss of this freedom has crippled more people,
possibly, than failure; it is—for all our secret yearnings toward a
limitless plenty—more painful than anyone who has never experienced it would likely dare to imagine. McGuane's Key West
neighbor, Tennessee Williams—we can see him huddled next to
McGuane in the photos of the *92 in the Shade* wrap party—knew
it when he wrote an essay called "The Catastrophe of Success,"

which describes how the rapturous reception of *The Glass Me-
nagerie* nearly killed him. In this essay, which should be required
reading for every aspiring American, Williams notes that people
are fundamentally built for conflict. Without it, "man is a sword
cutting daisies," he writes. "Not privation but luxury is the wolf
at the door, and . . . the fangs of this wolf are all the little vanities and conceits and laxities that Success is heir to." Williams
knew—he *knew*—exactly what the costs were (as did the other
man who flanks McGuane in those photos from the wrap party,
Truman Capote, although he surely failed to reckon with them
in the end), and he had known for decades. Did he whisper as
much to McGuane at the wrap party? Did he lean over to a man
who, grooving on a heady cocktail of drugs, starlets, and money
that seemed unlikely to run out anytime soon, might not have
listened anyway, and tell him, "Beware"? Surely not. Everyone

in the photograph looks quite contentedly bombed, clutching their rum drinks and grinning uncontrollably in their ascots and guayaberas. If anything, Williams's rapturous, beatific look in these photos is that of a disco king. Any second now, as soon as the flash stops popping, he'll scuttle for the restroom and chop himself another line.

◎

After *92 in the Shade* wrapped, McGuane flew to London with Kidder, who happened to be pregnant with his child. He and Becky filed for divorce, and—how's this for an O. Henry twist?—as soon as Oates and Fonda had split for Texas to make another movie together, it was *Fonda* who called up Becky and, with his friend Oates's blessing, begged her to marry him. He'd been in love with her all along! The circus rolled on (and if you're feeling cynical about love among the stars at this point, it's worth noting that Fonda and Becky would remain married for the next three and a half decades). But somewhere in the thick of all this, McGuane hung up Captain Berserko's cape and decided to get back to work. His real work. He took Kidder back to Montana with him, they had their baby, and he got cracking on the book he would come to feel was his best to that point: *Panama*.

Maybe a certain public resentment had crept in even before that book was published. Hollywood success, by which I mean money, but also mean *fun*, is a problem for folks, and I don't mean just for those who experience it. Somewhere in the puritanical American soul—even in my own, though I was raised to some extent by high-flying maniacs whose taste for ruin was matched

by one for excess—there lives a hatred of joy. God forbid anyone delight in their triumph, which may be why we've tended
to valorize our glummest and our angriest plutocrats, why we
elect them president, even, but can't stand the ones who love to
boogie. You think I'm joking? Check those black turtlenecks,
those drab Protestant uniforms worn by everyone from Henry
Ford to Mark Zuckerberg—another day, another fucking gray
T-shirt—and back again. Why do these people insist on hiding
their fortunes under a bushel? It isn't just because they're getting
away with something. (Although that too. Surely they feel, as we
do, the looming presence of the guillotine.) It's because we feel
it's vulgar, because *pleasure*—not money—is verboten.

McGuane put it this way, speaking with Renaud Mon-
fourny in 1990: "When I was in Hollywood, I took quite a lot
of drugs, I drank an unnecessary amount . . . It's this attitude
that creates an atmosphere of legend, because people think
you're going to die, *and that excites them.*" (Italics mine.) "But
if you don't die, that hurts the legend." An innocuous-seeming
remark, maybe, but we all know Americans might prefer leg-
ends to actual human beings—it's half the reason Hollywood
exists—and as for the sadism of hoping someone (anyone, let
alone one of our best living novelists) dies, well, consider the
piety with which we serenade our dead celebrities and wonder
whether mixed in with all that genuine feeling there mightn't
exist, somewhere, at least a tiny whiff of schadenfreude.

None of this is to say McGuane didn't act like an asshole. I
suspect he did, and showing up in lasciviously titled *People* magazine articles that talked about his lack of interest in marrying
the pregnant Kidder and how he was "practically wed to his

handcrafted rifles and fly rods anyway" might not have entirely stopped him from looking like one too. But *Panama* remains a great book, about a crisis undergone by someone who—like McGuane—has indulged every excess. Who knows to a T "the vanities and conceits and laxities that Success is heir to."

◎

Why bother, really, wallowing in every crappy review *Panama* got? John Leonard, in the *New York Times*, claimed the book was "[not] written; it is hallucinated," while Jonathan Yardley—the same man who'd fairly soiled himself with enthusiasm over the novel's three predecessors—was to call it "drearily self-indulgent . . . an exploitation of the author's new notoriety." Seemingly without exception, the reviews took umbrage not at McGuane's writing but at his choice of subject. To write about Chester Pomeroy, a faded rock star in the theatrical Kiss/Alice Cooper mode, and about the protracted symphony of regret that accompanies his retreat to Key West, seemed indulgent to many, an exercise in self-pity from a writer who ought to have known better. Maybe they're half-right—I suspect the book would be just as unfashionable now as it was then, as it could easily, and lazily, be misconstrued as a very case study in privilege. But McGuane's real concern isn't the travails of poor Chester Pomeroy at all; it is, rather, the conditions that have created them: the sizzling grid of American celebrity, which (surely no twenty-first-century denizen can doubt it) has come by now to ensnare us all.

◎

The first thing Chet Pomeroy does after we meet him—besides drag his coke-starved carcass up the streets of Key West for a quick visit with his stepmother—is nail his hand to a woman's door with the butt of a handgun. That this quixotic act of self-crucifixion is treated *lightly*, not as Grand Guignol but as minor mishap, is the point. Pomeroy's such a fuckup he doesn't even need an antagonist. All he has are ghosts. Of his father (who he claims is dead, despite having spoken with him recently on the phone), of Jesse James (upon whom he is fixated, believing he is alive), above all of his great love, Catherine Clay. Who happens to be right in front of him, but whom he can hardly *see*, in the blizzard of self-inflicted misery through which he staggers. Such blindness is in fact the point (one of many missed by the book's contemporaneous reviewers), but it's also, weirdly, *Panama*'s charm. Which is more elastic than that of the previous novels: less frantic, more profound. Because while *Panama* is indeed a comedy (all McGuane's books are: the tradition not of Hemingway but of Cervantes and Sterne), it's one that happens to be filled, too, with Melvillean howls of despair. "Even in the sun, all the world seems to contain a hollow wailing moan, long and drawn out, as though purgatory understood the meaning of not knowing what was next." If all the book had to offer was a wan sense of amusement coupled with grief, maybe it *would* be an exercise in self-pity. But it isn't, because McGuane—like Samuel Beckett—falls so deep into that horror he can't help but find it funny himself. And because he does so, too, within a uniquely American vernacular of both language and—this is celebrity we're dealing with here, our nation's greatest export—experience.

I was a simple occupant, the man the anonymous senders of junk mail have in mind when they buy the stamp. And it was only my ability to see something in the accretion of toothpaste on unscrubbed counters, the signaling stain from plugged eaves troughs, the smell of myself in fear, as unattractive and profound as the funk of unloaded clothes hampers, that propelled me into the public nerve net with the ability to terrify with a smile.

Man, that's weird. It might even be one-quarter nonsense (McGuane would later note that "the almost epidemic spread of cocaine throughout American society" was the fact most likely to make the book seem intelligible—indeed, "scriptural"—to a certain readership), but one can't miss the fact he's talking about the forces that create a famous person, rather than the travails of one. And one can't miss the fact he's describing a spiritual trauma, and that he must have known firsthand what it meant to be "the man the anonymous senders of junk mail have in mind." Because *Panama* was, by McGuane's own admission, the most directly autobiographical of his novels, the only one of those first four written in first person, and even from its opening lines ("This is the first time I've worked without a net. I want to tell the truth") a lapel-grabbing exercise in naked, if fictionalized, confession. It doesn't take a psychiatrist, or even the casual forensics of an armchair biographer, to see—and to feel—the link between Chester Pomeroy and his existentially tired, morally frayed (but unbroken) creator. "The occupational hazard of making a spectacle of yourself, over the long haul, is that at some point you buy a ticket too," McGuane writes, and one can be confident he'd lived that experience, both halves of it, all the way to the bone.[17]

◎

I wanted so badly to be him. Who am I kidding? I'd like to be him still. But not the man with the gold watch, the one McGuane almost surely isn't, and probably never was, but the one he is now, the man who passed through the eye of the needle and survived with his talent intact. *Success.* It may be a hollow bargain, but what's the other bargain, really? That you kneel at the foot of the mountain, waiting for permission to climb. Better, if you can survive it, to be the decisive man, the Thalberg man, who blows a tunnel through the hill just by thinking about it, who chops it down with the edge of his hand.

Not long ago, I went to Key West. I wanted to walk the same streets McGuane, and Chester Pomeroy, had walked; to stagger up Duval and along Simonton, have a drink at the Chart Room and a meal at Louie's Backyard. Beneath the tourist sheen that has accumulated along Duval Street—a smell of patchouli, windows full of lewd and stupid T-shirts, the same junk that encrusts Hollywood Boulevard—one can still feel something in the humid air, in the roosters who strut recklessly along the sidewalks, the paper airplane–sized bug that grazed my jaw as I stumbled back alone from one of these joints where the boys, Club Mandible, had assembled forty-odd years ago:

---

17. If he'd merely written about it, without necessarily living it—ahem, Don DeLillo, *Great Jones Street*—might the book have been better received? I suspect so.

some energy, some feeling of weird chance, a gravity that allowed all that crazy residue to collect *here*, at the southernmost
tip of America. The people are mostly gone now, even if the
places still remain: McGuane is gone, Harrison is dead. In Joy
Williams's guidebook to the Florida Keys, she describes Key
West as "a glittering, balmy, perhaps not terribly legitimate rock
beneath vast sea skies."[18] Perhaps it is less "legitimate" now than
ever. Now that one of its most vivid chroniclers has moved on.

These days, McGuane fishes and ranches and writes in Montana. Like many a landmark, he seems to hide in plain sight. Most
writers I have canvassed on the subject have read him . . . a little.
"*Panama*," they'll say. "It's been twenty years since I read that!" Or
"*The Bushwhacked Piano*. I used to love that book." It is, of course,
a product of luck for any writer to be remembered at all, just as it
may be an inevitable catastrophe for the one or two in a generation who become a Hemingway or Capote to find the weight of
public reputation so great there is nothing to do but eventually be
destroyed by it. Yet there is a sense in which McGuane's perdur-
ing, low-lying but steady presence in the landscape feels not just
optimal but intentional, as if he might have figured out what "success" actually means. In a sharp article published in the *Believer* in
2007, Mark Kamine writes about McGuane's "late style," how—
after *Panama*—he had kicked a certain antic quality to the curb
and had begun to produce writing of still-greater heft, in sentences that were plainer and more full of feeling and, at the same
time, still funnier, filled with a detached, rolling delight. "The

---

18. Williams also describes the fabled early twentieth-century construction
of a "bat tower" in the Sugarloaf Key, a fact that makes C. J. Clovis's pursuit
of the same in *The Bushwhacked Piano* seem a little less fantastical.

language has become more direct, the terrain more realistic," Ka-mine writes, but the work continues to carve out new shapes. "We have in his case something other than more of the same to look forward to." I wouldn't disagree. A novel like *The Cadence of Grass* or stories like those collected in the recent *Cloudbursts* all show as much. Once upon a time, the man wanted to climb the mountain. Like Fitzgerald, and like a million other writers before him, he thought Hollywood was a thing he could conquer, another dumb general—God, I've been one too—imagining that with enough forces behind him, creative or otherwise, he could blow a hole so wide he could do whatever he wanted. He could eradicate the distance between his septum and his skull. McGuane, flying down a Texas highway at some hundred-whatever miles per hour, would have felt invulnerable as he stepped on that accelerator pedal, as the car's engine revved and he reached over—wouldn't you?—to dial up the Rolling Stones on the stereo. Let's stay with him a moment: the gear stick vibrating, the air beaded with mist, a little winter sun cutting through, spraying prisms onto the pavement. In a moment that other car will come from nowhere, cutting him off—the sudden brake, the unsuccessful swerve—but just now he upshifts and accelerates. The Rita Blanca National Grassland spreads around him; somewhere in the distance, before or behind him, are the peaks: Guadalupe, El Capitan. He would've seen those snow-frosted spires and thought what so many of us do: *I'm going to climb that. I'm going to defeat it.* The obverse would eventually be true, because it always is, and yet for someone who knew, from sea to shining sea, *exactly* what the trouble is with our republic—he found out the hard way—he did the astounding in lieu of the impossible. He became the mountain, instead.

V

quasimodo
plays herself

tuesday weld

What business Quigg had being on that little bridge remains
a mystery. . . . Depending on whom you talk to, Quigg was
killed either because a nor'easter blew him off, or else by
his own careless hand. The matter was never resolved.

—D, "Among the Ended Causes" (unpublished novel)

MY FRIEND D left me a message. I hadn't spoken to him for more than a decade, but I checked my phone one afternoon and there it was: his voice, high-strung and excitable, dropping one word in a strangulated whisper.

"*Ffffreak!*"

Click. That was it, but it was all I needed. It meant D had quit drinking again, that inside the manic, beautiful cartoon of his being he'd found electricity and needed to share it. I called him back, but we found ourselves trading messages for a few weeks ("Freak daddy! It's me. I'm stuck in traffic, on my way to pick up the kid. Call me") before we finally connected. In the end, it would be worth it, although I worried for a while whether to speak would be to encourage him. His equilibrium had always been volatile. Even now, after another ten years have passed since I last heard it, his voice sizzles through my head—musical, exuberant, with a born raconteur's flair for the exaggerated pause—telling ribald and ridiculous stories about Orson Welles and Eudora Welty, Marianne Moore and Billy Collins, stories that didn't even have to be accurate to be true, somehow. There was no tracking D's manic enthusiasms, no way of knowing what song or film or novel he'd want to talk about at two in the morning, or four in the afternoon. But even after we spoke, I was concerned about him. He seemed lonely and bereft, and he was recently divorced, with a young daughter, just like I was. Then again, all the more reason to lean back into our friendship. God knows I needed someone to talk to.

I was living now where I had been since shortly before my mother died: the bottom floor of a duplex on Sixth Street, about a mile and a half south of 1448 on a line. A wide and quiet street, lined with Spanish-style houses and sycamore trees: a green oasis, far from the sign-cluttered chaos of the Strip. Here I tried, at last, to get my head straight: I cut back on my drinking and what had been, in the aftermath of my separation, an impulse to promiscuity, encounters that had left me—and, no doubt, other people—feeling empty. I woke up early and went running, took long walks around the neighborhood in the AM fog. A young woman in a knit cap strolled by me on the sidewalk daily, flanked by a pair of enormous Saint Bernards, her eyes wide like a Greek statue's. Watching her vanish back into the mist—silent, inexplicable—I felt half-apparitional myself, indentured still to my mother's ghost. Where had she gone? Where had I? On Sundays and Wednesdays my daughter slept over, and on the following mornings I would take her to school, holding her small, soft hand like an astronaut's tether as we padded across the playground. What did my feelings of "failure" even matter, as I listened to the rattle of kindergarten laughter, watched V trail away into her classroom, the reverse-Orphic joy, the ecstatic horror of seeing the person you love most disappear into the—future?

Hearing from D had shaken something loose in me. We'd met a decade and a half earlier, when we were both living in New York City and we both—I more insistently than he, I suppose—wanted to be writers. We were twenty-five, twenty-six: that age when wishful thinking bends a little harder into the need to execute your ambition. We'd hung around one another constantly, stayed up late, talking about everything under the sun—Philip Roth and Cormac McCarthy, James Baldwin and Toni Morrison, George Eliot and Virginia Woolf—and then he got married and moved back home to Richmond, planning to start a family. Last I'd heard, he'd gone to law school. And then we lost touch, the way it was easy to do in that pre–social media era. I'd heard rumors that he'd fallen on hard times, that he'd been diagnosed as bipolar, and may have spent some time in a psychiatric hospital. His alcoholism had come around to bite him in the ass. But the moment we spoke, I felt bound to him again as my secret twin.

◎

He wanted to talk and talk about many things, but the first things he wanted to say were about—Tuesday Weld.

"Have you seen her, Freak?" He hit me with a soft pause, which then extended. It was like he was modulating the silence even over the phone, controlling its qualities like all raconteurs do. "I mean have you *seen* her?"

"Yeah, man, I've seen her."

I had, but—where? Like a lot of Gen X-ers, I'd seen her on the front cover of Matthew Sweet's album *Girlfriend*, which featured Weld in a fur-lined hoodie, her skin the roseate pink of a glacier kissed by dawn; I'd seen her in Michael Mann's *Thief*, and in Sergio Leone's *Once Upon a Time in America*. I'd seen her in the 1977 adaptation of Judith Rossner's novel *Looking for Mr. Goodbar*, a film that had terrified me when I saw it as a teenager. I'd seen her, most recently, as Maria Wyeth, in Frank Perry's *Play It as It Lays*, but beyond this, a handful of apparitions, I was ignorant. Was there a story?

"What about her, Freak? Are there any essential Weld-daddies I should know about?" D and I had evolved this style of talking, an obnoxious paleo-beatnik patter, years ago, in New York. Why it should have persisted, I don't know. The silliness of it allowed us to amplify our enthusiasms, maybe, to turn our intrigues into manias. Like all geeks, really, we wanted personae through which to filter excitement, turn fandom's one-way love, ever shameful and lonely, into communion.

"*Lord Love a Duck*, man. *Lord Love a Duck* is the crucial Tuesday juice."

"On it." I knew he wasn't talking about Weld's physical beauty. He was talking about presence, some electrical quality that was also about him and me. Such is the trouble with masculinity, it seems: we are always hiding our love for one thing behind another. D would call and be wound up about Elizabeth Bishop or Joni Mitchell, and I would know he was trying to show me something, but also to conceal it. Pulsing inside his aloneness, like a firefly inside a jar.

◎

If you search for "Tuesday Weld" on YouTube, the first thing that comes up, alongside a few fan collages of stills from her films, is a 1971 appearance on *The Dick Cavett Show*. The clip remains—as it was when I watched it nearly a decade ago, as it surely was when it initially aired—fresh as tomorrow's breeze. Weld saunters out in big, tinted glasses and a blue peasant blouse, a long floral skirt and a shoulder bag big enough to hold groceries, plunking herself down between Dinah Shore and the seat where Milton Berle will eventually sit, fending off Cavett's lightly smug, lightly sexist patter with a smile and a stammering glow. Her manner is a bit like the young Diane Keaton's: conspicuously awkward, but also tender, and ballasted with a warm but unbending intelligence that is no less ferocious for being polite. What a drag it must have been, for someone of her obvious perceptiveness, to do publicity in the first place: to answer the same stupid questions over and over about her unusual name, her pedigree as a former Hollywood wild child, her private life, and about whatever picture(s) she happened to be promoting at the time—in the case of the *Cavett* appearance, Henry Jaglom's *A Safe Place*, in which she costarred with Jack Nicholson and Orson Welles. No matter how different the roles, the questions were practically identical. And yet to watch that clip is to feel the pulse of life itself, and also of an obvious falsehood that Hollywood keeps perpetuating: the sight of a person in her clear creative prime spinning out charm and graciousness, offering up a simple facade (absolutely, a lie: it's evident watching the clip that Weld is also in some sense merely holding it together, battling a fear and self-consciousness that might have easily crippled her) in which we nevertheless cannot help but believe. Her presence is transfixing. The rest of us are lucky just to bask in her glow, the luminous contrails that seem practically supernatural.

◎

How did she come by it, this grace? Given that her life—her young life, as it predates her emergence as an actress—was so difficult. She was born in New York City in 1943. Her father dropped dead of a heart attack when she was three, and Tuesday went to work as a child model at her mother's instigation. In an arrangement that was to seed a lifelong resentment, she became the family breadwinner, supporting her mother and two siblings. By the time she was twelve she'd landed her first role on television, and soon found herself in the movies. Because she was precocious, and because she was beautiful—her iconic early role was that of a clever gold digger named Thalia Menninger on the popular 1950s sitcom *The Many Loves of Dobie Gillis*—she wound up living a double life, a helix in which her cinematic roles (mostly kittens and boppers, sexualized adolescents who'd been scrubbed—barely—for public consumption) informed her public persona and vice versa. Was she really as louche as she appeared to be on television? She leaned into the role, the part of "Tuesday Weld," with abandon, and the tabloids ate it up. She drank, she smoked, she drove like a maniac, racking up tickets and abandoning her sports car with one wheel parked on the sidewalk, telling any reporter who'd listen how she didn't wear underwear and had suffered a nervous breakdown when she was nine years old, attempted suicide when she was twelve. She was, so far as it went, America's id, and although she was not yet eighteen, she was linked, at least in the gossip columns, to a series of older men: Elvis Presley, Dennis Hopper, Frank Sinatra. Allegedly Stanley Kubrick's first choice for the title role in his 1962 adaptation of *Lolita*, Weld turned him down because—according to a 1971 interview—"I didn't have to play [Lolita]; I *was* Lolita."

This story—not Weld's story but the story of a Hollywood that sexualizes and exploits young women and girls—is old, and it is not the less terrible even when someone manages to come out on top and become, against odds, a star. Because what Hollywood wants, I believe, is not so much a "star" but a *pending* star. A star is money already spent, whereas a person on the verge of becoming such—at the casino they call this "betting on the come"—can be sold more aggressively to anyone, not least to the ingenue herself. "Will Tuesday Weld become the next Marilyn Monroe?" The best possible starlet, at least for the purposes of Hollywood accounting, is the one who remains on the verge of becoming one . . . forever, and thereby is never afforded the luxury of becoming a mature and independent artist. Instead, she eventually becomes a symbol of her own broken promise. Never mind that this promise is nothing the artist ever made or agreed to, herself. "Whatever happened to so-and-so?" people say. "Is Tuesday Weld still alive?" (God knows, death would be more profitable, in a sense; would be the only possible fulfillment of this promise for the accountants.) The ideal star is someone forever preserved in amber, emblem of a hope that ultimately never came to pass.

Throughout the prime of her acting career, a prime that came later than the years of notoriety in which she found herself appearing in half-baked exploitation movies like 1961's *Return to Peyton Place*, or 1960's *Sex Kittens Go to College* ("You Never Saw a Student Body Like This!"), Tuesday Weld remained semi-invisible, whether ignored on the basis of her candyfloss reputation (as film historian David Thomson wrote, "If she had been 'Susan Weld' she might now be known as one of our great actresses"), or cast in films that were the victim of poor distribution, negative reviews, or just plain terrible timing. We might consider this a misfortune, although it's worth noting that . . . Weld herself never wanted to be famous. Some of her roles—the institutionalized actress Maria Wyeth in *Play It as It Lays*; the omnivorously ambitious high school student Barbara Ann Greene in *Lord Love a Duck*; even the sweetly sociopathic Sue Ann Stepanek in *Pretty Poison*—could even be construed as a sort of meta-commentary upon fame, and on the price of our aspirations toward it. Weld declared her ambivalence in public many times, and you can see it very clearly in that Cavett show clip. Beginning with her admission that this might have been her first-ever sober appearance on the publicity circuit (at least she tells Cavett it is, and in a profile by Rex Reed written that same week, she says, "I thought if I could just go on *Dick Cavett* without having to get drunk first, I could get through anything. . . . I just wanted to walk on the show cold and let it all come out"), the actress proceeds to shrug off questions about why she wasn't getting the roles she deserved, and why she'd turned down so many good ones. Asked, for example, about 1967's *Bonnie and Clyde*, a role she had famously declined and which went on to launch Faye Dunaway to stardom, Weld tells Cavett that she'd been nursing her infant daughter when the director Arthur Penn had offered her the part, "and I felt that there were enough movies to go on, but this is the one time I have a baby and I'm nursing and I [wanted] to do this [instead]."

Maybe she didn't want it. But what's clear from Weld's mature choices of roles, from both the great directors who wanted to work with her—the Kubricks and Penns—and from the formidable ones who did (John Frankenheimer, Sergio Leone, Michael Mann), is that Weld had the goods. She was *it*. Just about every scrap of film that features the adult Weld, no matter how incidental, is electrifying (shit, look at two silent minutes of her pottering around Roddy McDowall's beach house in 1965—a home movie—that can also be found on YouTube). So why didn't she blow up? Pauline Kael, the *New Yorker*'s film critic, was shrewd enough to wonder as much. In her 1968 review of *Pretty Poison*, Kael marvels at Weld's underratedness, finally deciding it's because her performances feel effortless, because "she's the kind of actress who's too natural." In a 1970 article entitled "Give Him Tuesday—Sunday, Monday, Always," the *New York Times*' Eugene Archer bewailed the commercial failure of the recent string of films in which Weld had given brilliant performances, comparing her to Carole Lombard and Marilyn Monroe. "Why . . . is an actress of such acknowledged gifts . . . still not a star?" The question remains valid, not so much on the basis of talent—actresses, and actors and writers and filmmakers, of "acknowledged gifts" fail to receive their due all the time—but on that of temperament.

What quality in Tuesday Weld—or in anyone, really—might have caused her to reject success outright, as she did over and again, turning down not just *Lolita* and *Bonnie and Clyde* but also *True Grit*, *Rosemary's Baby*, *Cactus Flower* (the same part for which Goldie Hawn won an Oscar), and *Bob & Carol & Ted & Alice*. In a 1971 interview with the *New York Times*, Weld put it bluntly. "Do you think I want a *success*? I refused to do 'Bonnie and Clyde' because I was nursing at the time, but also because down deep I knew that it was going to be a huge success. The same was true of 'Bob & Carol & Ted & Sue [*sic*],' or whatever it was called. It reeked of success. I may be self-destructive, but I like taking chances with movies . . . I'm happy being a legend. I think the Tuesday Weld cult is a very nice thing."

◎

I, too, think it's a nice thing. Not just because of her nominal artistic bravery ("I like taking chances with movies"), or because of her blitheness ("or whatever it was called"), either of which could be read as mere posturing, but because Weld's cool embrace of failure draws an aura of self-awareness around the whole topic of fame. Any old performer could—and did—hit the publicity circuit and blather on about artistic challenges and ostentatiously profess indifference to the even bigger hits that might have been, but Weld seems dismissive of the whole concept of success to begin with, even as she reserves just a sliver of it—the abiding, posthumous part—for herself. ("I'm happy being a legend.") Her position doesn't seem to be one of hardheaded iconoclasm, but neither is it merely one of unfiltered perversity, an impulse to kick against the Hollywood pricks. She wanted it, but she didn't want all of it. Just a part of it, the part that would have allowed certain perks while leaving her free to ignore whatever spiritual obligations came with the bargain. This may have saved her, but surely it undermined her too. And if she hated it so much—on the *Cavett Show* appearance, she speaks of her habit of retiring, noting that she hadn't done an interview in eight years—why did she keep returning to it? Having gone through the trouble of breaking free from the business, why did she keep deciding to start all over again?

◎

It takes energy to be a fuckup. I've learned this myself. You have to lean into it, it turns out, almost more than you do to become a success. You have to commit to the role. Well before D—whose ultimate message would be sent obliquely—fired off his final communiqué, I came to understand this. That failure is, too, a performance, unfolding before a convex mirror in the narcissistic theater of the self. To succeed you have to submit to something—even if that something is just luck, or privilege—whereas to fail you must struggle and fight. If you feel yourself like Quasimodo, you have to *be* Quasimodo. You've got to take it all the way. For some of us—the lucky ones, maybe—it is possible to both be the part and understand its fundamental unreality. For those people only, a gift for forgery is a blessing.

◎

Susan Ker Weld. Tuesday Weld's birth name is one of the few things her scant and refractory biography presents with perfect clarity. The rest one is presently forced to glean from the internet and a pair of middling-to-dubious sources, a 1995 clip job by Floyd Conner called *Pretty Poison: The Tuesday Weld Story,* and a bizarre, argumentative counter-memoir co-authored by Samuel Veta with Weld's mother, Yosene Ker Weld. According to Conner, Weld's nickname came about because she was herself unable to pronounce "Susan" properly as a tot and so her mauling of it ("Tu-Tu") begat "Tuesday." Per *If It's Tuesday . . . I Must Be Dead!,* as Veta's book is called, the original nickname was "Too-Too," "because she was just 'too' much of everything—too loud, too fussy, cried too much." It must be said that any attempt to square even the simple facts of Weld's life, beyond the ones offered by the sequence and existence of the movies she appeared in, is cluttered not just by the she-said, she-said conflict of the competing biographies (Conner's assembled if not with Weld's cooperation, then at least largely from her own words, whereas Veta's seems mostly a defensive and untrustworthy screed), but also by Tuesday's habit of leading the press along. Or, as she puts it on her *Cavett Show* appearance, of lying. "Did you lie to those [reporters]?" Cavett asks, when he expresses his own confusion over the myriad contradictions contained in Weld's press clippings over the years, and the actress merely giggles. "All the time." She did so, she explains, out of boredom. "I have a problem with interviews, which is I hate to say the same thing over again." For which one can hardly blame her, but one wonders what this guardedness actually signified, or what she was trying to protect. As I thought about tracking her down and trying to interview her myself—a mutual friend told me that though she rarely speaks to reporters, she occasionally makes an exception, particularly when the interviewer is a man—my heart sank. What might she tell me that wouldn't be contradicted by something she'd told someone else a decade, or three decades, before? Weld hasn't acted since 2001, and hasn't given a detailed, on-the-record interview in longer. What would be the point in raking up old memories in a cloud of fresh distortions? I thought of Yosene Ker Weld's book, which is titled after an incident in which the actress told an interviewer her mother had passed on, despite Yosene's being very much alive. It is, for all intents and purposes, unreadable, stacked with so much resentment against Weld it's a wonder the actress survived. If this was what she was up against—this indignant, bullying, self-pitying nightmare—no wonder Weld preferred to lead interviewers along. Better a simple, entertaining falsehood than an ultimately intolerable truth.

◎

Are you never really ashamed of lying?

This was my friend D's favorite quote from Tolstoy's story *The Death of Ivan Ilyich*, something he reminded me of in an email, not long after we'd started talking again. He was living now in an unincorporated Virginia suburb—I tried to picture it, those riverine, tidewater greens and blues he must have moved through every day—and he'd taken a job in a law office in Richmond, doing personal injury work. He wasn't excited about it. "I desperately needed an infusion of cash, and p.i. is a good way to do it," he wrote, and he mocked a colleague who was "whooping and hollering and talking legal strategies, and I said, 'Will you never be ashamed of lying?' He said, 'It's all about weighing risks and benefits.' I couldn't even muster the energy to shame him into his bowl of chili."

I loved D, then as now, for his vivid and sardonic prose style—his emails could've gone on forever, so far as I was concerned. But I was aware, too, of an impulse toward embellishment, a tendency—as may have been the case with Weld too—to twist the facts into myth. He claimed to be sober. I hoped this was true. He certainly seemed so, although there was no way of knowing from a distance. When I'd met D, he was a book editor, a rail-thin twentysomething who seemed almost a burlesque of what you once would've imagined an old-school, Maxwell Perkins–style "editor" to be like: rumpled and elegant and quick, with a cigarette lighter in one pocket and a Penguin paperback in the other. He cared more about literature than anyone I knew. More, certainly, than he did about the law, a profession I suspect he entered because of its theoretical gravitas only to find what he did in the email quoted above: greed, calculation, ethical flexibility. He shared with me too an overbearing father: his dad was a federal court judge. D and I first met two weeks after I'd moved to New York in the early nineties, a moment—possibly the last moment—in which I found myself riding high. I'd gone to work for an actor, a man who was the king of Lower Manhattan, his spirit brooding over the whole of downtown; I'd been hypnotized by his films since I was a teenager, watched him prowl the streets of Little Italy, drive his cab through Times Square, bulk up sixty pounds to play a prize fighter so violent it gave me nightmares. To work for him was a dream, and further, this gig opened doors, allowing me to glide from room to room with callow impunity, on a cushion of comped drinks and free theater tickets. One night I attended a party where I knew not a single soul, a crowd of journalists and media people, and was soon captivated by a guy who seemed like electricity in a bottle. Long-limbed, rubbery, with a habit of emphatic gestures—finger snaps, jabs—and a maniacal, bug-eyed smile, the dude was a human comic strip, Roger Rabbit redrawn as a man. As he filled the air with quick-witted opinions and ridiculous tales, stories of drag-racing with famous, but stoned, American poets and snorting up drugs with National Book Award–winning novelists, I let his charm overturn my skepticism. I knew a bullshit artist when I saw one—the type of bullshit artist whose stories are all built around an irreducible grain of truth—but I loved him right away. His enthusiasm was contagious, and he had a palpable kindness and vitality. I drifted off from our conversation about whatever topic he was holding forth on when I decided to refill my whiskey glass— William Styron, maybe, or Robert Lowell—and marveled that New York stood a chance of being decent, if this was the sort of live-wire human being I was likely to trip over at a party and then, I supposed, never see again. The next morning, I stepped into an elevator in the Tribeca Film Center, eighty blocks south, and—there he was, with an office, it turned out, directly upstairs from mine. We quickly became friends, *real* friends, and soon struck up a habit, as twentysomethings do, of spending a lot of time in bars. Sometimes at night, and occasionally during the day: at lunch we'd go down the block to Walker's, and if D had a tendency to order one—or two, or four—chardonnay(s) too many, I barely noticed. He had a seasoned drinker's ability to keep his glass full, ordering almost invisibly, flagging the waiter like he was James Brown conducting his band, but he also never seemed, to my scrutinizing eye, anything other than lucid. It didn't occur to me that he might have left his previous job at a large literary publishing house involuntarily, or landed where he was, the book imprint recently fired up by an independent film studio, for want of a better alternative. Maybe he hadn't. It's only the long story, my knowledge of how it all turned out, that makes me scour the history here for clues.

◎

Why Tuesday Weld? I spent a lot of time wondering, in those weeks after D and I started talking again, why he chose to come in waving his arms over this particular enthusiasm. Not that it mattered, such was our friendship, and such was D, so who cared what lit him up enough to call me out of the blue? I was happy just to have him back. He never said much about the places he'd been, the travails he'd suffered in the years—more than a decade—since I'd seen him last, and I didn't press. But he seemed different, when we spoke on the phone: calmer, less manic. He spoke of his sobriety without proselytizing, and even as I gathered the last couple of years had been particularly brutal, I got the sense that he had come through. Our daughters were roughly the same age, and we talked a lot about our kids, about their steadying influence, and about how our marriages had come apart. (D blamed no one but himself.) Chastened by failure, saddened by his divorce, trundling along in the shadow of a successful father, utterly delighted by his daughter, and at odds with his day job, he reminded me of someone else, namely myself, and so whenever we talked, I would feel refreshed. I felt understood, and in some sense *seen*, if not exactly vindicated. D had arrived at a certain sanity, I thought, of the sort only a real maniac can possess, because there is a clarity of thought—or rather, a clarity of understanding—that comes from burning yourself down to the wick. I loved D more than I ever had even when we were younger, because he'd turned his former chaos into wisdom, balanced the scales, it seemed to me, on the whole game of success and failure.

Was this why Weld? Because (with the benefit of hindsight, at least) she seems to have balanced them too. On the *Cavett Show*, freshly sober (though she is careful *not* to define herself as alcoholic; "I could have been," she says when asked if she has ever identified as such, "but I stopped"), she seems cool as a matador when invited to perform the crooked dance of publicity. She is at once guarded and open, defended without ever quite being defen*sive*. If the game of fame involves being both naked and invulnerable—the "game" at least as defined by those who get to set the rules, the spectators—then Weld is playing it perfectly. If it involves, rather, feeling like a human being instead of a fat-ted calf, well, then, who knows, but it's worth noting that Weld retains her poise, and more importantly her sharpness, all the way through the interview. When the next guest, Milton Berle,

shows up and bloviates confidently, boringly, with all the entitlement of a male celebrity who's used to being listened to, Weld
interrupts him with an observation that seems telling. They are
talking about Orson Welles, the question of whether the great
director really enjoyed acting (having just done so alongside
Weld in *A Safe Place*) or if he was merely slumming. Berle opines,
naturally, that Welles must have enjoyed it, but Weld demurs.
"I think he doesn't even like himself for liking to act," she says.
Maybe he can't help but be sucked into it a little bit, she adds,
but "I just have a feeling he has that little argument with himself.
I've never met an actor—an older actor—who was happy with
himself, and his life."

She says these words with a bright smile, as if she is just making an observation, but of course she would have been speaking
from experience. There is that soft odor of self-loathing that so
often trails the perfume of charm. That "little argument" would
have been ongoing for her, as it was with D, and as it is with me
too. A director assembles films. A writer composes them. But
an actor, whose whole life can feel like an exercise in impostor
syndrome—there is the exhaustion of suspecting that you might
be a fraud, which any creative person feels, and then there is
the need to enact a performance of authenticity with your entire
body before you can even let this possibility have its due—knows
this quarrel, I would imagine, better than anyone.

◎

Weld's first real leading role came in 1966's *Lord Love a Duck*.
Which came after she'd been working for more than a decade,

after she'd been catapulted to a certain sort of stardom by her one-season turn as Thalia Menninger, the money-hungry temptress on the wildly popular television show *The Many Loves of Dobie Gillis*, and had come, thus, to occupy her position as America's reckless young sweetheart. *Lord Love a Duck* is, it must be said, an exceptionally strange movie, one that anticipates by a good twenty years such pitch-black Gen X excursions as *Heathers*, but Weld lights up the screen from go in the service of a part that—not for the last time—addresses themes that would have been significant to her: Svengali-ism, fame and ambition, image manipulation and control. The story of an emotionally disturbed high school student named Alan "Mollymauk" Musgrave (played by Roddy McDowall) and his friendship with a striving female classmate (Weld), the film is at once a lighthearted parody of American International Pictures' Frankie-and-Annette-starring teen movies—*Beach Blanket Bingo*, *Bikini Beach*, etc.—and a deranged Faust narrative that takes clear-eyed aim at consumer culture. At one point Weld's character, seeking entrée to a clique of popular girls known as "The Cashmere Sweater Club," persuades her estranged father to take her shopping. The scene that ensues is, to put it bluntly, nuts, a consumer fantasia in which Weld whips herself into a sexualized frenzy by trying on a series of brightly colored sweaters. As she writhes and squeals in various shades of angora ("Pink put-on . . . papaya surprise . . . periwinkle pussycat!"), her "father" leers and trembles, rooting her on until he is positively bug-eyed with lust. It's disturbing, upsetting—as lurid as anything in the Kubrick rendition of *Lolita*—but the scene travels so far over the top it hits like nitrous oxide: discomfort slides into shock and then straight-up hilarity. The movie might not know quite what it wants to be (by the time Weld's character gets married and then attempts, at Mollymauk's instigation, to off her dim-bulb husband, we've left both realism and the zany, *Hard Day's Night*-style poptimism of the film's opening far behind), but it's exhilaratingly perverse. And frame for frame, Weld's performance is magnetic: no matter how weird things get, or how tonally confused the film becomes, you can hardly take your eyes off her. The same

can be said of 1968's *Pretty Poison*, which many consider to be
the actress's best—and certainly her most representative—film.
Weld herself claimed to dislike the movie—she'd clashed with
director Noel Black, and as she later told Cavett, she was incapable of enjoying a film she hadn't found pleasure in making. If
anything, *Pretty Poison* is even more messed up than *Lord Love
a Duck*. Anthony Perkins plays a paroled arsonist who moves to
an industrial New England town and soon gets mixed up with
Weld's wholesome-seeming high school girl. Thematically, the
setup is practically identical to *Lord Love a Duck*, with the film
playing on an association with Perkins's role in *Psycho*, only this
time . . . it's Weld's character who turns out to be the malig-
nant sociopath, more deviant by far than her opponent. She's
not only immune to the hapless arsonist's manipulations, she's
several steps ahead of him the whole while. It's a strong performance, as Pauline Kael was the first to note, but it's also one that
imbalances the film that surrounds it a bit. Weld is so radiant—
it's hard to imagine a *sunnier* presence onscreen than she was at
this juncture, and the movie maximizes this by kitting her out
in majorette gear the first time we see her, turning her into an
emblem of American wholesomeness—where the film itself is
melodramatic and downbeat. In its way it resembles the Perrys'
adaptation of *The Swimmer*, training its queasy, psychedelic-era
lens on the decidedly pre-psychedelic world of rural/suburban
New England, without quite deciding which side of the divide
it belongs to.

In a way, the very ambiguity of these movies, their ambivalent split between a mainstream cheer and a subversive
violence, mirrors Weld's own position: too sunny for the

burgeoning counterculture, I suspect, and too sour for the suburbs. Yet there is such delight in them. A near-total absence of vanity, and a superabundance of joy.

◎

Recently, I had lunch with a friend, an actress whose career has been rather more successful than Weld's. We sat in the windowless gloom of an Italian restaurant near one of the studio lots, a place we both like because it is echoic of the older LA, in which she and I grew up—and because it is largely empty most of the time: there are few other diners, and not many people likely to bother my friend who, I would suppose, is used to fending off paparazzi and autograph seekers anyway. We talked, as we always do on those infrequent occasions we see one another, about writers and books, films and Los Angeles—anything except "the biz," which she seems to dislike as much as I do—and at a certain point she let slip a comment that surprised me.

"I wish I had worked more," she said. "When I was younger, I turned down so many things."

"Did you?"

I sipped my glass of midday chianti. I suppose I was startled to hear this note of regret creep in. I'd thought my friend had done pretty much exactly what she wanted, which was pretty much exactly what *anyone* would have wanted. Her filmography was stellar, filled with nominations and awards, to say nothing of performances any actress would be proud to have given. What hadn't she done? I wondered. I studied her face, its pensiveness: the subtle workings of all those nerves and muscles—she surely

didn't even know she was doing it—creating shades of meaning and emotion I could myself scarcely name, even at rest. It
was a face I'd watched for decades, playing guileless high school
students and drug-ravaged criminals, wisecracking molls and
tormented theater actresses. Now it was deep in the role of her
own private self.

"I turned down _____," she said, naming a movie that had
won multiple Oscars, not least for its now-iconic performance
by its female lead, as a sleep-haunted detective. "I just couldn't
get my head around the script."

"Wow."

"I turned down a whole bunch of things," she said, then
rattled off a slew of titles—*Pretty Woman* was one; *Thelma and
Louise*, another—that suggested an alternate history, not just
for her but for the last thirty-odd years of Hollywood. I saw
this history pass before my eyes—her star glowing differently,
other careers diminished or eradicated, or enhanced by different roles they had taken instead—as I swapped her into one
film and then the next. There was the disorienting question
of whether the pictures themselves would have been better, or
worse, if she'd appeared in them; if even a superior performance
could have led somehow to an inferior movie.

"Do you regret it?" I said.

"No." Her eyes narrowed. (*I* regretted it. I would've enjoyed
seeing her in those roles.) "I just wish I had taken on more. I
don't regret the things I did, or the things I turned down. But I
feel like I missed something."

Surely, we all feel this, eventually. Surely, we all feel the negative weight of lives unlived, alternate paths not taken. But I

recall this conversation now not just in thinking of Tuesday Weld (does she regret, now, all those storied roles she turned down?), but also in thinking of D, who walked away from something he cared about—books—in order to forge a career pursuing something he did not. Did he ever regret it? Would it have made a difference, ultimately, if he had stayed in New York to chase his original dream?

D and I spoke often, in those months that followed my mother's death. I had no sense of anything wrong, insofar as he seemed only moderately unhappy—with the same middle-aged aches as anyone, I thought—and because, above all, he was so funny about it. "How goes I?" he wrote, in one of the endless skeins of emails we volleyed back and forth. "Melancholy, prodigal, dishonest, true, lustful, ascetic, happy, mean, angry and free, as Montaigne said." He launched into a story about a "knife-wielding goon" (a "pimp") who arrived on his doorstep one night by mistake, only to be disarmed by the promise of a bowl of soup ("store-bought tomato, for God's sake"), and wound up falling asleep at D's kitchen table. He wrote, "I am so tired of overserious men who think they are actually relevant. I had a wild, very traditional dream recently where Chrissie Hynde wrapped her eight-foot legs around me and started strangling me like a boa. Then she insisted I only eat wheat germ. It was weird."

Did I regret anything? My divorce was final; my career as a feature writer remained on hold—or perhaps was over—and I was alone. I had my daughter, which of course reduced all questions of "regret" to mere hypotheticals, but: Did I? Even as I played the role of screwup to the hilt—chronically befuddled, underemployed, given to forgetting what day of the week it was if V wasn't there to remind me—I knew I did not, because in my secret heart, the one that beat beneath my deepest dissatisfaction, I was not unhappy. And as I rattled around the bottom floor of my duplex—I'd scored a good deal on it, thanks to a sympathetic landlady—listening to the stork-like clopping of my upstairs neighbor, a journalist, in her high heels, I wondered what it meant that I didn't feel such regret, if even this might suggest, somehow, a lack of imagination. If your life has taken on water, aren't you at least supposed to dream of the things you might have done to make it better? ("I feel like somewhere my life got infected by failure," D wrote, and I certainly understood this feeling acutely.) What did it say that I couldn't even get that far? Instead, I marinated in a sadness that clutched at me like quicksand, even as I knew at the root that I was doing all this to myself: that it was simply, in the end, another role I may have been born to play.

◎

During those weeks, I lost a lot of sleep. As the weather warmed toward spring, I tossed and turned into the small hours, never knowing exactly why. Living where I did, on the southernmost fringe of West Hollywood where it starts to bleed into the anonymous corridor of the neighborhood called "Mid-City"—where the marginal glitz and pallid sleaze of the Strip gives way to something quieter—I could only wonder whether I had found my way into a kind of purgatory. Los Angeles has always been a place where people come to chase their dreams. No matter how

ancient this observation seems—no matter how close it drifts
to cliché—it remains true. And yet my neighborhood, and my
apartment, seemed devoid of any signs that dreaming was even
possible. "The eternal Los Angeles is composed of infinite in-
tersections full of nothing remarkable," writes Sam Sweet, in his
excellent monograph *Hadley Lee Lightcap*. "Each one offers a
similar but always slightly different combination of peeling signage, concrete pathways, and buildings painted and repainted
in so many layers of nameless color that it's no longer possible
to tell whether they're new or very old. These places don't ask
to be discovered and are rarely remembered. Here the city is so
devoid of historic significance and attraction that you wouldn't
know its tempo unless you deliberately attuned yourself to it."
This was the LA I inhabited now—flip side of the one where
everyone dreams of being discovered, that other, also indelible,
Los Angeles that has nothing to do with "Hollywood," and
which promises only oblivion. The air that spring was heavy
and wet; the avenues were silent. At night a glaucous moon—or
was that only a streetlamp?—glowed vague and gaseous beyond
the blinds, painting the wooden floors with a toxic gloss. Those
nights, the ones on which I didn't have my daughter, were filled
with doubt and uncertainty, a vicious insomnia that alternately
launched me from my bed and nailed me in place. I paced the
tiny kitchen in circles, or stretched on the ragged rattan couch
in the living room and read; I lay flat and waited for the windows to brighten, the bars on the outside solidifying into being
so I could experience this place for what it was, both fortress
and prison. The furniture was haphazard, secondhand, scattered
in such a way that only emphasized the gaps: a couch, a lone

armchair, but no table; shelves, books, but no desk. This was the room I'd occupied when my aunt called to say my mother had died, the one in which I lay awake, now, and dreamed of Tuesday Weld. Nights spent squinting at bootleg DVDs and grainy YouTube streams; long hours of contemplating the void. When a Tuesday Weld, or any public figure, fails to live up to our ridiculously inflated hopes for her, we call that a tragedy, or at least a shame. When a middle-aged wannabe, a civilian, fails to live up to his inflated hopes for himself, that's no tragedy, it's adulthood, an education that arrives better late than never. Sitting in that room in the dark, sprawled on that couch like Marat in the bath, I thought of D, my doppelganger on the East Coast, and I made my peace. If I wasn't quite ready to tattoo BORN TO LOSE on my shoulder just yet, I knew I'd been born to stumble. Just like everybody else.

◎

After *Pretty Poison* flopped, Weld's career still seemed to stretch out brightly in front of her. A thirteen-year industry veteran, she was, incredibly, still just twenty-five years old. It felt like she'd been doing this forever. Even as the tastemakers, like Kael, stood up for her, and she nabbed a runner-up for 1968's Best Actress from the New York Film Critics Circle, she was stuck pushing up the Sisyphean hill of her sex bomb reputation. If people had only been able to see the film—it was in and out of theaters overnight, as the producers couldn't find a distributor—it would've been a hit. Or maybe the cult of Tuesday Weld is its own self-perpetuating machine at this point, doomed to overrate her performances in movies that don't quite come off. Maybe the movies aren't that good; maybe I, now a card-carrying cultist, myself, overrate them, and this effort to resurrect an actress who is still very much alive is just a fool's errand. But her later performances—in films like 1981's *Thief* and 1978's *Who'll Stop the Rain*, or in Sergio Leone's *Once Upon a Time in America*, which is best seen in its 1984 international version, rather than in the bowdlerized one that was released in the US—all suggest Weld as a poet of failure, someone who was inexorably drawn to parts that showcased deterioration and disappointment, unhappiness and collapse. And whether one watches her in a great movie (like *Once Upon a Time in America*) or a lousy one (like 1971's *A Safe Place*, Henry Jaglom's "experimental" dreck-fest that wastes her along with Jack Nicholson and Orson Welles), a functional one (say, 1970's *I Walk the Line*, which casts her oddly opposite a sluggish Gregory Peck) or a good one (1965's *The Cincinnati Kid*) in which she's just not given enough to do, the effect is the same: like seeing a figure that could as easily be spun from liquid gold and moonlight—a goddess of stardust and cream—seem persuasively, ineffably *natural* on camera. The problem was never that Weld "didn't get the parts she deserved," nor even that she turned so many of them down. The problem was that the movies barely deserved *her*. She could make even the technology that created her, somehow, seem common.

◎

For the most part, I am uninterested in Weld's personal life, in combing its contours—three marriages (the latter two to actor

Dudley Moore, from 1975 to 1980, and to the concert violinist Pinchas Zukerman, from 1985 to 1998) and two children—for clues. For the most part, the information isn't available anyway, but there is one moment that intrigues me. It came just after her first marriage, to a screenwriter named Claude Harz, had fallen apart. In 1970, Weld and her infant daughter decamped to London. She seems to have split from her husband amicably, at least as these things go. She waived alimony, telling the *New York Times*, "I don't see any reason for Claude to have that hanging over his head. . . . If he has the money, I'm sure he'll give it to me." Then she fell into a period of drift, of windblown wanderlust that may have been—if you've ever had this feeling, you know—a form of clinical depression. Or maybe she had always been this way, her life in chaos even when she was a small child, moving from coast to coast and school to school as Yosene jerked her around and forced her to go to work as a toddler. "I feel so misplaced everywhere," she told the *Times*, on the eve of yet another departure, getting ready to set out now from London to Paris. "Sometimes I just walk the streets at night, for hours and hours. I'm incredibly restless." Her restlessness came to an end only when, while she was home for a while in Los Angeles, her car broke down—a beloved Porsche roadster she'd purchased at Elvis's recommendation when they were shooting 1961's *Wild in the Country*—and then one night, when she was visiting Catalina Island alone, her house caught fire. Racing home to Malibu, Weld found herself stuck on the ferry for several hours. Santa Ana winds had knocked down the telephone wires, and the actress had no idea where her daughter was. She arrived the next morning to find her child safe—she'd been spirited from the blaze by her nanny—but everything she owned, everything, had been burned to ash: her furniture, her journals, those years of writing she'd been saving for an eventual memoir, the paintings she'd done, her memorabilia, her clothing: all of it was gone.

What did it feel like? I wonder. Having lost all of her possessions, whatever spoils she'd amassed, did the actress feel disconsolate? Or did she—picking through the wreckage with the cold surf pounding behind her—did she, rather, feel free? "I went to look at the ashes, but I didn't cry," she told an interviewer. "Aside from [my journals], none of it mattered." Later, she said, "I'm suspended, floating. I'm not happy, and I'm not sad." Profiles from that year, 1971, describe her nomadic lifestyle. A Rex Reed piece, written while the actress was doing publicity for *A Safe Place*, invokes the chaos of her New York City hotel room, its door propped open with a cardboard box, the floor strewn with "notebooks crammed with jottings in soft lead pencil . . . a portable radio, vitamin pills, bottled water, ashtrays filled with unsmoked cigarettes," Weld herself presiding in a ratty red sweatshirt stamped with the *Superman* logo. Like she had nothing and wanted nothing and maybe, just maybe, actually preferred it that way.

◎

Did my friend D feel free? Did I? There is something to be said, after all, for ground zero, for that place where, as the famous song puts it, one has nothing, and so nothing to lose. When I lost my mother I felt encumbered; having lost her as a responsible guardian decades before that, I was left to reckon with the weight of that previous absence, which was suddenly as heavy as cement. When I'd lost my marriage, I felt turned inside out, like I needed to unwind, also, an entire identity. But thinking of Weld, I felt secretly elated. If this book is an effort to reckon with a legacy of parental failure, a legacy as vivid as the wildest dream of success, then it is itself foredoomed to fail. You cannot mourn what is already too long missing. But dreaming of Weld and talking to D, exchanging calls and emails at all hours of the night, I began to see a way forward, to tug a little bit free of the inertia that had clutched at my heart. Love, after all, can do this. And fandom, even if it isn't love, can do this too, by offering a sort of template for living.

Art invites identification. When we are young, and sometimes when we are not, we make the mistake of identifying with the artist, crucifying such people for perceived sins and deifying them in projected glory. I have a friend who spent her teenage years making bracelets that said WHAT WOULD JOAN DIDION DO, as if we don't already know the answer. (She would have done exactly the thing that is tragically unavailable to the rest of us: written the very books that made her Joan Didion.) My friend D tried to lay out his own path. Years after he left New York, during that period he and I were back in touch, in fact, he managed the first ten thousand words of a novel. They were good, at least as I read them, but still the impulse petered out, the way it sometimes does. Weld's career didn't exactly "peter out," as she kept working for another three decades after *Play It as It Lays*. If the parts got smaller, they also, you could argue, got stronger for a while. Her work beginning in the later part of the seventies—all the way through to 1984's *Once Upon a Time in America*—is her best: searching turns that are the more appealing for their scarred humanity, the fact that the characters involved are all, one way or another, losers of a kind. I don't believe my friend D was a loser—no more than I was, really—but I know he identified with them. ("My heart will always be with the loser," he wrote. "Always.") As do I. Falling in love with Weld was like falling in love with my friend. In both of them, I saw vistas, the wide sweep of understanding that comes only with loss. D wrote, "I realize now I did not seize all the opportunities the '90s offered. I sat idly by and dreamt." He wrote, "Your father has been very successful, and I wonder if the end symptom of that, in men especially, is self-absorption—a conviction in oneself, which I never have too much of." He wrote these things and I thought he saw the world all the way to the bottom. That he understood the meaning of disappointment, and that his gift to me now—sudden, unexpected, like a rabbit yanked elegantly from a hat—was that I finally did too.

◎

He called me. One afternoon while I was driving, the phone rang, and I picked up.

"Freak." D's voice sounded slow and slurry, like a vinyl record playing at the wrong speed. I was winding my way through an unfamiliar city: Detroit, where I was visiting friends. "Freak, I messed up."

"What is it?" I jerked the wheel left, then right, searching for parking as I circled a block in the shadow of Wayne State University, in Midtown.

"I fell off the wagon."

"Oh?" I wasn't paying attention. Listening, but not really listening. My mind was on other things.

"I really, really screwed up."

I can hear it still: the sludge of despair in his voice, a heavy, medicated quality.

"Where are you?"

"Hospital." The word rolled off his tongue like a boulder. "I'm at the hospital."

What did I say? I'm too ashamed to remember, really, the platitudes I must have spouted. *It's OK. You'll get better. You've got this. It's fine.* Outside, the day was cold and overcast, the city strange and alluring. A few isolated flakes fluttered down out of the milk-pale sky. The brownstone university buildings looked romantic to me, like castles compared to the low-lying, palmy sprawl of Los Angeles.

"It's all right," I said. How many times had my mother gotten sober, over the later years of her life? Did I assume this was just a little slip, a misstep that could be corrected with a bit of effort, a willingness to start over?

"You'll get sober again, Freak." (Sadly, I did, offering up the most wilted platitudes.) "One day at a time, right? Isn't that what they say?"

"Yeahh."

His voice sounded so far off its regular, exuberant pitch. Like he was underwater, warbling in from the depths. I didn't really hear this until later, though; didn't process what it meant until I'd almost forgotten this call ever happened.

"I love you, Freak. You'll be OK. I promise."

As if I understood the first damn thing about this kind of alcoholism: chronic, severe, the kind given to blackouts and hospital trips. My mother's too frequently functional variety of it had taught me nothing, or at least had omitted from my education those things I so dearly needed—in this case—to know.

◎

That was the last time I heard his voice, although I look back over our subsequent emails and see messages about new medications, restored sobriety, articulations of hope ("I'm doing swell, man") and vitality ("Thank God I'm not drinking. It's worse than cancer"). I check my receipts and see—can this possibly be right?—the night before he phoned me, he'd also emailed me a poem he'd written and a link to a blog where he'd posted the first chapter of his novel: the stirrings of a fresh creative burst. The record is mysterious in its absence of any real expressions of doubt, let alone despair. In one of the last emails I have from him, responding to an instance where I'd been complaining about something or other, he wrote, "Cheer up, dude, I love you. Doesn't that mean anything? The quality of life depends on who's walking around in it, and while I'm not walking around in your life, I am, so to speak, walking in it over Interspace." Indeed, he was. In a sense he still is, nearly a decade later. Like all of us in "Interspace," he is at once forever nearer and infinitely farther than he appears.

◎

The call came on a Sunday morning. It was our mutual friend P from Charlottesville, who'd known D even longer than I had.

"Hey," I said. Sweating, a little flushed, I was just back from a run. "What's going on?"

She and I had gotten to know each other through D—the two of them had gone to high school together—and we'd fallen into the recent habit of talking, flirting. I was ready to tumble into the vortex of our regular conversation: punk rock, the lives of people we'd known together in the nineties, sex.

"It's D," she said. "Something's happened. He fell."

"Fell?"

"Off a roof," she said. "He jumped or he fell. It's not clear."

"Is he—"

I hesitated, because—

"He's dead," she said.

I set the phone down a moment, because I couldn't speak. After I picked it back up, she walked me through what happened: he was up on top of his apartment building, for what purpose who knew, and had leapt or slipped. There was no note, and his body had lain undiscovered in an alleyway between his building and the adjacent one for three days. For a moment, we were willing to believe it was an accident. Or maybe she was just generous enough to let me think that. After we hung up—she, too, had thought his life was getting better, she said; she'd believed in his recently restored sobriety—I sat looking down at my hands as they rested on the edge of my wooden dining table. They looked *old*, I remember thinking: rough and cracked and knotty. But it was just a trick of the light. I moved them, and they looked like themselves again: uncommonly smooth for a person of my age. As if I could change them just by shifting a little, dream them in and out of youth the way I am trying to do, right now, with my late friend too.

◎

I don't know if D ever saw the run of movies Tuesday Weld did in the late seventies and early eighties, but I imagine he would have loved them: the lapsed Catholic older sister she plays in *Looking for Mr. Goodbar*, the ragged waitress in *Thief*. I found myself turning to these movies in the weeks after he died, scouring YouTube for clips. A scene from the latter—ten minutes long, one uninterrupted take—she plays against James Caan in a diner, both of them pouring forth their dreams and disappointments in a way that would not quite be credible if their performances were not so moving. Weld's face clouds with tears, Caan stammers and struts and pleads as his character—a safecracker who has spent a decade in prison—pulls a collage from his wallet, a composition he's pasted together from pictures in magazines, to show her the shape of his life, the one he wants as well as the one that has befallen him. She is lovely, in this scene, as ever: her eyes flashing and dark, her face crumbling in on itself a dozen ways, one for every hesitation, as she hunches in a gray fur coat. Until she succumbs, the way we almost always do, to her desire, that feeling that will, eventually, ruin her life.

Maybe D never saw it. And Weld, operating on the other side of the one-way glass that protects people in the movies from the ones outside them, never saw the two of us either.

A few months passed before I learned the things that made my friend's death appear a little more legible, before P decided I was ready to know the truth. She said his time in the hospital was not voluntary—when he called, he'd been committed, not checked in on his own steam—and I heard stories of riotous disturbances, police calls, cells with padded walls and restraints; I heard there were books left among his effects that had pages stained by Listerine, the high-alcohol mouthwash he'd reduced himself to drinking, after his bottles were taken away. I understood I didn't *know* anything, that the friend with whom I bantered and sparred so thrillingly over the years had undergone, and no doubt also inflicted too, pain I would never have dared to imagine. If I say I loved him more than anything, which I did, that doesn't make either one of us any less of a monster, now does it?

In one of D's favorite novels, Walker Percy's *The Moviegoer*, Percy talks about "the search," which he defines as "what anyone would undertake if he were not sunk in the everydayness of his own life." The search, he says, is that thing that defines us, the existential wakefulness—and restlessness—that keeps us moving, ahead of despair. Indeed, the movies *are* the search, he implies, that space where we dream and chase, only—"they screw it up." A movie ends with the restitution of everydayness, that torpor from which we are fighting to escape to begin with. "The search always ends in despair."

I find myself thinking of this, not because I believe it—I'm not sure I do—but rather because I believe art and life chase each other. Tuesday Weld glows before us onscreen like the very Grail and we take off in pursuit, hurtling after her like dogs chasing a tennis ball across a dappled field. But I believe the people deprived of ordinariness, those poor, broken folks who achieve their dream of immortality, if only for a moment, are chasing something too. And when the lights come up, they go on searching. The search ends in neither fulfillment nor despair: it stops, only, in death. D's search now is finished. And the actress—retired, these days, living somewhere in the Hollywood Hills, having not appeared in a movie since 2001—rises in the morning to confront that regular life, that everydayness that belongs to all of us, but perhaps even to her most of all, now that she is free, at last, to live inside it.

VI
the cadaver and the search

warren zevon

It's all one case.

—ROSS MACDONALD,
The Zebra-Striped Hearse

I FELL IN love with a television writer, crucifying myself one more time—the last time, I hoped—on the altar of the motion picture industry. I performed every romantic gesture—letters, flowers, playlists; a chain of clever text messages that went on sometimes for hours—until I barely recognized myself; until I *did* recognize myself, as the scared adolescent I once was decades earlier. "Love hurts," the song goes. It hurts more when you decide, simply, to skin yourself alive.

I met Q on a dating site. My first mistake was to take everything at face value. We went to dinner at a place on Highland Avenue, sat under golden lights that made her look—large-eyed, heavy-lidded, with a smile that spread across her cheeks like wine sinking slowly into fabric—like a Jewish Italian goddess. I adored her disproportionately, placed speculative bets on a future even before dessert, which neither of us wanted to eat, arrived. We sat for three and a half hours, after which I kissed her on the street as she leaned against a streetlamp.

"I'm seeing someone else," she said. The air around us was halogen-rich, glowing. She leaned forward to kiss me again. "I don't think I like him very much."

She smelled like God's laundry: a pheromonal trap. I drove home ten minutes later, car stereo blaring. It was as if I had been injected with a slow-acting poison, a paralyzing agent that wouldn't take effect for a few days. *I don't think I like him very much.* These words rang in my head the next morning. (*Then why are you seeing him?* I might have asked, if I were not—then as always—slow to heed an internal warning.) She had waited almost four hours to tell me that. *Ah, well.* I texted her anyway. And when we went on another date, and then another after that, the same thing happened: little remarks like fishhooks, tiny cruelties that slipped beneath my skin without pain until it was too late, until I was bound in place like Gulliver tied to the shore by Lilliputians.

"I love you," I said.

"I think I might be falling in love with you too."

Six weeks, maybe, had elapsed. Six weeks of flirting and chasing, of lurching pursuit; six weeks of kissing and, more recently, sex; six weeks of waiting, always a little too long, for our text thread to resume, declarations of ardor (mine) and of half ardor, semi-ardor, that were just enough to keep me going.

"I hope you do," I said, but what I meant was, *I'm going to make you.* We all know how that turns out. The sex was desperate, a little messy. I felt like I was trying to climb a mountain with webbed hands, unable to gain purchase with someone who—this was the core of it—just didn't like me as much as I needed to be liked. I never asked about the other man again, just assumed, in my narcissistic blindness, that had come to a full stop. Maybe it had. But after another few weeks of this, of my hard-charging pursuit and her lawyerly caution, she called.

"I can't see you."

"No?" My voice leaked out of me like helium fleeing a balloon: a tinny, infantile squeak. "Are you breaking up with me?"

"I don't have the feelings I thought I'd felt."

I don't remember what I said next. I was too stunned by what I sounded like: a Smurf or a very young child. I was visiting a friend in Topanga Canyon, staring out the window at our daughters on his sun-swept patio, with the blue glitter of the Pacific far, far below. In a space a lot like this one, almost thirty years earlier, I had decided to become what I was: a writer. But I had no words for what I was experiencing: a murderous distress that revealed me for the weakling I was, too. Life with my mother had been like this, when she was at her most wild and abusive and I was just a helpless teenager. But there, I was living with an addict; here, I was just chasing another human being who happened to want—no matter how much it pained me—something else.

◎

"Did someone tell a joke?"

I was sitting on the floor of my living room, weeping. The front door was open and my neighbor, the journalist with the loud heels, peered inside as she was unlocking the adjacent door to her own, upstairs, unit.

"What?" I looked over at her with blind eyes, face wet with tears.

"Oh." She hesitated, gracefully. "I'm sorry. I thought you were laughing."

Have I made it sound like the experience was all disappointment? We'd gone to dinner parties in the hills, thrown by her friends and mine; cared for each other when we were sick, making soup runs to Factor's Famous Deli; after our third date we'd shared a joint and kissed all over again, drinking smoke from one another's lungs. It was a lot. And what made it so painful to lose, besides the aching second adolescence into which I'd blundered at forty-two years old, was how close it had seemed to real: how what had evaporated was not a relationship but rather a series of signs that pointed toward one. I had crawled like a thirsty man in the desert, still reeling from my friend's death too—*If not now, when?* I'd told myself as I'd decided to start dating again, to pull myself out of a lonely hole—only to see it evaporate in front of me, this dream, alas, of water.

"Ever had a relationship that seemed like it was made entirely of mixed signals?" (For there was this too: the artful way she'd said from the beginning, *I like you, I think; come hither . . . now stop.*) I looked up at my neighbor from my spot on the floor where I sat with my legs stretched into a V, weeping. I still wasn't over it, even a few weeks later.

"Hmm." She had a kind face. Indeed, she might have been Q's older, cooler, more merciful sister: dark hair and large eyes, with a similar quattrocento beauty. She was still standing with the key in the lock of her front door, one slender heel lifted like a flamingo's. "I may have, yes."

"Really?"

Her face cracked open into a smile. I'd left the door open, because it was spring, and because I'd wanted the evidence that the wider world went on without giving a damn about my foolish feelings. Now here it was.

"Honey." She shook her head. "You have no idea."

◎

Thus, my neighbor and I became friends. I'd been living here for the better part of a year already, and though we'd met, glancingly, on several occasions, this was the moment it crystallized. "Come upstairs for coffee," she said, and so—I did. I liked her. Like me, she was home almost all the time; unlike me, it was because she was busy, a freelance journalist whose days were filled with deadlines. I could always knock: some days I dragged my laptop up there so we could cowork, and because her place was full of sunlight. She had a New Yorker's directness—she'd moved out here two and a half decades earlier and had retained almost all of it: the accent, the winter pallor, the allergy to bullshit, including my own—but also a surplus of kindness. I would knock and she would summon me in, usually from the kitchen in back where she was working. I'd wind my way through her apartment, which was laid out differently from mine, following the sound of her voice. The front room was lined with books, and filled with the kinds of bric-a-brac—scarves, candles, matchbooks, photographs, letters, LPs—that marked an analog life, the type of entrenchment you see more often in Upper West Side apartments, where rent control and the sheer weight of one's material possessions can keep a person anchored for life. I'd step inside and feel transported, like to a library, and to a different time and place. I'd follow the sound of her back to where she sat working, perched at a small table with a lipstick-smudged coffee cup and some other talisman—a pencil, a notebook, a copy of *Just Kids*—by her elbow and her laptop in front.

"What do you need?" She looked up at me without irritation, even though I am sure I was, in those days, irritating in the extreme: playing music too loud at odd hours, sitting up at night getting drunk in my kitchen. I was a mess.

"Who was the bad boyfriend?"

"What?"

"The one you told me about." She'd mentioned him a few times now, the one she'd come out years ago to meet and who, I surmised, had broken her heart. This was the man she'd referred to on the stoop, a musician.

"Warren Zevon."

"What? Get out!"

"That's who it was."

"Really?"

I don't know why it hadn't occurred to me to ask sooner. I knew it had to be someone: she'd been writing for *Rolling Stone* magazine as a staffer and been sent out to interview him, the musician for whom she'd, instead, never left. She'd told me that before and I hadn't pressed, maybe assuming her heartbreak, though ancient, was somehow as raw as my own.

"Why?" She smiled. In the incongruous white cube of her kitchen—linoleum floors, steel appliances, gas stove—she looked, still, like a painting: her dark eyes liquid and quizzical. "You like him?"

"Yeah," I said. "Well, no. He brings back memories."

"That about sums it up."

"No, I mean for me."

"Oh." She looked at me with interest, like I wasn't just—suddenly—some blithering idiot here to get drunk on wine or to cry on her shoulder. "What's the story?"

◎

Years ago, when I was a boy, my father sometimes used to take me to school. This was just before I could drive myself, in the days when my parents were still together—the marriage was barely hanging on. He'd give me a lift so I didn't have to take the bus. Occasionally in the afternoons he'd pick me up or, if it was summer, give me a ride to my job instead, which happened to be at his office, where I worked in the mailroom. I was a teenager, stuck in that nexus where suspicion of your parents runs much deeper even than love, but I looked forward to these drives. In those days, our moments in the car were as close as we got. One thing about my father was that he'd always had good taste in music, uncommonly hip for a middle-aged man of that era, and so we'd listen to cassettes that I'd made him or vice versa while we cruised through Beverly Hills or Century City: Talking Heads' *77* on one side, *Remain in Light* on the other; Lou Reed's *Transformer* and Mott the Hoople's *All the Young Dudes*. Occasionally we played the California seventies stuff that he liked—Fleetwood Mac, Steely Dan, the Eagles—and I was snotty about it. One place where we achieved détente was a tape that had Jackson Browne ("These Days") on one side, and Warren Zevon on the other. I no longer remember which of us made that cassette, whether I did or he did, but I do know that I loved that one side, the Zevon side, unreasonably. I loved the mania, the perversity, the songs about mercenaries and "lawyers, guns, and money." I even liked the stupid one about werewolves, because it referenced Trader Vic's, a restaurant I had been to God knows how many times with my parents, and which I could actually see from the windows of the building where my father and I worked. If you know Zevon's music even a little bit you know what I'm talking about: the guy was a literary writer without being a *literary* writer, pulpy, zany, irreverent, and unpretentious, romantic in the Raymond Chandler sense, where any impulse to prettify things is clouded by disappointment. I liked him. And what I remembered was driving home one particular summer evening with my dad—it would have been June, because the fog was so dense by the time we got to Santa Monica, we could as well have been inside a cloud—and he was behind the wheel of his convertible, one arm stretched out and the music just *blaring*, Zevon's great song about being an "excitable boy." There was a disconnect between this romping, stomping tune—almost music hall–like—about biting theater ushers and cutting up young women, and the weather, which wrapped itself around us like a substance; and also between the song (ridiculous, violent, but, y'know, jolly) and my father's silence. He wasn't saying a word. We pulled up in front of the house, the one in which we all, at that time, lived, and sat for a second, letting the song play out. I bobbed my head, trying to harness its mood, hoping I might be able to lift him out of his funk.

"Aren't you coming?" I said finally.

My dad sat stock-still behind the wheel, staring at the street. The top was down, and I was freezing. I just wanted to go inside. The fog was so dense—we lived seven blocks from the beach—I could barely see the house, which was not thirty feet from the curb where we'd stopped, and my father's shirt (white) and the hood of his car (also white) all seemed to blend into a milky stew. It was like we'd gotten lost, like we were piloting a biplane through a thick layer of clouds.

"Dad?"

He turned up his palms helplessly. Zevon's voice roared in my ears, gave shape to those inchoate feelings—rage, grief, and dismay—that were forming even in response to the moment.

"I'm not coming in," he said.

"No?"

"Your mother and I are separating."

I can't remember the exact words that followed this. I know I asked why, and he didn't quite tell me. There was a girlfriend nearby and—he was going to sleep at her house, not just tonight but on all of them. I don't believe the word "divorce" was used, but I understood what was happening. I'd heard my mother sloshing around drunk in the kitchen, and those late-night fights that had spiked between them over the last few weeks, but I hadn't put it together until just now. Whenever they started arguing I'd strap on headphones and smoke a joint, blowing clouds out the window until I could roll over and go to sleep, but now the penny dropped.

"I'll see you next weekend," he said. Like he'd planned it all out—this perfectly ordinary suburban crime—but I wasn't ready. I knew that going inside would leave me and my younger sister alone now with our mother's mountingly erratic behavior, a brute reality for which I was, at fourteen, unprepared.

"Yeah."

I got out and started up the front walk. Halfway up I turned and looked back at the street. My dad still sat at the wheel, bobbing his head slightly, the car—a bone-white Mercedes with a blood-colored interior—jutting from the curb at an odd angle. The curbside palms shot up into the fog and vanished, so that the tops looked like leviathans: shadowy octopi hovering in the murk. He reached over to turn the radio back up—Zevon still, a disco tune now; "Nighttime in the Switching Yard"—and then pulled away down the street, his taillights and that wild California sound receding, until I was left alone with the cold mist and the silence.

◎

What's the story?

That was the story, as my neighbor had asked: Zevon's music had soundtracked one of the most emotionally uncomfortable moments of my adolescent life, one that, as I found myself living in a house now with an abusive parent but no rules, catapulted me into an isolation that would dog me the next few years. I didn't "like" Warren Zevon for the same reason one doesn't like pushing on a bruise. I admired it, but I found his music painful to listen to.

Then again, everything was painful to listen to, as I sat in my living room and played certain songs—David Crosby's "Everybody's Been Burned," Donna Summer's "On the Radio"—that both summoned and blotted the seasickness of my breakup with Q. Surely I'd been heartbroken before, several times, so why was this one so much worse? Why did I sit there some nights in my pajamas, drinking whiskey or wine straight out of the bottle, pitying myself and listening to records—13th Floor Elevators' feral, gnostic *Easter Everywhere*; the numbing gospel shimmer of Spacemen 3's *The Perfect Prescription*—that weren't going to make me feel any better? I was so ill I began taking aspirin, simply because I read somewhere it might be good for a figurative, as well as a literal, broken heart. I dragged that heart around inside me, where I could actually feel it burning, heavy as a boulder. Why was this so much worse even than my divorce, why did my mind keep returning, even as her reality began to dissolve—if I ever saw her again, I knew, I'd be shocked, as if I were looking at a stranger on the street—to the idea of a person who had never even liked me that much to begin with?

"What was it like," I asked my neighbor, "when you were with him? Was it good, at least at the beginning?"

She thought for a while, and then nodded. "He was so smart. He made me feel smart."

I nodded back. I understood this. It was part of the seduction.

"Was he kind to you?"

She snorted. "He wasn't very kind to himself."

Yeah, yeah, I thought. I understood this too. Did I really "like" Q, myself? The thought had occurred to me that in fact I did not, that the waves of a near-physical craving that shook me were more like a desire for nicotine: the wish for a toxic, and in fact unpleasant, substance that could kill. Once, we'd been walking home to her apartment after dinner and she'd said, "I think I'm smarter than you. You're a better writer, but I'm much smarter." Aside from wondering why she would care, I'd stared down at the street and thought, *I see you*. I'd fallen in love with a bully. I understood that now.

"Can I borrow these?" My neighbor had vinyl records, including several of Zevon's, taking up shelves on one wall of her living room. I knew I could stream them, but I wanted to relive my original encounters with the man in an analog format. I wanted to press the bruise as directly as I could: to feel not just the ache of more current suffering but also the pain that lay behind it. "I'll take good care of 'em."

"Knock yourself out," she said.

As I carried the records downstairs—with a couple of CDs as well, things he'd recorded during the time of his relationship with my neighbor—I thumbed their ragged cardboard edges, flipping through so I could view their covers. It seemed to me he was more like a writer or, in his mind, at least, an actor: the jackets were all images of himself, sometimes tricked out (as on one album called *The Envoy*) in a tableau that looked like a scene from a film. Zevon had never done any soundtrack work, nor had he ever, with one exception—a western called *South of Heaven, West of Hell*, released in 2000 and directed by Dwight Yoakam—appeared in a motion picture either. But he remained a creature of the industry, I could tell even at a glance. The movies had made, and unmade, him too.

◎

One thing about Los Angeles, since as I have just noted, Zevon belonged to it as truly as anyone ever will: this city is small. As a municipality, of course, it is massive, with at least eighty-four neighborhoods spread across 503 square miles, but as a myth? Zevon was born in Chicago, with family roots stretching back a generation into the Ukrainian shtetl, but he knew: this town is tiny. Particularly when you're engaging with the more storied elements of it—the rock joints, the restaurants, a literal geography that might stretch from the Sunset Strip to Joan Didion's Franklin Avenue house to Trader Vic's to Malibu Beach and back again—it is genuinely petite: barely more than a neighborhood. You see the same people, encounter the same names and faces all over, even as the old hot spots vanish (Ports, La Scala, the Hamburger Hamlet, Morton's, Jimmy's) and newer ones blossom (Giorgio Baldi, Wally's Santa Monica, the Grill on the Alley); even as people disappear and somehow, still, their essences remain: you can walk into a brand-new room and feel like you've been there dozens of times, never mind that you can smell the fresh paint. This is the mirage of Hollywood, the aspect of this place, frequently mislabeled as "ahistorical," that is like an all-night casino, in which every gesture has the force of desperation while remaining, at the same time, fundamentally lighthearted. *This* is the Los Angeles that the writer Eve Babitz, at one time Zevon's paramour and later his sponsor in AA, describes, and the one Zevon, who died a half-dozen doors down from where I am now writing, in an apartment on Kings Road in West Hollywood, belonged to. He ate his breakfasts at Hugo's on Santa Monica Boulevard, and did his shopping—oodles of it—at the excellent Book Soup, where he bought novels by writers who would later become his collaborators: Carl Hiaasen, say, or (I can't say I was surprised to see his name listed among *The Envoy*'s credits, as I scrutinized the sleeve) Thomas McGuane. When he lived up on Horn Avenue—walking distance from Kings Road, just past the shell of the original Spago, opposite Tower Records on Sunset, in the place he'd christened "Cat Piss Manor"—he bought his groceries at the Ralphs that was just up the block from the Troubadour, where he'd once ("once"—ha!) been arrested for public drunkenness. All of this forms a tight regional geography, of places that are largely not on maps, un-ogled by the busloads of tourists that still cruise the Strip and the curving passages of Sunset Boulevard that wind toward the sea. It is, in essence, a proletarian place: pretty but seedy, down-at-the-heel but also a little hopeful, like drinking a cheap mimosa on a hotel terrace where one can smell, always, the distant traces of last night's vomit. The signage is peeling, the tattoo parlor across the street—no matter which way you face, it's always there—is closed. If this sounds like I am describing the setting for a detective story, it's because I know Zevon would have liked it that way. Because he was a person who fought to romanticize his own experience every step of the way (the way addicts often tend to), and who could never outrun his consciousness of guilt. Because he was the kind of detective, in other words, who was also the cadaver and the search.

◎

He came to LA for the same reason all the others did—Browne and Lindley and Henley and Frey, all those Eagles and high-flying troubadours who were quicker than he was to make it big—though he didn't know any of them then: didn't know the members of Fleetwood Mac who'd eventually play on his records, or Linda Ronstadt, who'd help build his career by covering "Hasten Down the Wind" a decade later, either. An itinerant kid—there'd been schools in Fresno, San Pedro, and San Francisco, before he finally decided to live with his dad in Culver City and finish at Fairfax High—he came to play music. He already had a band, called lyme and cybelle (lowercase intentional), a folk duo who recorded a clutch of singles in 1966. Only: there's no way to talk about this without addressing the elephant in the room first. Before we get to any of the meaty stuff about Zevon's life and times, it seems important to note that he was a drunk, a violent and abusive alcoholic. The singer's ex-wife, Crystal Zevon, confirms as much in her raucous and surprisingly forgiving oral history *I'll Sleep When I'm Dead*, wherein she describes an incident in which he beat her until her entire face turned black and blue. He was a serial philanderer, negligent toward his children when they were young; he was unkind and occasionally ungenerous with his cowriters, for instance Roy Marinell, whom he apparently screwed out of royalties for "Werewolves of London." He was, in short, a real prick. So it's fair to wonder, here in the more enlightened twenty-first century, why write about him? The one thing we seem to be able to agree on these days is that people like that should be, y'know, canceled. Why dig up his grave (death having "canceled" Zevon pretty effectively a good twenty years ago and left him, at most, with the marginal status of a cult artist) only to insult his rotting bones? His writing is good—great, even; great enough that Bob Dylan, Bruce Springsteen, Neil Young, Stevie Nicks, and the Pixies, among many others, were all huge fans—but his story is miserable from one end to the other. It offers neither redemption nor much in the way of contrition nor, well, anything, really, beyond chaos and disorder and a stretch (at least there was that) of bristling sobriety. So is there any good reason one should opt now to tell it?

I won't answer that. Or rather, I won't answer it yet. Like any good prosecutor, and any good public defender, I'll let the facts speak for themselves, hammering them only when necessary. I have people—let's call them figures of moral authority, and sometimes of mercy—ready to testify on either side.

◎

Zevon's father was a gambler, a card shark nicknamed "Stumpy." All his life, Zevon would surround himself with nicknames—there was Duncan Aldrich, for example, his road manager, whom everyone around Zevon called "Dr. Babyhead"; "Klook Mop," a.k.a. "Klooky," his most frequent songwriting collaborator, Jorge Calderon; "Scorpion Boy," as he called novelist Carl Hiaasen; to say nothing of the various "turd handlers" and "mud jugglers" who handled the business end of his career—but somehow this ur-figure, his father, seems even a little more important than usual. Zevon told some people that Stumpy—née Willie, who owned a carpet store on Wilshire Boulevard—was a mobster, so right away you see the impulse to self-mythology.[19] Zevon was a prodigy, of sorts. He drove a white Corvette, wore a long leather

---

19. Maybe he was a mobster, at least by association. He and his kid brother Hymie did some work under the aegis of legendary mob boss Sam Giancana in Chicago, in the forties, shortly before Zevon was born.

coat and a gunslinger's hat; he played classical piano, which he'd learned, in part, at the feet of Stravinsky. He was, in short, a *figure*, even in midsixties Los Angeles where the absurdly gifted freaks—Captain Beefheart, Lowell George, those top-hatted and pointy-bearded figures who proliferated along the Strip— tended to collect. He reaped some serious royalties long before he himself ever had a hit (not that he was to have many, or any, really, besides "Werewolves") when the Turtles, his friends, put a song of his called "Like the Seasons" on the B side of their 45 of "Happy Together," which of course sold millions. One day he pulled his car over to the side of the road to pick up a hitcher, a girl he knew from San Francisco named Marilyn "Tule" Living- ston, and before long they were shacked up. But it wasn't Tule he went on to marry—not even after they had a child together, a son named Jordan—but rather Crystal, whom he met a few years later when he was touring with the Everly Brothers, acting as musical director for their band. All of this . . . well, it isn't "pre- history," exactly, but it's the setup: the staging of a life in which he was to act like a real rock 'n' roll asshole, never really "having it all" (certainly not; while his friends Jackson Browne and the guys in the Eagles were having hit records, Zevon was struggling along eating cheap burritos in Echo Park, gathering more appre- ciation from his peers than actual tangible evidence of success), but never altogether *not* having it either. At the beginning of his career, there was promise, the golden hope of a person whose immense talent was incontestable. At the end—and it was a long end: many years of records released by labels who knew how gifted he was, and that it might be a crime *not* to release music by someone as good as that, but who also knew how few units he actually shifted—there was acceptance, I think, of what it meant to be a cult artist. In between, there was "Werewolves of London," a novelty song—a goof, at least, because Zevon didn't do "novelty," but he also had the guts not to take himself too seriously (imagine Jackson Browne, or Bruce Springsteen, or even Lindsey Buckingham, any of his peers, being willing to write a tune that was basically the thinking person's "Monster Mash")—which took off to become a huge hit. Not nearly his best song, not even among his top thirty by my lights, it is completely irresistible, loopy and charming and dumb, "dumb" in that way that only a really intelligent thing, sometimes, can be. It is still probably the only piece of music he ever made, cowritten in this case with Roy Marinell and the guitarist Waddy Wachtel, that truly pleased his label bosses, at least in a commercial sense, that made David Geffen sit up and think, *Hey, there's money to be made here.* Only . . . that was it. Which left a good twenty-five years or so for Zevon to soldier on as Mr. Disappointment, the Talent Who Never Really Broke, the Great American Songwriter who might also, in the end, have been little more than a footnote.

◎

The life story, as I say, is sordid. There's a reason I'd like to get it over with, and it isn't just to give him a pass. As with a lot of artists, the work is more engaging than the life (one gets the sense that all that drinking and staggering and stumbling he did was largely to mitigate the *boredom*, the sense of everything else being fundamentally intolerable to him), but you can't just skip over it. Hardly. But let's assume you know, or at least can imagine, the basics: groupies, sexual exploitation, alcoholic blackouts, ruinous behavior onstage and off—the night he was reluctant to leave New York City because he wanted to see his friend Bruce Springsteen live, only to be told the show had happened the evening before, and he'd in fact been in attendance; the Christmas in Spain he came home and decked his wife before kicking her out of their hotel room, along with their infant daughter; the night he shot up his bathtub with a handgun, in pursuit of imaginary cockroaches—the callousness, the eventual sobriety, when it finally took after multiple failed attempts, the years of leaping from girlfriend to girlfriend (each seemed to last approximately two years) like some sort of extraordinarily rough-skinned frog moving among the lily pads. His friend Tom McGuane described Zevon as "a kind of lost child. But, because he's such a prickly, complicated person, he's not the kind of lost child you give a hug to." Fair enough. I won't hug his corpse either.

Let's assume, as the record shows, Zevon was a lousy human, who caused a fair amount of suffering. Let's assume, too, that the people who loved him did so for reasons greater than just the lure of his genius, or his charm. The novelist William Gaddis wrote, "What's any artist, but the dregs of his work? the human shambles that follows it around." This may be true, although it seems to me equally backward: the work is just the residue, the precious gunk that collects, so to speak, in the mesh of the pipe. But let the complexity of the life here be something of a given, then, and let's attend, instead, to the rest of it. By which I mean not (just) the work but the people, the other human beings— you could call some of them "apostles," or "interpreters," though you won't find too many apologists—who collected around the man, who suffered and glowed in his wake.

◎

Zevon's favorite novelist was Ross Macdonald, the great crime writer who defined a certain view of Southern California in the 1950s and '60s. There were others (scan the various biographies, not just Crystal Zevon's book but James Campion's *Accidentally Like a Martyr*, George Plasketes's *Warren Zevon*, or the best and most recent of the bunch, C. M. Kushins's *Nothing's Bad Luck*, and catch the various references to Paul Bowles, James Crumley, Norman Mailer, Joyce Carol Oates; Zevon may have read like a mid-twentieth-century litterateur, with an unfortunate emphasis on white dudes, but read he certainly did), yet Macdonald retained pride of place. Indeed, even beyond the confines of influence, the writer would play a small but determinant role in Zevon's life. When Zevon and Crystal decided to move to Montecito, California, in 1978, they did so in part because they thought (don't the addict and the enabler always think) that getting away from the "temptations" of LA would be good for Zevon, but also because Macdonald, who was Zevon's absolute hero, happened to live there. The *Rolling Stone* journalist Paul Nelson, who was another hero of a kind thanks to his advocacy, the truly tireless work he put in fighting for those artists in whom he believed, wrote about Zevon's encounters with Macdonald. In a long, harrowing, and slightly depressing profile Nelson wrote about Zevon in 1981—harrowing because it describes in close detail the intervention Nelson and others staged to get the musician into rehab in 1978, along with the behavior that led to it; depressing because it somehow retains a rather moist and worshipful stance toward its subject even so—the journalist recalls Zevon's awkward first meeting with Macdonald at the Coral Casino Beach Club in 1976.[20] He describes too how a few years later, when Zevon was fresh out of a Santa Barbara hospital and teetering on the lip of real catastrophe, beset by hallucinations and manias, it was Macdonald who showed up on Zevon's doorstep as an angel of mercy, to coax him back over to reason. It is almost impossible, for me at least, to think about Zevon without thinking of these two men: Nelson and Macdonald, whose real name was Kenneth Millar. Together they form a trinity: the songwriter, the journalist, and the novelist; the addict, the enabler, and the rescuer; or, if you like, the Father (Macdonald), the Son (Zevon), and the Holy Spirit (Nelson, I guess). Their involvement, so far as it went, was brief: Nelson, who met Zevon shortly after the release of his second, self-titled, album in 1976, was out of his life by the mid-1980s, while Macdonald played only a peripheral, if crucial, role in Zevon's biography at all. Still, they need each other. As—Macdonald certainly understood this—we all finally do . . .

◎

---

20. The magazine ran the article only in radically abridged form, but the complete—and superior—piece can be found along with many of Nelson's other writings in Kevin Avery's excellent compendium *Everything Is an Afterthought: The Life and Writings of Paul Nelson* (Seattle, Washington: Fantagraphics, 2011).

Macdonald was the third in the line—after Dashiell Hammett and Raymond Chandler, respectively—of America's great twentieth-century noir writers, the inventors of the hard-boiled style. As Hammett had Sam Spade and Chandler had Philip Marlowe, Macdonald had Lew Archer, the private eye who featured in eighteen of his novels, starting with 1949's *The Moving Target*.[21] Hard-boiled fiction seemed to Macdonald to offer a very specific set of literary possibilities: it allowed both the reportorial freedom he'd seen in his all-time favorite novel, *The Great Gatsby*, and an opportunity to interrogate problems of morality and civic power. Macdonald was a great writer, not just of "crime fiction" but of fiction, period. His greatness resides less in any particular

---

21. Initially John Macdonald, the author's pen name became John Ross Macdonald with the publication of the second Archer book, *The Drowning Pool*, and eventually—with 1956's *The Barbarous Coast*—became simply Ross Macdonald, remaining so for the thirteen books that followed.

stylistic gift, although his bare, unadorned prose is unfailingly accurate, and prone to land upon the sharpest possible detail, and more in his moral density and precision: the Henry James of crime novels, in this respect. At least as valuable to California writing in particular as Chandler—who hated and resented him, and went out of his way to belittle the younger writer throughout his career[22]—Macdonald had something that distinguished him to the next generation of enthusiasts and literary wannabes, that made people like Zevon and Nelson and their peers (music critics Dave Marsh and Kit Rachlis were two more high-profile fans) clutch his books to heart in a way they didn't, quite, with Chandler's. It had something to do, I think, with empathic range, with that quality—the Archer novels, particularly the late ones, are suffused with it—Keats called "negative capability."[23] For people like these, who came of age in the sixties, Macdonald seemed like a kindred spirit. In the introduction to Kevin Avery's wonderful assemblage of Nelson's conversations with the novelist, based on the nearly fifty hours of tape the journalist compiled with an eye toward an oral biography of Macdonald that never happened, Dave Marsh recalls, "You did not feel a generation gap.... [Macdonald] had an empathy with the dilemma of young people like very few other [writers] in his generation." Nelson felt the same,

---

22. Chandler's backstabbing letters, which are included in the collection *Raymond Chandler Speaking*, accuse Macdonald of, among other things, "a lack of some kind of natural animal emotion."

23. Again. One wonders what star-crossing forces—or what long arm of coincidence—may have tangled Macdonald's fate, like Fitzgerald's, with the date of Keats's letter, December 21. The title of an autobiographical narrative Macdonald struggled for many years to finish was *Winter Solstice*.

but it wasn't because Macdonald was "hip." It was, rather, because he was almost priestly, because there was something in his fiction—and, one surmises from Nelson's and Zevon's accounts of him, in his person—that oriented toward forgiveness. One sees it in his books over and over, the laying bare of motives that aren't strictly venal: behind the instigating art theft in 1976's *The Blue Hammer*, say, or the twenty-years-dormant murder in 1963's *The Chill*. People in Macdonald's cosmos commit crimes to protect themselves, or to stay hidden around questions of identity and personal freedom. Children and spouses go missing, but where the Chandlerian web tends to unfold in the present, Macdonald's plots, in the later novels especially, open doors to the deep past. And through it all moves the forensic hand of Lew Archer, who's more of an enigma than Sam Spade or Philip Marlowe, but whose fundamental loneliness (because this is a hard-boiled detective, after all) is edged out by fathomless empathy. As Archer thinks in 1956's *The Barbarous Coast*, "The problem was to love people, try to serve them, without wanting anything from them." Try to imagine Marlowe—or any other noir detective, really—thinking that.

Zevon the reader loved him. Zevon the man did too, after Macdonald showed up on his doorstep out of the blue. "It was like a dream come true," he told Paul Nelson. "At the lowest point in my life, the doorbell rang. And there, quite literally, was Lew Archer, on a compassionate mission, come to save my life." Zevon was in awe, where for Macdonald, whose response to Zevon's music isn't recorded—Nelson had given him an album, but Macdonald predominantly loved jazz—this was just the sort of merciful visit you performed for a person, *any* person perhaps, in trouble. The sort *he* performed, at least. Zevon wasn't to remain a part of his life. It was just a fan encounter, a stray kindness. Of the kind one tends, often enough, to forget.

◎

Did Zevon deserve it? The musician didn't get sober for the long haul until the better part of a decade later, and so what I'm wondering is . . . is it wasteful to offer this type of kindness to someone who might be considered something of a monster? Not that Zevon can be summed up quite so easily. My upstairs neighbor—who dated him during one of the final periods of active addiction, after his Santa Barbara crackup in '79, but before 1986, when he was rescued by a stalwart record label executive named Andrew Slater and shepherded, successfully at long last, into sobriety—would not describe him as anything of the kind. For her, he was just a crummy boyfriend. "I've had better and I've had worse," was how she put it when I pressed her, hoping I might find a corollary to my own experience. But once we start lining up a person's lapses and misjudgments, when we begin poring over his or her biography to catalogue all the terrible behaviors we find there—Zevon's inventory being approximately a hundred times longer than most people's—it's hard to stop. So why should *anyone* have treated him kindly?

It's no real answer to seek refuge in the work, or to note that Zevon never released a bad record. The whole great-artist-but-lousy-person thing went out with the twentieth century, and Zevon's failure was failure of the lowest possible order: the sort that glorifies itself, over and over and over, in a futile attempt to escape the persecutions of shame. If you read Nelson's 1981 profile of Zevon in *Rolling Stone*, it's hard not to cringe. Not just because the piece, which is titled "Warren Zevon: How He Saved Himself from a Coward's Death," is inaccurate, as Zevon would not "save himself" from the "cowardly" alcoholic death he claims to have been spared from for another several years yet, but also for the way it inadvertently endorses Zevon's most transparently self-dramatizing claims. Wading in with the usual malarkey about how fit and trim and together he seems, how clear-eyed and clearheaded—the classic terms of the Sober Celebrity Puff Piece, down to the new girlfriend (actress Kim Lankford, of the then-popular TV show *Knots Landing*) by his side—Nelson proceeds to allow Zevon to proclaim there's "nothing romantic . . . about drinking," and then to evoke a whole battery of romantic touchstones (F. Scott Fitzgerald, Clint Eastwood, Sam Peckinpah, the New York Dolls) in describing Zevon's boozy, nomadic history. It's not really Nelson's fault—he's a wonderful writer, contagiously passionate, and the piece derives immense power from its intimacy—but the article offers an awfully friendly theater for Zevon's self-mythologizing. Perhaps all celebrity profiles do as much. But this one, in which Zevon speaks of heading off "to Morocco with a bag filled with Valium, vodka, and Fitzgerald," suffers from the same willful self-magnification as Zevon's hero's "The Crack-Up," insofar as the "vulnerability" and "self-knowledge" proposed are largely a pile of bull.[24]

---

24. According to Zevon's most recent biographer, C. M. Kushins, one of the singer's early nicknames for himself was "F. Scott Fitzevon." *Nothing's Bad Luck* (New York: Da Capo, 2019), 50.

But as I hunkered down with my neighbor's records, I slowly grew to love them, and Zevon, without apology. In part because it's just this manner of hedging—the creation of multiple persuasive personae, from the brothers in 1976's "Frank and Jesse James," to the nearly naked, fig-leafed singer of 2003's "Keep Me in Your Heart," a song that puts forward, I suspect, a slightly more repentant figure than the songwriter actually was—that makes Zevon so great. It allows the work to carry so much feeling, to remain clear-eyed while conveying both a sense of ridiculousness and profound feelings of grief. "The days slide by / Should have done, should have done, we all sigh / Never thought I'd be so lonely," he sang in "Accidentally Like a Martyr." And, in "Trouble Waiting to Happen," "I woke up this morning and fell out of bed . . . / Should have quit while I was ahead." As someone who had become suddenly radically reacquainted with his own haplessness in the face of a mighty despair—I had never felt so foolish as I did that spring, losing my mind over a person I had known barely three months—those records cut me to the bone.

◎

"Am I a terrible person?"

She'd asked me this once. I no longer remember where or when, but Q had turned to me—it was after a fight, or rather after one of the argumentative sparring sessions we engaged in constantly—and said this. I couldn't tell at the time if she meant it rhetorically, the way we do when we ask after some tiny misdemeanor, a social faux pas ("Am I a terrible person if I say I hate vanilla ice cream?"), or whether she meant it genuinely.

"That depends," I said.

Two lines, plucked from oblivion. My response was passive-aggressive, pointy, calculated to annoy. I no longer remember what she said in answer to this either. But I remembered this exchange—boiled down to its essence, it was almost koan-like—as I immersed myself in Zevon's music, and in my feelings of regret, which led me too to scrutinize my motives. Why had I fallen so hard for someone who was basically a cipher to me? It wasn't her work or her intelligence I'd loved, it was her charm, which anyone who's ever met a sociopath knows is but a veil. Q certainly wasn't that, but as I swam through the murky and, it seemed, ever-deepening currents of my feelings, I began to wonder too about my own performance. *Am I a terrible person?* Was I a good one? Because it bore itself in upon me that the things I had done, the late-night runs for chicken soup and the trip to the animal hospital and the walking of her dogs when she was tired, the things that were meant (I'd thought, at the time) to be considerate, were really just bullying efforts too. *I'll take care of you.* (Was that really what I was saying? Or was it, rather, *I'm irresistible.*) *Love me.* Well, you can never compel another person's love. We all know that. But of course, that rarely stops us from trying when the opportunity arises. An opportunity that was not, as I had believed, about adoration; it was about self-hatred, and about my own gnarled feelings of inadequacy.

I loved Zevon's music because those feelings didn't hide. A song he'd written about my neighbor, "Angel Dressed in Black," began with a description of waiting anxiously for her to return: "Sitting on the sofa / suckin' a bowl of crack." Yet even when he was fanning these emotional knots out among various characters—headless Thompson gunners and junk-bond traders gambling in casinos, apes breaking out of captivity and diplomats flying into Damascus—he was singing about himself, and when he was singing about himself, naked confessional songs like "Reconsider Me" or "Let Nothing Come Between You," it was always, also, about other people. Was Zevon a terrible person? It began to seem, somehow, the wrong question. He was terrible to many who were close to him—when Paul Nelson had gone to the mat for him, had flown to California on his own dime to usher the singer into rehab; when he'd fought tooth and nail for *Rolling Stone* to run the piece he'd written over his editor in chief's objections, a fight that ultimately cost him his job, Zevon just dropped him, and stopped returning his calls—but generous in his art. And art is effectively a person too.

I wasn't done wallowing. I spent a long time—too long—wringing my hands and stewing, scrutinizing Zevon's lyrics like a Talmudic scholar and reading, over and over, the novels of Ross Macdonald. There was a song called "Splendid Isolation" that I loved. The song was obviously sardonic, with its lyrics about wanting to live in the desert, about wanting to wake up alone, and obviously sincere: he was telling someone, possibly an ex-partner, that he wanted to be left by himself. I wanted to want this. Once, that spring, I was driving along Third Street, listening to Zevon as I glided between traffic—the song on the stereo was the hit, with its delicious, alliterative lyric about the "little old lady" being "mutilated late last night"—when a car, a white Prius, pulled out in front of me.

"A-ooooooh! Werewolves of—"

Oh, fuck. I recognized her car. And as I stepped on the brake, to let her merge, and then watched her accelerate, pulling away from me in both time and space—into a life that had nothing to do with me—I felt my body grow cold. I turned a corner and swung the car to the curb, then cracked the driver's side door and, I swear, vomited onto the street. I felt numb, dissociative. I'd never had a panic attack, but this was what I supposed one was like: an involuntary bodily response, more like a flu than an emotion. My temples flushed and my sinuses throbbed. I shook for about ten minutes, hanging out the door so I could suck some air. Then it passed and I was able to drive home.

Zevon was no help. Art was no help—I was barely able to concentrate sometimes to read, let alone to write—but he would have understood these feelings, I'm sure. You have to hate yourself a lot to make a record like *Bad Luck Streak in Dancing School*, to name but one of his self-loathing opuses; you have to beat yourself senseless and then—or rather, also, at the same time—be willing to laugh at that too. Maybe that was something. Even as I reacted to the very rumor of Q (was that her car? I wasn't sure I'd had the license plate right, afterward) like someone being pulverized by a disease, I felt like I was cleaning myself out. Like I was working my way free of something and it was working free of me: a splinter that had lived far too long under the skin.

◎

How do we forgive those people who've done their damage so close to home?

As the weather warmed—it was almost summer now—I turned this question around in my mind, thinking of my mother, and of D and of N: the little crimes, and the larger ones, that make up a life. Was I supposed to remember my mother for her cruelties, only? Was I supposed to judge N for a single act of infidelity?

Zevon was rough on the people closest to him. His relationships never lasted, not just with the girlfriends but with everybody else. The close friends, the collaborators, the family members, the label bosses—even a stalwart supporter like Jackson Browne, who'd bent over backward to land Zevon his first record deal—got sick of him, exhausted by the curmudgeonliness, the caretaking, the irrationality, the betrayals: all the things anyone who has ever loved an addict knows, surely, too well.

"Did you ever forgive him?"

I asked my neighbor this question once. By now our friendship had moved on to other things—we often sat together with our laptops, working, in a companionable silence that could stretch out sometimes for hours—and so she looked up at me blankly.

"Who?"

(By now I had heard the story of their relationship, how their first date began with her meeting the ostensibly sober musician, recently out of rehab, at the Sunset Marquis and ended with him drunk in a bathtub, empty vodka bottle cradled to his chest; how they'd lived together for two years in the apartment up above Sunset, "Cat Piss Manor," before he'd decided one afternoon to cut her unceremoniously from his life.)

"Warren."

She stared at me a moment. As if to say, *That's the wrong question.*

"I never thought of it that way."

It was hot. I remember looking out the window at the yard we shared but never used: a little square of dry brown grass, a glass patio table. We were upstairs in her kitchen.

"Didn't you?"

"No!" She waved her hand barely, just flicked it. The question didn't require further thought. "He was just a person."

Maybe this was it, for her: when they'd met, I knew this too, he was a *genius*, a poet, a rock star; when they broke up, he was a human being, with the usual boring eccentricities and daily habits. But so it goes with every relationship, really.

As I made my way downstairs, later that afternoon—down the metal fire-escape-like flight that led behind the house from her unit down to mine—I found myself frozen as I glanced over at the lawn: someone's idea of utopia, surely, this little neglected patch that had fallen into disrepair. My brief encounter with Q was like that too: a bright idea, an imagined green space—oasis, dream—that had outlived its utility. That had died on the verge of its very construction.

The person you are, and the person you wish to be. The life you have and the one you merely wish you did, free of all those dismaying compulsions and idiosyncratic behaviors, those alarming intrapsychic spirals I suspect we all trace. There is a gap between these things, just as there is between the person you love and the one you merely hope to. In a strange way, the latter can, sometimes, be harder even to lose.

Warren Zevon was the same person, the same artist, from one end of his life to the other. He was a reckless, drug-fueled maniac at the beginning—an "excitable boy," as the song has it—and a prickly, Mountain Dew–fueled one after that. "People change," we say, but what we mean is that our perception of them changes, or, sometimes, that their perception of themselves does. I spent that summer getting back to work, taking breaks occasionally to listen to Zevon. My favorite record was still his first one, the self-titled album that came out in 1976, but I listened over and over again to the later albums, 2000's *Life'll Kill Ya*, 2002's *My Ride's Here*, and 2003's *The Wind*. Not because they offered any stirring conclusions but because they seemed somehow plainer: a little less gonzo self-mythologizing, a little more humility in their approach to private suffering, and to the actual world.

> *Some days I feel like my shadow's casting me*
> *Some days the sun don't shine*
> *Sometimes I wonder why I'm still running free*
> *All up and down the line*

Perhaps I was mistaken (after all, Zevon had been singing about crimes committed and consequences that could not be outrun—"Keep on riding, riding, riding"—since "Frank and Jesse James" at the beginning), but it felt that way. Just as it felt I was returning my own attention to that actual world too.

◎

In the summer of 2002, Zevon was playing a gig in Canada. He walked offstage and felt—dizzy, like he was going to puke.

"You OK, Warren?" his guitarist asked him.

"Fine."

"You sure?"

Bent over, with his hands on his knees, the singer found himself gasping for breath.

"Y—yeah," he said, as he straightened up finally. "Just a little altitude-sick."

That's what it was, right? It happened again the next night. But when you played these shows in the mountains, you got winded, Zevon figured. Or maybe these were panic attacks, just like he'd seen Tony Soprano have on TV. He didn't want to think about it, really. Would you?

I want to linger here for a moment, in this place where Zevon was yanked up against his most profound terror. I want to see if there's anything to be gained in paying attention—just like I was that spring—to the moment when the clock stopped. "My songs are all about fear," Zevon had remarked, back in 1989. And yet the next batch of songs, the ones he would write for *The Wind*, are no more so really than the ones he'd written before this: they ring with the same mordant exuberance he seemed to discover everywhere else. But a feeling of mournful sweetness—something a bit gentler, I think, than on other efforts—moves through them like humidity, saturating them, softening things just a touch.

He flew home from Canada. Tony Soprano, right? That was the explanation he liked: the one where life—at least, his life—resembled something from the movies.

"You should go see a doctor." His friend Jorge Calderon made the suggestion. "If something's wrong, get it checked out."

"Nah," Zevon said. "It's OK, really. I'm OK."

"You sure about that?"

◎

In fact, Zevon hadn't so much as visited a physician in decades. *Life'll Kill Ya* closed with a song entitled "Don't Let Us Get Sick," and—by the crooked logic that seemed to govern the man's thinking here—maybe you couldn't get sick if you never went to see someone who might conceivably say you were. In a life that was riddled with superstitions and phobias—Zevon could barely cross the street without ascribing an arcane meaning to the number of cars he counted—doctors were the worst.

"You'd be so proud of me! Guess where I am!" He called Calderon one morning from a pay phone. "Guess!"

"Warren, I have no idea."

"I'm at the cardiologist! You told me, right? Here I am!"

Maybe he thought that would do it. Pleasing his friends like it was a trick he could perform that would let him off the hook. He went back upstairs. The doctor ran a series of tests: chest X-rays, angiograms. When Zevon called Calderon back three hours later, he didn't sound so bright.

"It's not good," he said. "It's ... not good."

Indeed it wasn't. He had mesothelioma, which unfortunately they had just caught late. According to the doctor, Zevon had approximately three months to live.

◎

Did he *know*?

The cover of the album he'd released only a few months earlier, *My Ride's Here*, had portrayed him gazing out the side window of a hearse, as if it were a premonition—but of course he didn't. That was just a dark joke, the same one he'd been playing almost from the beginning, when he'd sung about a pair of doomed outlaws or about finding things to do in Denver when you're dead. Back in '89 he'd written one about how he was "gone to Detox Mansion / Way down on Last Breath Farm." But this was something else: the joke without a punch line, or the one in which the only punch line turned out to be yourself.

What would you do, given this news that all of us will, in some form or another, face eventually? Would you attempt to outrun that, too? The singer did what he had always done, confronted with a deadline: he went to work. Given the choice between some arch-romantic misadventure (with his ex-wife, for a moment, he discussed going to India so he might die at twilight in a boat along the Ganges) or an idiotic nineties-style Hollywood boondoggle (his record label boss sent him to meet with Deepak Chopra, so that he might pay through the nose for the privilege of dying in a "spiritual" context), Zevon decided, instead, to make an album. To do exactly what he would have done anyway, only faster.

When my mother was diagnosed, she kept a journal. If I had known a little better, when I'd visited her that final Christmas, I would have understood her reticence to engage with V and me was an expression of terror, a retreat into the silence that threatened to swallow her mind. Zevon had always been full of fear. He suffered from an obsessive-compulsive disorder that told him some things were "lucky," but others weren't. Pants, pencils, groceries, guitar picks: *everything* that passed through his hands became the object of an alarmed scrutiny. Prowling his favorite department store, Fred Segal on Melrose, he would spend hours sifting through packets of gray, always gray, T-shirts or underwear, trying to fathom which of the identical items weren't going to hex him. The same with other basics. My neighbor remembers going to the supermarket one afternoon with him in 1987 and seeing him reject carton after carton of milk. "This isn't the lucky one. We need the lucky one!" His friend Ryan Rayston, a writer he befriended late in his life—a rare close, platonic friendship for him with a woman—recalls the same, that he would sometimes call her to ask, "Nothing's bad luck, is it?" Rayston, who had OCD herself, understood. I suppose that I, too, understand the cast of that particular nightmare, the sense that life itself is a set of codes you hack or a roulette wheel you spin and then brace yourself, infinitely, against a bad outcome that remains inevitable. I'm only intermittently superstitious, but I *do* get this, the mind's attempt to cast a grid of rigid but opaque reasoning over events it cannot control. Zevon's terror, the one that had stalked his art—and his life—from the very beginning, would have found itself weirdly liberated here, able to impose a little order.

Like anyone, I hope one day to face my own death bravely. Writing remains one of my only hedges—a rehearsal space of sorts—against that fear. For Zevon, recording *The Wind*, which he did not at his home studio on Kings Road, the place he'd dubbed "Anatomy of a Headache" and where he'd recorded the album's three predecessors, but at Sunset Sound Recorders at 6650 Sunset Boulevard, would have been the same: a way of managing his panic, the threat of a pending oblivion. His friends who came by the studio—Bruce Springsteen, who played guitar on one song and sang backup on another; Tom Petty, who sang on "The Rest of the Night"; the other usual suspects who were on hand for the proceedings: Billy Bob Thornton, songwriter Jorge Calderon, Jackson Browne, Dwight Yoakam, drummer Jim Keltner, various Eagles—all noticed Zevon's exhaustion: he seemed pale and frail and a little bit drawn. But his musical capacities were undiminished. He sang and played as well as he ever had, his voice still resonant and warm. It was never his strength, the singing, but it wasn't really a weakness either: his was a storyteller's voice, affable and sardonic. Some of these studio guests, too, noticed what Zevon wasn't trying very hard to conceal: the bottles of liquid morphine he carried now in his pockets, in part, of course, to keep down the pain. In part.

This record sounds like a wake, rowdy and casual. You can hear the singer's friends—Browne, Thornton, the great country artist Emmylou Harris, too—leaning into it, their contributions standing slightly apart, feeling not so much integrated into a band sound as passingly spotlit, tributary. Zevon's own performances—the spoken exhortations that sometimes open a song, or coax a solo—feel the same, warty in a way that makes the record seem at once disarmingly intimate and a little unfinished. The songs about prisons and disorderly houses, the one about the singer's "dirty life and times" and the cover of "Knockin' on Heaven's Door"—perhaps the only time Zevon ever chose to perform one whose meaning and implication were obvious—aren't mysterious in their sentiments. Neither are the love songs, of which there are several. If, on *My Ride's Here*, recorded only a year earlier, there were songs called "Lord Byron's Luggage" and "Hit Somebody! (The Hockey Song)"—lyrically busy tunes he'd cowritten with Carl Hiaasen, Hunter S. Thompson, the Irish poet Paul Muldoon, and others—*The Wind* held "Please Stay" and "Keep Me in Your Heart," songs that require little interpretation even though they are, also, without trace of mawkishness or self-pity. The mop-topped and bearded figure who stares forth from the album cover is the same one pictured on the sleeve of *Excitable Boy*—thinner, sure, but not particularly "ravaged." He looks handsome and unrepentant, like a guy who might have designed it all to go out looking precisely the way he'd always hoped to: like a Byronic gunslinger, the romantic antihero who haunts nobody's twenty-first-century dreams any longer.

There were the farewell performances—no live dates, he wasn't in good enough shape for those, but a final appearance on his friend David Letterman's late-night show and a documentary shot for VH1, which tracked him through the recording of *The Wind*—and there were the private milestones too. He'd said he wanted to live long enough to see the forthcoming James Bond movie—under the circumstances, its title, *Die Another Day*, tickled him—and so the producers arranged a private screening. He wanted to witness the birth of his grandchildren, twin boys, and he did that too. *The Wind* was released in late August 2003, almost a year to the day after the doctors had offered up his final diagnosis. On September 7, his friend Ryan Rayston came by his apartment to fix him lunch. He was bedridden by then, thankful for the company. She made soup. Then she sat with him awhile, talking.

"Nothing's bad luck, is it?"

She knew what to say. "Nothing's bad luck."

He closed his eyes. "I'm just gonna rest a minute."

When he started to drift off, she stood to leave, knowing he liked to be alone while he slept.

"Please stay," he murmured. Like the song, the one he'd recorded just a few months earlier.

She sat. Listening, perhaps, to the traffic hissing along Kings Road at intervals; to her friend's ragged breathing; to that silence that would have filled the room as surely as the afternoon's swell of sunlight did, until she realized his breathing had stopped.

◎

All deaths are, in some sense, alike. Not just in the obvious one—the stopping of a heartbeat, cessation of breathing—but in the holes we leave for our loved ones and in their essential privacy. I think of Zevon, that cad, that genius, that father, that failure, that paragon, that lover, that friend, that person who was probably terrible to live with but wonderful to know, that husband, that adversary, that alcoholic who was sober for fifteen years, that *wit* and that dandy, that . . . folk singer, is how he wanted to be remembered, but I'm inclined to settle upon human being. *He was just a person.* He died in the middle of everything: even if his album was finished and released, there might have been more: the symphony he'd always hoped to write, the detective novels he'd hoped to someday manage too, about a gumshoe named Whip S. Bug. The books on his shelves—the camera stops briefly in the VH1 documentary to pan lavishly across them—the other songs that remained unwritten, performances that never happened, jokes that were never told. But the distinction was all in the *life*, that thing (Zevon was fond of quoting Schopenhauer on how "buying books would be good if we could also buy time to read them") that stopped short. And if you'd prefer to contemplate one that was a little less hurtful, at least once upon a time, to its bystanders, feel free. Only—

I cannot help but think of Ross Macdonald, who died of Alzheimer's in 1983, haunted still by the daughter he'd lost early to drug addiction. I cannot help but remember the phrase that resonates through *The Zebra-Striped Hearse*, which became for Macdonald a kind of maxim. "It's all one case." I cannot help but think of Paul Nelson, too, who died destitute in an Upper Manhattan apartment, having sacrificed his career on the altar of Zevon's talent. In Macdonald's novel, Lew Archer is doing as he does, tracking a runaway child from San Francisco to Mexico and back again, tying the obscure movements of the past to the enigmas of the present, but the words, too, are the writer's benediction spoken over his own profession, over his *and* Archer's. As he told Paul Nelson, the phrase "reflects my feeling that we're all members of a single body, to degrees that we have no idea except in moments of what might be called revelation . . . we live or die together." This feeling, which was at its root a religious one, is of course nothing new for a writer. It goes back to John Donne—"No man is an island"—at the very least. There is a bonus layer of irony, I suppose, in applying this notion to Zevon, who sang with cheerful cantankerousness of his "splendid isolation," who lived stubbornly alone, albeit with a rotating crew of lovers a phone call away, as he got older. But not really. Because Zevon's body of work was, in its own way, also religious. Even at its most profane, it remained abundantly generous, profuse not just with metaphor and narrative—and energy, madness, absurdity, perverse delight—but also with unconcealed feeling. The people who loved him, of whom there were many, surely did so not *despite* or *although* he was difficult; they loved him *because* he was, for exactly that impossible person he happened to be.

I walk by his house almost every day, the apartment building on Kings Road where he lived and where he recorded *Mutineer* and *Life'll Kill Ya*, the rooms in which, though I didn't know it until recently, he died. I like to think that those walls that were so lined with books by Ross Macdonald and others—those blocks of pages read and unread—are lined with them still. And I like to think that when he passed there remained some ineffable trace— for he and the critic had once been so close they'd enacted an archaic ritual in which they'd cut themselves and mingled their blood, "blood brothers"—of Paul Nelson, still, in his system, that these two other highly moral and beautiful human beings, each of whom died broken and in despair, each of whom deserves mercy if anyone ever did, surrounded him. That they were inside his heart and mind and body, and by his side, on his night table, and that their voices and their memories—that steam into which we will all someday vanish—filled his lungs and his inner ear, the way Zevon's—like F. Scott Fitzgerald's, and like Tom McGuane's, like Carole Eastman's and Eleanor Perry's, like my old friend D's and my former lover Q's—now fill mine, and like I, breathing out now from the bottom of a well, like I now fill yours.

VII

kings,
killings, etc.

hal ashby and
michael cimino

Once, I had a dream of fame.
Generally, even then, I was lonely.

—DAVID MARKSON, *Wittgenstein's Mistress*

I MET A MAN on Fifty-Seventh Street, once. This was during my high-rolling days in the 1990s, when I worked for the actor in Manhattan. Days filled with expensive meals, with an illusion—the one illusion that "success" really buys— of a seamless consubstantiality, as if I myself comprised the same expensive material that made up the Italian suits of half the people I dined with, the overpriced food on the superstar athlete's plate, the brightly painted walls, the filtered light and air, the bonhomie, which was really just money, that swirled around the rooms I passed through. Though I am ashamed to admit as much now, these are sweet memories: I was young, and Manhattan felt (as it did to others too in those econom-ically prosperous days) illimitable, an endless storehouse of cathedral-bright afternoons and honey-lit nights, nights spent shoveling myself in and out of taxicabs and beyond cur-tains and velvet ropes on the other side of which were things someone else had already paid for, all the useless perks that come when you can already afford the things you actually need, and plenty of those you don't. I cringe to think how much I enjoyed it, all this collateral crime. How could I, or anyone, have believed such extravagances were justified, that each free meal, paid for with a credit card that dipped straight into a multinational corporation's coffers, didn't rest somewhere on the back of a whole set of systemic atrocities? "Hi, Derek Jeter!" "Nice to see you, Sharon Stone." I'd like to imagine I wasn't an asshole, but there is no way to encounter a life like that even briefly—I walked away before the decade was over, sure it was killing me—without being fundamentally implicated. And when I look over my shoulder at my younger life's brightest hour, I can't help but shudder. But on this afternoon I am thinking of, one on which I was still too young to know any better, I recognized the man on Fifty-Seventh Street, and though I had never met him before, I walked over to introduce myself, like I was the president and he was the mayor. In those days, I didn't even think I needed a reason to present myself to someone like this, like I was some sort of an—instrument of fate.

"Are you Charles Burnett?" I asked.

The man, older than I was, no more famous to the general public then than he is today—less, surely, than he should be—seemed surprised. "I am."

"*The* Charles Burnett?"

He laughed. "I'm definitely one of them."

I was on my way in to a meeting, and he was—I assume, as the building we were standing outside housed a talent agency—on his way out of one, a conference of some kind with people who would have been helping him put together a movie that likely never happened, since Burnett has directed only two feature films in the last twenty-five years. But I can remember standing on the street, greenly, and oiling him with my enthusiasm, as sincere in my intention as he was in his affect: he fairly radiated decency, humility, kindness, charm. Then, as now, I considered Burnett one of the very greatest living American filmmakers, a giant whose relative obscurity was a crime. But as I drifted away from this brief, friendly encounter, one in which I foolishly assumed Burnett's greatness might be reward enough in itself, I failed to take the warning. I thought we were two kings, or one king and one princeling, merchants on the road to Smyrna, and not a wise man and an idiot, a great artist who'd retained his humility ("I'm one of them") speaking to a fool. Still. All these years later, I think on this encounter, which couldn't have lasted more than five minutes, and wonder if it might hold a sort of skeleton key; if it contains, in its way, everything there is to say about American ideas of success, and about how to survive it.

◎

I never wanted to be a filmmaker. Even as, growing up in Los Angeles, I came to understand the director was everything—thanks to a thrillingly evangelical film studies teacher who'd bathed our teenage eyes in Hitchcock and Buñuel, who led my high school classmates and me to sit in the darkness of LA's handful of revival houses and watch Nicholas Ray movies, Wim Wenders, Fassbinder, Godard—the idea never appealed, for reasons unknown. Movies were made by people (too frequently male and white, although this systemic tic wouldn't be plain to me until later) who were headstrong enough to overwhelm the system that arrayed itself against the making of quality cinema. This was the myth, incomplete at the very least, that hung itself over the world in which I grew up, during the aftermath of the chaotic, auteurist, and fabled "New Hollywood" of the 1970s. That there were other stories, and other myths—that a filmmaker as preternaturally gifted as Burnett could make films as lucid, appealing, and humane as 1978's *Killer of Sheep* or 1990's *To Sleep with Anger* and still be marginalized within the commercial establishment largely because (ahem) he wasn't white—wasn't yet clear to me, but even so. This was the central tenet of the American success narrative. An artist, or an entrepreneur, has an idea. This person brings the idea to market, and, with any luck (and with whatever forces align with that luck, be they talent, hard work, or simply privilege)—voilà! Success! Acclaim! Awards! It's a crude oversimplification of both process and result, but now as then it's the filmmaker who wears the glory, just as the writer does with the book, the musician with the song, etc. And if this model has come to seem a little exhausted, the product of a late capitalist, and very American, obsession with individual accomplishment and excessive private reward . . . that doesn't mean it isn't still secretly titillating. If "the function of freedom is to free someone else," as Toni Morrison said, then what is to be done with that other type of putative freedom, the freedom to do whatever it is you like? There is the famous story, recounted in Peter Biskind's *Easy Riders, Raging Bulls*, of filmmakers Francis Ford Coppola, William Friedkin, and Peter Bogdanovich pulling up in their limousines alongside one another at a traffic light on the Sunset Strip and hectoring one another, each man leaning out the window to quote his glowing reviews and list his Academy Award triumphs ("Eight nominations and five Oscars, including Best Picture!" "The most exciting American film in twenty-five years!"), before squealing off in their separate clouds of dust. Just because I had stopped being an asshole doesn't mean I didn't dream, at least occasionally, of what it might be like to someday become a bigger one. What was it like for these people—what was it like, when Hollywood was at its peak—to have the world, or at least Los Angeles, on a string? To have had the vision and the money and the license to execute, to do, at least for a moment, whatever they damn well pleased.

◎

I was watching a lot of movies, still. As the days stayed long and the weather got hotter yet, the bright, dry days of August, I prepared myself to move yet again. I wasn't going far—once more, just a few blocks away—but I needed to leave the room in which I'd received the news of my mother's death, the space in which I could feel the clinging specters of alcoholism, heartbreak, and suicide. I started boxing up my belongings, pausing in the thick of it to pant and sweat and breathe in lungfuls of cardboard dust. Occasionally I took breaks to fire up the DVD player, zeroing in on a pair of discs that were my mother's old favorites: 1979's *Being There* and 1978's *The Deer Hunter*, which were directed by Hal Ashby and Michael Cimino, respectively. I'd been too young for either when I'd first seen them, as a thirteen-year-old boy sneaking behind my parents' backs to watch them on cable. But they were part of my family's history too. My father had known Cimino at the beginning of the director's career, when he'd been script-doctoring and putting together his first feature, 1974's *Thunderbolt and Lightfoot*. He'd known Ashby a little also, when the director had cast Bruce Dern, my father's client and longtime friend, in 1978's *Coming Home*. This last film had cast a spell over my childhood: Jon Voight's turn as a paraplegic Vietnam veteran and Jane Fonda's as a newly awakening war widow, and—above all—Dern, who played Bob Hyde, a conservative soldier who comes home to discover his wife is having it off with another man. I'll watch Dern in anything—even as a small boy, I'd been entranced by his work in *Silent Running*, a 1972 dystopian thriller cowritten by Cimino—but throughout my adulthood, I realized, I had come to identify with the actor as well. Not just because of his knack for playing clueless cuckolds (besides Hyde, he'd also played Tom Buchanan in the 1974 adaptation of *The Great Gatsby*) but because his career, illustrious as it was, still feels defined by what might have been. The actor feels defined by films, and roles, that are under-seen and slightly underappreciated: 1972's *The King of Marvin Gardens* and 1975's *Smile*; 1989's *The 'Burbs* and 1976's *Family Plot*. All movies that are erratic but compelling, and all featuring—as do many others—excellent performances from Dern.

Besides this, though, there was something else. As I dug up *Coming Home* and watched that too, I found it fiercely moving, a romantic drama of three people—children, they all seem to me today—bound up in the repercussions of a war they ought not to be fighting. Under Ashby's gentle gaze, it seemed less conspicuously operatic, more thoughtful than other Vietnam movies like

The Deer Hunter, Apocalypse Now, or *Full Metal Jacket.* But also, it evoked so sharply a private world, one that is now long gone: my mother in Malibu, unravaged as yet by alcohol, my father young and clean-shaven, my sister and me wading at the surf's edge, playing with Dern's German shepherd, Sergei, while the adults drank wine or margaritas or, in Dern's case, Pepsi out of a long glass bottle, telling jokes that went well over my sun-bleached, seven-year-old head. It was personal, to watch this movie, or *Being There* (the author of whose source novel, Jerzy Kosinski—another suicide—had likewise been a friend of my father's), or any number of films from this era that offered an opportunity to see the once-invisible pain of the adults who populated my childhood translated into performance. Was this what I wanted? I couldn't help but wonder also, as I cracked back to work on still another script, a television pilot this time, whether all this was just an effort to revert back to the source. It feels embarrassing to confess this, that I had stared at some of these high-water marks of seventies cinema like they were home movies, private runes, but I did. Like anyone who's ever lost a parent, I found myself overwhelmed by a whole concordance of feelings: sadness and disappointment, nostalgia and grief. But because I can see the pieces of that vanished world rise before me again, can hear the recorded voices—as consoling as lullabies—and watch those youthful faces play before me, I am lucky, more so than most. Luckier too than these players were themselves, even as they lived the most glamorous dreams of their era.

◎

Ashby and Cimino. Cimino and Ashby. Two filmmakers, of that storied class that had sprung up during the late sixties and early seventies—Steven Spielberg, Martin Scorsese, George Lucas, Robert Altman, Francis Ford Coppola, Peter Bogdanovich, and others. A class that, for all its demographic flaws—it ought to include, in greater abundance, the work of Elaine May, Barbara Loden, Polly Platt, Eleanor Perry; it ought to include Melvin Van Peebles and Gordon Parks with the same types of studio budgets and creative freedom afforded their white contemporaries—remains as gifted as any Hollywood has ever produced. And if these two filmmakers, Hal Ashby and Michael Cimino, are effectively polar opposites—Ashby a dope-smoking flower child who took the sixties ethos to heart and ran with it; Cimino, strangely, a reactionary, a political conservative whose work was militaristic and aggressive—they nevertheless seem of a piece, two preternatural talents who found a way to take their brilliant careers and end them prematurely. Two, from that bright harvest of New Hollywood auteurs, who might at this very moment be sitting together in cinema heaven, in order that each might turn to the other and say, just like Peter Fonda's Captain America to Dennis Hopper's Billy the Kid at the end of *Easy Rider*, "We blew it." Who might commiserate forever in their twinned failure.

◎

Of the two, Ashby is the more lovable. He is certainly the more knowable, being the subject of both a detailed biography (Nick Dawson's *Being Hal Ashby*) and a recent, excellent feature documentary (Amy Scott's *Hal*), both of which allow the director's warmly generous, if complex, nature to float to the fore. Cimino, by contrast, was a recluse: after the storied failure of his *Heaven's Gate* in 1980—a failure that not only bankrupted a movie studio but inspired a best-selling book from the executive who oversaw this disaster, so that Cimino's folly was broadcast even beyond the coastal watering holes and gossip columns—he directed a handful of films, but for the most part lived in seclusion until his death in 2016. The man was such an enigma that even the fundamentals of his biography remained in doubt all the way to the end. Like Tuesday Weld—like a lot of people in Hollywood, really—Cimino had indulged in some selective mythmaking throughout the course of his career, lying about his birth date, blurring the lines around his family history, his education, even his military service. After the director told the *New York Times*, during the making of *The Deer Hunter*, that he had been a medic and a Green Beret in the Vietnam War, Universal Studios head Thom Mount shot that inexact claim down, saying, "He was no more a medic in the Green Berets than I'm a rutabaga." The facts, such as they were, remained fuzzy. Indeed, they still do. Cimino's and Ashby's lives intersected most notably at the 1979 Academy Awards, where *The Deer Hunter* was nominated for nine Oscars (and won five, including Best Picture), and *Coming Home* was nominated for eight (and won three, including Best Actor, Best Actress, and Best Screenplay). The films offered competing visions of Vietnam that showcased different political views, different aesthetic approaches, and different ideas of what it meant to be an American. Still. The two men shared an affinity, or at least an appreciation, as Cimino was one of a few people whose remembrance was aired at Ashby's funeral. And whatever else, they shared a fate, as filmmakers whose stock in Hollywood would plummet sharply, vertiginously, at precisely that moment of their greatest success.

◎

Ashby was raised in Utah. His parents were lapsed Mormons, and his father died by suicide when Hal was twelve—the one event from his childhood that would make itself felt, definitively, in several of his films. Otherwise, Ashby's background was generationally typical: born into a crucible of midcentury conservatism, educated unhappily at a naval academy, Ashby found himself married at seventeen, and, realizing only months later this had been a mistake, he lit out on the road. After a few months working railroad construction in Wyoming, he headed for California. In other words—his background was Kerouacian, that of a classic wannabe beatnik. He and a childhood friend hitchhiked six hundred miles to the corner of Santa Monica Boulevard and Vermont Avenue only to arrive broke and to discover that Ashby's paternal uncle, on whose presumed largesse they'd intended to rely, had died a few years earlier. It took a while for Ashby to find his feet. There were a few months of living on onion sandwiches, a story he would enjoy telling later about the day he bought a candy bar with his last dime and stretched it out to make it last three days. Eventually, he slunk back to Ogden again—not before marrying a second time—only to return to Los Angeles just months later, in early 1950. He didn't know what he wanted to do (he knew what he *didn't* want: to be a Ward Cleaver–style husband and provider; his second marriage, to a woman he'd met in Las Vegas, lasted not much longer than the first), but he was drawn, rather abstractly, to the movies. When the State Employment Office was able to help him land a job operating a mimeograph machine on the Universal Studios lot, he jumped at the chance. From there, he could see what he wanted. Being a director seemed to Ashby the best gig on the lot—the most prestigious, the most attractive. It would take him a long time to realize this dream, including, among other things, an eight-year union apprenticeship as a film editor, but he could see it. The rest was just hard work. And smoking weed. If there was a formative influence on Ashby's career, it was this. Drugs were of course all over fifties Hollywood—who *didn't* smoke weed, behind closed doors?—but Hal's intake was prodigious even in the bohemian circles he ran in.[25] Well before there was anything resembling a hippie movement, before anyone wore their hair long, or knew what a "flower child" was, Ashby was a walking hash clump. He was stoned pretty much all the time.

And Cimino? His drug habits were most probably nonexistent. He looked at the sixties—both the 1960s and, in the opening sequences of *Heaven's Gate*, the 1860s—through a seemingly prelapsarian lens. His wasn't the Vietnam that spawned an awakened consciousness, it was the one in which steelworkers from a Rust Belt town would enlist voluntarily, and would come home

---

25. Ashby kept some hip company. One of his traveling companions in those years was Sammy Davis Jr., himself a few years shy of becoming an established entertainer, member of Frank Sinatra's Rat Pack, etc.

from the war (some of them, at least) to sing "God Bless America" around a kitchen table, their patriotism unshaken even as their lives had been blown to pieces. If that makes Cimino sound like a right-wing square, well, fair enough, but the subversions and discomforts that leak through the cracks of his first three films—the three he made before his career skipped the rails—are compelling enough unto themselves. Where Ashby was a genial, anti-authoritarian humanist, whose characters are always (successfully or otherwise) kicking against the rigid hierarchies that surround them, Cimino was an opera singer whose heroic librettos were composed with a certain perversity, a formalist whose heroes (perhaps predictably, John Ford, Akira Kurosawa, and Luchino Visconti) were never as noisy, as freakishly sensational as he was. Born to more privilege than Ashby (or so it appears; Cimino was as indirect about his parentage as he was about everything else), he went to private school in Old Westbury, New York, and received both a BFA and an MFA from Yale. His father was a music publisher, his mother, a clothing designer, and in one of the scattering of interviews he ever granted that would even address the topic at all, he pointedly announced that he didn't want to discuss his family. ("It was like a Eugene O'Neill play," he said. "Every part of it hurts.") What little he did offer describes them in terms that are starkly aristocratic (his father "was a bit like a Vanderbilt or a Whitney") and suggests he'd been raised as a child prodigy. To that same interviewer, Cimino flashed a passport that indicated he'd been born in 1952, thirteen years after his actual date of birth, so maybe these utterances too should be taken with a grain of salt. What *is* known is that Cimino worked in advertising in the 1960s, that he came up as a commercial director and began writing screenplays. He cowrote *Silent Running*—that Dern-starring ecoterrorist thriller about a rogue botanist who decides to off his colleagues on a space station rather than obey orders to destroy the fauna they've cultivated—and then soloed on 1973's *Magnum Force*, the second in Clint Eastwood's line of *Dirty Harry* movies. The latter earned Cimino that actor's patronage, and he was able to direct his next script as Eastwood agreed to star alongside Jeff Bridges in *Thunderbolt and Lightfoot*.

◎

Filmmakers, of course, are not competitors, outside the ginned-up context of awards ceremonies. It's pointless to stack up Ashby's career next to Cimino's (by 1974, when the latter was just getting started, Ashby would have been gearing up to direct his fourth feature, 1975's *Shampoo*), as if they were a pair of hot rods, gunning their engines on the Strip. Still, there is a way in which the world of either director makes the other's stand in stark relief. Cimino's debut is a buddy film, a road movie in which a seasoned convict (Eastwood) and a young hustler (Bridges) go on the run from a group of vengeful bank robbers before the whole crew teams up to stage a heist all together. It's weirdly classical—a lot closer to *Adventures of Huckleberry Finn* or to Melville's *The Confidence-Man* than it is to the airiness of more traditional Hollywood caper films—and while it's nominally a comedy, the film is sober-sided and sad. It's also a valentine to the Old America, to one-room schoolhouses and country churches (we first meet Eastwood disguised as a preacher, peddling snake oil behind a pulpit), to amber waves and blond fields that are presented almost as ravishingly as they are in Terrence Malick's *Days of Heaven*. In a way, the movie seems a rebuke to *Easy Rider*, as Bridges's dying outlaw tells Eastwood's not that they blew it but rather that "I don't think of us as criminals, you know? I feel we accomplished something. A good job." It's hard to think of a sentiment less countercultural than this, which proposes its twin fugitives not as romantic antiheroes but as something more like workaday Americans. But *Thunderbolt and Lightfoot* is a love story: the heist itself hardly matters. Bridges's Lightfoot wants Eastwood's friendship, his affection, and if this is almost always the unconcealed subtext of a Hollywood buddy movie, here it's the text itself—he says as much. Bridges spends a good chunk of the movie—longer by far than is necessitated by its plot—wearing a dress: as this fact is played for laughs, it's the sort of reflexively transphobic Old Hollywood yuk-yuk that feels antiquated today, but it somehow adds to the film's unmistakable tenderness. This tenderness feels a little rough because you can't quite see the flinty Eastwood embracing it, but the film remains warm and engaging, in part because of some knottiness, some yearning Cimino can't quite bring to the surface.

Ashby, by contrast, let his countercultural flag fly high from the beginning. An inclination to tweak the complacency and self-regard of the middle class ran through the center of his debut feature, 1970's *The Landlord*, but it achieved full flower in the following year's *Harold and Maude*, a startlingly carnal romance between a teenage boy and an octogenarian woman. The latter is a renowned cult classic, easy to take for granted in its witchy idiosyncrasy, and yet when I saw it again recently, the sheer discomfiture of its central relationship, the sight of postcoital, death-haunted teenager Harold (Bud Cort) in bed with dotty old Maude (Ruth Gordon), still struck me as shocking. Even Ashby was a little freaked out by the relationship as he made the film, which is based on a script by Colin Higgins. When the director's method-acting star, Cort, asserted that he and Gordon should actually have sex on camera, Ashby flinched, and begged Cort to take a more soft-focus approach: "Please don't tell me this!" But it works: the film's weird blend of anti-military, anti-materialist, anti-Nixon sentiment with both winking nihilism and genuine heartwarming affection is hard to resist even today. Commercially, the film was a flop—pity the poor marketing executives trying to flog an erotic love story between an odd-looking suicidal teen and a nutty geriatric— but aesthetically? It's a masterpiece, even if it could have been shot on a different planet from any of Cimino's movies. Ashby's free-love aesthetic, present even in the military setting of 1973's *The Last Detail*, couldn't be further from Cimino's sweaty, honor-and-discipline fanaticism, for which the latter would find even greater extension in the films ahead. But you can't have one without the other, and the story of a Hollywood failure—or of *any* failure, really—is incomplete without its twin.

◎

My father served in the army, briefly, during the Korean War. He was closer to Ashby in temperament than to Cimino; though he was never overseas, his decision to enlist would also have been a poke in the eye to his own dad, my grandfather, with whom he did not get along. That grandfather—Grandpa Reuben—once filled his pockets with rocks and walked into the Pacific, distraught over a failed business venture, although he changed his mind at the last minute and swam to shore before he could drown. My mother, too, attempted suicide when she was a young woman, although the family record is murky on the circumstances: sleeping pills were the instrument, the reason is unrecorded. When she was a girl, just eight years old, her father had dropped dead of a heart attack at the kitchen table. My grandmother's response was simply to cross the room, have a seat at the piano, and begin to play hymns, without saying a word. My family on both sides is the opposite of self-dramatizing. If a bomb were to fall on a house occupied by any member of it, the survivor would probably brush off the dust, fix a sandwich, and sit down in the rubble to eat. My parents and I have wanted, I think, different things, as I have sought self-expression and each of them sought "success," even if that search was overtaken in my mother's case by a romanticized impulse toward oblivion. But romance dissolves in the face of information. The more you know about anything, or anyone, the less "romantic" it becomes. The paradox of my family—a Hollywood family, although this is probably true of families all over—is that no one knows anything, stories become anecdotes and anecdotes become myths and the myths themselves become hot to the touch, because the pain that underlies them is intolerable. Did my mother's mother *really* not say a word to any of her children after her husband collapsed? My mother isn't around to ask, although my aunt, who's nearly ninety now, tells me it's so. My father, well, he never talks about anything—it isn't a matter of taciturn machismo;

more one of Jewish neurotic self-effacement—so when I ask him about my grandfather's suicide attempt, he deflects like a politician. "I don't recall. Maybe." So here I sit, in the thick of a mythology composed of rumors and crudely outlined facts, facts I can neither elucidate nor explain. No wonder I have devoted so much of my life, practically all of it, to dreaming . . .

Bob Hyde (it is impossible almost to separate the image of Bruce Dern's character in *Coming Home* from that of my father, somehow: the two men were inseparable then) runs on the tarmac of a military base, the heat shimmering in waves in front of him, while the Rolling Stones' "Out of Time" plays on the soundtrack. On a fogbound beach, he takes off his wedding ring and his dress blues and he wades buck naked into the Pacific, swimming deliberately, decisively toward his doom. Is it wrong to see in this film's bookends a family history, my own unavailable life rendered legible to me? Is it wrong to see the same when Robert De Niro jams a pistol to his head in *The Deer Hunter*, grimacing—the joy of rolling the dice, the ineffable *delight* of knowing you could die in an instant—as he pulls the trigger and wins, lives to play (as he will have to) Russian roulette another day? Assuredly, yes, but it's all I have. And this is why we make—and consume—art in the first place.

◎

Ashby's father shot himself in the barn behind the family's house in Ogden. Although that suicide took place on dry land, Ashby's films often seem to rehearse suicide around water, not just in the conclusion of *Coming Home* but in those too of

Harold and Maude (wherein Harold's final attempt, after he has staged so many fakes over the course of the story, takes place on an ocean bluff) and in 1979's *Being There*, wherein Peter Sellers's Chance Gardiner strides out onto a pond and—miraculously fails to sink. Cimino may not have been haunted by suicide at all—in his filmography only Christopher Walken's Nicky, in *The Deer Hunter*, could be said to die this way—but he was, again, so tormented by his family he refused to speak of them in the first place. Neither man retained too much in the way of a tie to his parents: Ashby remained casually in touch with his mother—she visited him a few times in LA as his career warmed up—but she disapproved of his multiple marriages and viewed him with what could only be described as a loving detachment, writing to him that she was proud, but that he was, to some extent, a stranger. "I feel like I have never really known you since you were a young boy." Cimino's father died young—or so the director claimed—but of his mother he noted that she reached out to him only once after the success of *The Deer Hunter*, when his name was used as a clue in the *New York Times* crossword puzzle. ("Now I know you're famous," she said.) Such are the wages of success, perhaps—or such is a certain temperament, the kind that would live in flight from a family history of pain, that is so dogged in pursuit of them. Maybe there was a moment for each—for Ashby, as he carted away his armloads of Academy Awards (none of them, sadly, for Best Picture or Director) for *Coming Home*; for Cimino, as he bought yet another of the fleet of cars he kept behind the gates of his Beverly Hills manor, up Coldwater Canyon—where he wanted to shriek, "Top of the world, Ma," or where he felt, at last, his parents truly loved him. But that moment, if it came, would have passed only too quickly. Indeed, that moment would be, for each, but the beginning of the end.

◎

For Ashby, it began with an apprenticeship. Eight long years as an editor, working under the warm eye of the director Norman Jewison; eight long years in which he'd discovered his true love: those relentless days in the darkness of an edit bay tangled up in film stock, hanging around him like a woman's long hair. Any film editor will tell you it's an obsessive task, sifting through the untold yards of raw footage frame by frame, the exhausting task of putting an actual movie together, but Ashby was nothing if not obsessive. He worked so hard it would have killed him, if he didn't enjoy it so much. He got married again (wife number three, Mickey Bartron, was a painter, a freewheeling bohemian, and a dedicated weed smoker much like himself), and again (Mrs. Hal number four, Shirley Citron, was likewise an apprentice film editor; she was also a single mother, something Ashby embraced—until the structure of family life overwhelmed him), and—yes—a fifth, and final, time to the actress Joan Marshall, whom he met in 1969 while he was shooting *The Landlord* and divorced only a year later. Thereafter, the director would confine himself to good old serial, non-matrimonial, monogamy. His career as a filmmaker hadn't even begun at this point—though he'd won an Academy Award for editing, for 1967's *In the Heat of the Night*—but it's telling that his ex-wives all seemed to retain great affection for Ashby through the long decades ahead. The director may have been passionate to the point of exclusion about his work, but he was no callous rolling stone. He was a lover's lover, a fact underscored not just by the content of the films—even at his most sardonic, as in the Restoration-comedy-by-way-of-California-satire of 1975's *Shampoo*, for example, he is never *cold*, the way certain of his me generation peers could be—but also by the life, by the testimony of his friends that asserted as much. "Have you ever said *no!* to anyone in your life?" the actress Margot Kidder, one such friend, wrote to him while he was finishing *The Landlord*. "You are a man with five times as much goodness in you than most men . . . a goodness that we are all taught to strive for." If anything bedeviled him it was, simply, self-doubt. Where most directors are confident to a fault, Ashby fretted in a way that made studio filmmaking a torture to him. And yet one can imagine the films themselves were all the better for it.

Cimino, on the other hand, well . . . he seems not to have suffered from any such humility. There are no detailed portrayals of him as a swinging dick, exactly—the sort of tub-thumping macho ass you'd expect after watching *The Deer Hunter*, or from his mufti of ruggedly unbuttoned denim shirt and thickly coiffed Italianate glare, which telegraph more cowboy swagger than should be necessary for anyone whose job isn't the actual roping of steers—but the ones that *do* exist depict nothing but confidence. In his book *Final Cut*, Steven Bach—the executive who green-lit *Heaven's Gate* to begin with—describes Cimino at their first meeting as soft-spoken. The director had "a self-assurance that radiated reliability. He was calm reason itself. . . . His tone

implied confidence, not arrogance, and if there was a ruthless-
ness, it stemmed not from recklessness but from conviction." Of
Cimino's physical appearance, Bach says he was "solid ... pleasant
and smiling," with a "head that recalled an antique bust: a young,
slightly pampered Roman senator perhaps." There is a trace of
venom in this description, of course, the kind of passive insult
at which Hollywood executives excel ("pampered," you say? He
comes not to bury this senator but to praise him ... faintly), but
Bach's book is excellent: one of the most engaging chronicles of
art versus commerce ever told. And if it was Cimino's monoma-
nia that would lead him to defy his financial backer and make
a film as long and oblique as *Heaven's Gate*—his Waterloo, the
wreck of his career from which he would never recover—the
writing was on the wall a lot earlier than that.

◎

1980. What a year. It was notable, I suppose, for any number of
reasons—in my own private theater of family pain, it was the
year in which my parents' marriage started to fray, in which my
mother's drinking increased to levels that would soon prove
unignorable—but it was also, even leaving aside the Chrys-
ler bailout, the assassination of John Lennon, the election of
Ronald Reagan, the whole knot of symbolic and political ca-
tastrophes that told us the hippie era was over, an aesthetic
bellwether. The drab solipsism of late-seventies Hollywood—
Kramer vs. Kramer, *Ordinary People*, those intimate but faintly
slick family dramas that had packed the multiplexes during
the final part of the decade—might persist for another year or

two, but there was a notable turn for the slicker still, a sense that the more ambitious, more ambiguous, more nakedly personal and yet broadly reflective style that had defined the "New Hollywood" of the previous decade had come to its end. So, too, for Ashby and Cimino. Not two years after the men had faced off at the fifty-first annual Academy Awards with *The Deer Hunter* and *Coming Home*, their respective careers were basically finished. Neither would direct a satisfying—or successful—film again.

For Ashby, the decline was steep and sudden. The run of movies he directed in the seventies—starting with *The Landlord*, then continuing with *Harold and Maude*, *The Last Detail*, *Shampoo*, *Bound for Glory* (his underrated 1976 Dust Bowl drama, starring David Carradine as a young Woody Guthrie), *Coming Home*, and then culminating in 1979's *Being There*—is as satisfying a run as I can think of, a straight flush as compelling as (say) Preston Sturges's in the early 1940s, or as Billy Wilder's a decade later. If Ashby didn't quite get the same level of attention as some of his peers—he was never lionized as decisively as Spielberg or Scorsese would be—the fact remains there isn't a clunker in the bunch. *Shampoo* is, by my lights, the best; *Harold and Maude*, the most endearing. But because, I suspect, Ashby brought a subtle and empathic eye, rather than a cynical or an operatic one, to questions of race, gender, and—especially—class, his contribution has been slightly undervalued. The writer Sean Fennessey has described Ashby's work as "a monument covered in scaffolding." There is an obliquity, an unwillingness to tackle loud subjects (the Vietnam War, or presidential politics) with comparably loud filmmaking. And Ashby himself was so gentle-tempered, so collaborative by nature—not just with actors, writers, film editors, and cinematographers but also with outsiders like the musicians who scored his pictures (Cat Stevens on *Harold and Maude*; Neil Young on *The Landlord* until legal hassles intervened)—he was occasionally pushed around on set by more egotistically minded cohorts. (This was rumored to have been the case during his three-headed collaboration with Warren Beatty and Robert Towne on the set of *Shampoo*.) But what did him in eventually was not a passive nature or a sense of being underappreciated: he didn't have a specific grudge to work out. Nor was he, all rumors to the contrary notwithstanding, just an unregenerate drug addict incapable of working harmoniously with others. (Ashby certainly enjoyed his weed, his periodic mushrooms, and his less periodic cocaine, but in those days, who didn't?) It was studio filmmaking: a bad deal he entered into with Lorimar Pictures, at what was, otherwise, the height of his career.

It should have been easy. Three pictures. The contract had promised Ashby, as these things always did, a better shake: creative control, greater profit participation. He'd battled enough with United Artists during the production of *Coming Home*—a movie that began shooting with only a third of its script complete—and so when Lorimar, a television company with ambitions, came knocking, he was ready to listen. Imagine the relief he must have felt—weirdo, beardy Hal, a gentle man with an anti-authoritarian streak, as tender as a Trappist monk—finally being offered that promise every filmmaker wants: the promise of being left alone. The movies he'd done so far had been good, but he wanted to do his own sort of picture with his own people, unmolested, not bicker with the studio nabobs about casting, about story, all the creative choices the filmmaking process is heir to. He started shooting his first movie for Lorimar, based on a script that had been kicking around Hollywood for nearly a decade called *The Hamster of Happiness*. *The Hamster of Happiness*—let's call it *HOH* for short—was written by Charles Eastman, Carole's brother, and, if anything, the legend of Charles Eastman is an even more fascinating tale of half-realized talent than his younger sister's. It's certainly no less odd. You can catch a glimpse of the man, as I've noted, in Monte Hellman's *The Shooting*, and you can catch a glimpse of the talent in the 1970 motorcycle-racing drama *Little Fauss and Big Halsy*, which is the better of his two produced movies. For a long time Eastman's reputation rested upon a single unproduced screenplay called *Honeybear, I Think I Love You*, which circulated around Hollywood for decades and earned him a fervent cult.[26] Eastman's script for *HOH* may have been comparably brilliant—there's certainly evidence of an interesting talent at work—but the movie, which was titled *Second-Hand Hearts* upon its 1981 release, is a disaster. Starring Robert Blake (best known for his turn in the seventies cop show *Baretta*, and for his terrifying, apparitional role as the Mystery Man in David

---

26. Robert Towne remarked that *Honeybear* "was the first contemporary screenplay I had read that . . . opened up what you could put into a screenplay in terms of language and the observations of life," and there were others who felt the same: that *Honeybear* was one of the greatest Hollywood movies never made.

Lynch's *Lost Highway*[27]) as Loyal Muke, a hapless Texas auto mechanic who wakes from a bender to discover he has married a cocktail waitress named Dinette Dusty (Barbara Harris), the film is a vinegar-and-baking-soda combination of actors working in completely different tonal and emotional registers. Blake sputters and yelps, Harris drawls and sighs: as a portrait of nominally salt-of-the-earth people, *Second-Hand Hearts* is condescending and sloppy; as a romance between oddballs, it's abrasive and unenjoyable. The film's two stars hated each other, the studio and the participants alike couldn't quite decide whether the film should be a comedy or a drama, and Ashby, possibly recognizing what a dog he had on his hands, distracted himself by plunging into *Being There*, a massively superior movie he began shooting immediately after he wrapped *Hearts*, but which would ultimately be released a year and a half before. Still. Isn't every artist entitled to the occasional dud? Particularly Ashby, coming off such a string of pure golden strikes, of which *Being There* constituted the seventh. Peter Sellers's deadpan, surreal performance as a baffled lifelong shut-in who emerges into the world in middle age—everything he knows, he's learned from watching television—to become a powerful Washington insider is perfect, and the film very nearly is too. In a way, it's an ideal bookend to *Harold and Maude*, with which it shares a gently acerbic surrealism, a blend of personal bewilderment and social outrage. It's also the last good film Ashby ever made.

---

27. Blake is also known, of course, for a murder case in which he was accused of shooting his wife, an actress named Bonnie Lee Bakley. Tried in 2004 and early 2005, the actor was acquitted.

◎

How did it go bad so quickly? Was it ego? Intransigence? Exhaustion? Because *Second-Hand Hearts* would prove to be not just a misstep but the beginning of the end: what came next was arguably only worse. And while Ashby's glum run of eighties failures—the "best," such as it is, is probably *Lookin' to Get Out*, an offbeat drama about a pair of gambling buddies in the vein of Robert Altman's *California Split*; the worst, surely, is 1985's Neil Simon adaptation *The Slugger's Wife*, a listless sports comedy so lousy, I have tried and failed three times to get through ten minutes of it—suggests a talent so depleted the films could have been made by a different person, it all seems to come back to that fateful deal with Lorimar. The company and Ashby clashed, first on *Second-Hand Hearts*, then again on *Lookin' to Get Out*, on which the director's relationship with the suits upstairs grew so argumentative and sour they locked him out of the editing room, recutting the movie over Ashby's passionate objection. After that, as you can imagine, things were never right again. Even after he'd extricated himself, thank God, from his relationship with Lorimar—three pictures were only three pictures, it turned out, even if they'd been miserable experiences for him one and all[28]— Ashby soon found himself tagged with that all-purpose Hollywood epithet, "difficult." Hal Ashby was "difficult." Even if his cast and crew, the people who were in the trenches with Ashby, fervently disagreed. They adored him—"You've treated me with

---

28. Even *Being There*. Although the film was a critical success, Ashby felt it had been mis-marketed and poorly released by Lorimar, and blamed the company for its so-so performance at the box office.

more courtesy, warmth, understanding, and friendship than any other director for whom I have worked," Andy Stone, his assistant director on 1986's *8 Million Ways to Die* wrote to him after the film had wrapped. "The entire crew would march into battle with you anytime"—but this was how the financiers saw it. Those rumors about his drug use, the ones that insisted he was fairly *living* on blow and mushrooms, LSD and weed ("We would hear his Mercedes, and we would say, 'Here comes Captain Wacky to the bridge,'" one of his late-period editors said), were allegedly started by the disgruntled muck-a-mucks at Lorimar, to pay him back for being such a pain in the ass on *Hamster*. And whether or not these happened to be true (any number of others claimed Ashby was no different from how he'd always been, an enthusiastic pothead whose creativity only benefited from a responsible ingestion of substances), Ashby didn't help his case by jet-setting around with his buddy Mick Jagger, with whom he codeveloped an idea that ultimately never went anywhere—an intended adaptation of Gore Vidal's novel *Kalki*—and directed a feeble documentary of the Stones' 1981 tour, *Let's Spend the Night Together*, which came out just as enervated as the director's career, all of a sudden, was. Whether or not he was one, he *looked* like a drug fiend: white beard and stringy hair and emaciated frame, crooked teeth and sallow complexion. One night during the filming of the Stones' tour, recovering, according to conflicting reports, either from an overdose or a severe bout of flu, he croaked out his orders on set from a gurney. Three years had passed since his Academy Award, yet he seemed to have aged fifteen. He had passed straight out of his prime like *that*, overnight.

◎

Here comes Captain Wacky to the bridge. I'm trying to imagine what it must be like, to have the world in the palm of your hand, then to wake up abruptly and find this gone. To emerge from a period of power, as Cimino did too, and find that it has just disappeared. It's not that either of these people, or anyone else in their predicament, quite deserves our pity—poor Michael Cimino, pottering around in his exile, trying to decide which of his cars to drive, should he opt to leave the grounds of his Beverly Hills manse today—but still: how human it seems. To be old, or past one's prime—it can happen early, or late, but in the fullness of time it happens to everybody—and to be discarded, thus. I'll never know how exactly my mother felt, in this respect, what it was like for her to pull up her stakes and move from California to the Pacific Northwest, discarded by an industry she might never have wanted that much to do with from the start; I'll never know what it was like for my grandfather to walk into the ocean, thinking he might prefer to drown than to keep on breathing, or for my friend D to climb up onto a rooftop in Richmond, Virginia, and then to—plunge from its edge. I have only my own feelings of failure, small but persistent, to guide me, which indeed they do. But these two men, tender Ashby and arrogant, brittle Cimino, light my way too. The Ahab-like obsession that drove them both, the hours on sets and in editing bays, is known to me, as, alas, are the empty hands and empty days at which they both arrived. "Nothing will come of nothing," but to nothing we all finally come. Everyone knows that. But what, if anything, would have made that time between—that fragile moment when Ashby and Cimino felt like kings, with their fleets and their killings, their ability to do as they liked—last longer? Could either have done still more with his talent, or found something to do with it besides piss it down the drain? Success may come to you too, sure. But what makes you think it would ever come to stay?

◎

Sometimes, when I had lunch with my father, I wondered the same thing. When I was a high-rolling man, myself—when I'd worked in the same version of the industry he did, if in a different quadrant of it, that version that had to do with deals, more than with art—I'd thought it might: that "success" had an aspect that was adhesive, and once encountered, was likely to stick. I knew better now (though I understood too that some part of it *did* stick: the corruption of it; that if money or entitlement had ever descended upon you, you might scrub and scrub without ever being clean), but I wondered if my dad felt the same way. I'd known wealthy people all my life, but my father was no soulless plutocrat; he was a decent man with a surplus of empathy and a conscience.

"So?"

We'd meet for lunch in one of those light-filled barns he'd always favored, a place like the Grill on the Alley in Beverly Hills, or Giorgio Baldi: rooms where he was known and loved, or at least recognized, where his name had a weight and value it might not have elsewhere. It was a vanity I could forgive, even if I still wondered.

"What are you writing?"

He was always the one with the questions, somehow. I could never turn the tables and say, *What is this like for you? Do you still feel hungry, or is it enough?* I'd stare at his watch, as heavy as a manacle; read the weave of his dark jacket or his salmon-colored shirt, the crispness of its collar beneath his soft-chinned face. He seemed to live in a world of pure matter, but it wasn't one that rejected kindness. He wanted me to succeed also.

"First draft of another novel. And that pilot pitch I sold."

I'd go on to talk about it, to translate these vapors of my daily life—scenarios that were unfinished, characters that mightn't have names—for him the best I could, but what I wondered was, *Is this enough?* My dad, bless him, had no cruelty in him. Venality, sure—you don't make money without wanting it more than you should—but not meanness, whatever his many additional faults. Success never made him cold. We'd always been close, through my adult life and career, in a strange way: I'd call him sometimes for advice, though more often keep a certain firewall between his interests and mine.

"That's good," he would say, once I had finished talking. "A writer writes."

Ah. He would smile to let me know he was kidding (a talent agent who'd represented writers, he understood how often this famous tautology proved untrue), but it seemed to me he was sincere, also. He was that man, the Thalberg kind, for whom the world and its obstacles were physical or logistical; for whom the other style of impediment—crises of the mind, or of the heart and spirit—might be harder to apprehend.

"You want coffee?"

He'd offer and I'd drink it with him, watching him lean forward opposite me in the booth like a jockey, like he couldn't wait to reach whatever finish line was waiting for him. Always the same ritual for him every day—a pair of espressos, one after the other—and as he drained the cup and set it back upon its saucer, I took it all in: the immaculate white linen, the waiters darting around like minnows, the other tables, crowded with power brokers all, gossiping and haggling, their murmurous voices all building somehow toward a sound that felt like—serenity, whatever isolated despondencies were hidden behind it. I'd wanted this once, I thought, or at least I'd believed I did. It seemed like hell to me now, predicated as it was upon an untruth. I knew I'd leave and feel shabby again, standing out on the sidewalk in my tennis shoes. But I'd look at my dad, that moment of stillness before he practically vaulted out of his seat ("Back to work!"), and think, *This is his element. He belongs to it and vice versa.* His eyes scanned the room one last time, casually. When I'd mentioned that I'd been watching a lot of Ashby's movies, he'd just shrugged. Not out of indifference, but—what could you learn from someone who'd flamed out? Why would you try?

"Love you, Son." The same words, too, each time as we stood on the street and the valet arrived always with his car first. My problem was never Cimino's or Ashby's in this respect either. My father was not withholding. But as I watched him climb into his car—peeling a bill from a gold clip to tip the man who'd brought it, wind and sunlight buffeting the silver corona of his hair—I knew this was still his own bent. He thought it would last forever.

"Love you too."

Watching him pull away, the dark, metallic sheen of his sleek vehicle—new, of course, since I saw him last—almost painful to look at, I wanted to believe this too. But I couldn't, even as I closed my eyes a moment to listen to that forceful roar of a German engine as my father gunned away from the curb, fading to a purr before it—too—vanished into the wind.

◎

There were, of course, the choices, those turns at which either of them would have arrived at a different career. Before he blew it with *Heaven's Gate*, before that film's endless shoot and ballooning budget—like Colonel Kurtz himself, Cimino holed up with his crew on their set in Kalispell, Montana, and refused contact with the studio altogether as they shot hundreds of thousands of feet of film. The director had a different project in mind. He'd wanted to direct an adaptation of Ayn Rand's *The Fountainhead*, and if it's difficult to imagine that ungodly monument to a libertarian architect's ego turning out any better, or any less overblown, than *Heaven's Gate* did, we'll never know for sure. At the very least it might not have gone so far off the rails if he'd been able to get one of his other projects off the ground: the intended adaptation of André Malraux's *Man's Fate*; the biopic of Dostoevsky from a script by Raymond Carver. If he'd managed to hang on to direct 1984's *Footloose*, instead of being fired in preproduction at the last minute, maybe we'd remember him differently. Ashby's biography, too, is riddled with the films he never made: an earlier approach to 1975's *One Flew Over the Cuckoo's Nest*, which Ashby lost when he pushed for Jack Nicholson—at the time, the studio didn't want him—to star; 1982's *Tootsie*, which Lorimar prevented him from taking; an adaptation of Saul Bellow's *Henderson the Rain King*, also with Jack Nicholson; a Richard Brautigan–scripted "gothic western" called *The Hawkline Monster*; an adaptation of Erica Jong's *Fear of Flying* with Dyan Cannon. Both directors were at one time or another involved in a proposed adaptation of Truman Capote's questionable, but gripping, "true crime" story "Handcarved Coffins." But both men, like all of us, were stapled to their respective temperaments, and that temperament, in Cimino's case, happened to be at once visionary and vague, stubborn—yes, of course he needed to build that nineteenth-century roller rink from scratch in the middle of Wyoming, and people it with hundreds of extras who'd all be taught, meticulously, to skate—but shy. Contrary to its commercial reception, *Heaven's Gate* is a beautiful film, largely unprecedented in its depiction of the American West not as a sequence of panoramic vistas (those wide-open plains against which the solitary semi-heroes of John Ford or Howard Hawks were always moving) but as a space filled with tumult. The vast clouds of smoke and whirling dust, the thronging shots of frontier towns that crowd the movie are still thrillingly alive. But contrary to its recent revisionist stature as a masterpiece, *Heaven's Gate* is also, it must be said, painfully boring, a movie whose dramatic core is swept away by set pieces, interred within a structure that, if whittled down, reveals itself as wispy and weak. Cimino couldn't cut the story if, as I suspect, he didn't really know what it was, and so the movie was pilloried upon its release—most famously, Vincent Canby in the *New*

York Times compared it to "a forced, four-hour walking tour of one's own living room"—and it lasted exactly two weeks in theaters, pulled after it had earned just a tick over $1 million. It had cost forty-four times as much to make.

◎

Again, so what? Most of us will never sniff a fraction of $44 million over a lifetime, let alone blow as much playing cowboy games for a year in Montana, so who gives a damn about Cimino's folly? Yet—failure is failure. We've all lost jobs, or relationships, seen our high hopes go awry. We've all experienced those humiliations, that sinking feeling that occurs when something we've anticipated skips the track. Cimino arrived at *Heaven's Gate*'s New York City premiere ready for triumph. It was only afterward, as he milled around the theater lobby, that he clocked the crowd's muted response.

"Why isn't anyone drinking the champagne?" he whispered to his publicist.

"Because they hated the movie, Michael."

At least the publicist gave it to him straight. But as his gaze swept the room, the muttering people in tuxedos, the untouched flutes full of liquid gold, he must have wanted to vomit. It's a moment that seems oddly human, Hollywood budget or no. And while Cimino took the fall for the studio's subsequent collapse—the $37 million loss United Artists took on the picture drove them to the verge of bankruptcy, ultimately forcing its parent company, Transamerica Corporation, to sell it off—the director might have come out of it a better artist, and perhaps even a better person. If only he hadn't been so damned intransigent. If only his ego ("Michael was a little crazy up there in Montana," his producer, Joann Carelli, told *Rolling Stone* magazine. "He won those two Academy Awards and really believed they meant something") hadn't run so out of control.

Ego, of course, undoes so many people. And there are ways of responding to success, or to failure, beyond throwing a protracted tantrum. (How did Tennessee Williams put it? "Not privation but luxury is the wolf at the door.") But Cimino never recovered: none of the projects that followed *Heaven's Gate*—over the course of his lifetime, four features, one short film, and two novels, both published only in French—seem anything to write home about. Whatever merits inhere in Cimino's late work, all of it lacks the expansiveness, the intensity, the unmitigated (and yet also mitigating) gall of his first two films. And if Cimino put on a brave front, claiming in those few interviews he gave not to have been affected by the vituperative reviews *Heaven's Gate* received (asked in 2015 if he felt vindicated by the revisionist applause the film had garnered, Cimino puffed up his chest: "I didn't need vindication. . . . I knew what I had done"), well, it's fairly obvious this isn't the case. Unless you think he merely withdrew to his gated mansion and decided to spend thirty-five years in Norma Desmond–like seclusion for the hell of it. The later work is interesting here and there for all the wrong reasons (the queasy-making racism of 1985's Chinatown-set *Year of the Dragon*, which was remarked upon even at the time, seems to forecast aspects of Trumpism; at one point Mickey Rourke's bigoted cop lights into his journalist girlfriend, telling her, "You wanna know what's destroying this country? It's not booze, it's not drugs . . . it's media"), but by and large it's punishingly dull.

Given this, and given the at best contradictory knot of his politics (right wing in many respects, yet *Heaven's Gate* is an unapologetically leftist movie, one that valorizes the battle of immigrant cattle thieves against plutocratic land barons), why waste even a speck of empathy upon this man? *Racist asshole!* Why bother, right? But—I suspect Cimino, more than Ashby, more than most people even, was tormented by things that had little to do with failure or success, and even less to do with the movies. I suspect he was uprooted in some pivotal respect, unmoored within himself; that he was not merely "unhappy" but fundamentally estranged.

◎

"So why did you have the surgery?"

It was a reporter from *Vanity Fair* who wanted to know about Cimino's jaw, about his hair and about his face. Why did the director look so different, when he granted a rare interview to the magazine in 2010? Everyone gets older, and no one's appearance stays the same, but Cimino looked like an entirely different person: the meaty-featured Sicilian boychik of yore replaced by a whittled, frail-seeming sylph.

"I didn't have the right alignment of my jaw," the director explained. A doctor had needed to rebuild his mouth, fix his teeth, which then altered his cheeks.

"So, inadvertently, you got yourself a new face?"

The rumors had swirled in Hollywood for years; they would follow Cimino all the way to his grave. The *Vanity Fair* article is otherwise an intriguing puff piece, a disinterring of its so-called "Howard Hughes of Hollywood," but the moment is a little uncomfortable, as the journalist gently prods the director around a question he does not want to answer— the question of whether Cimino was transitioning—and the director repeatedly denies it. In the *Vanity Fair* article, Cimino credits fasting for weight loss and blames the misleading photographic conditions of earlier pictures for a change in his hair color ("I was always a blond") before pivoting grossly to his long-standing reputation as a ladies' man and his squeamishness about knives to offer evidence that he isn't, y'know . . . *like that*. Viewed from a contemporary perspective, this response is appalling, but viewed in situ, I guess—leaving aside questions of the director's own transphobia and the traces of clumsy macho swagger that wind through the profile even besides—it feels rooted in a profound, and even relatable, self-estrangement. Cimino doesn't deny, he *deflects*, which is a whole other thing, and he does so, even, with attempts at humor, waggishly telling the journalist people might have him confused with the heavily made-up musician Gene Simmons (of Kiss), who'd happened to live for a while in a ranch house on Cimino's property, and suggesting that he's finally prepared to offer the question a straight answer, but "if you don't believe the straight answer, then I'll tell you a lie. How's that?" Indeed, the article contains what might be the definitive Cimino utterance, at least when it comes to questions about his private history. "When I'm kidding, I'm serious, and when I'm serious,

I'm kidding," the director remarks, addressing the multitude of rumors surrounding not just his identity but his eccentricity, the radical, Garbo-like privacy into which he'd retreated. "I am not who I am, and I am who I am not."

◎

I am who I am not. Where would Hollywood—where would *America*—be without that? F. Scott Fitzgerald knew it, when he headed west. He knew it even before that, when he wrote that defining novel of the earlier twentieth century, the story of little Jimmy Gatz who changed his name in order to become Gatsby, the tycoon. Holden Caulfield, ranting about "phonies" in *The Catcher in the Rye*, was probably abreacting to Hollywood, which codified the American impulse to flim-flam, and gave it a place to go. When the director strung that interviewer along, and even as he tried both to metabolize his failure ("Nobody lives without making mistakes," he said. "It's not how you handle the hills, it's how you handle the valleys") and to reinvent himself, to present as unbowed, Cimino was trying to do what we all do, one way or another: to construct a public face he could live with, and cultivate a private one that remained alive. It's an impossible errand—if we were honest we would spend most of our time together naked and sobbing, outdoors—but what crucified him, ultimately, was success, that "bitch goddess" that led Marilyn Monroe to swallow a handful of barbiturates and Elvis to die on the john. There is no prison like the one of getting everything-you-ever-wanted-plus-a-bunch-of-stuff-you-didn't-know-came-with-that, and if Cimino's triumph, the brief, flashing moment after *The Deer Hunter* in which he was crowned king of the world, was short-lived, he evidently inhaled it for all it was worth. And understood that the real core of the American story is loneliness, of which fame, that whorish distortion of subject-object relation—one person is always ninety feet tall and the other remains invisible—is the consummate avatar. "This is a lonely country," Cimino told the *New York Times* in 1978, "and people die of loneliness as surely as they die of cancer."

This is true. And Cimino enacted that loneliness as comprehensively as possible, withdrawing from public life for thirty-odd years while at the same time trying to manipulate an image before an American public that had stopped caring long ago. Look at those later photos of him and see a seventy-three-year-old man who looks—not "youthful" exactly, but obsessively tended in a way that is perplexing: wrinkle-free and dewy-lipped, with glossy, salon-fresh hair and coyly tinted sunglasses. It's a transformation akin to the late Michael Jackson's, the look of a person for whom surgery must have been, finally, a way of life. He wanted to appear younger. He wanted to *be* younger, apparently—check that fraudulent driver's license in his pocket—but if there's anything we can surmise from all this hocus-pocus, all this hustle around his age and his identity and his family history, at least one of which is none of our business, it's that Cimino's impulse to endless self-invention was rooted in a profound feeling of alienation. And nothing he owned and nothing he accomplished—no mansion and no automobile, no accolade and no flop, no private glory and no public shame—would mitigate this for him in the end.

◎

"Once, I had a dream of fame," the novelist David Markson wrote in *Wittgenstein's Mistress*, a book that was rejected by fifty-four publishers before it found a home. "Generally, even then, I was lonely." Ah. "Even then." *Especially* then, I would think. But whatever Markson's narrator, who believes herself (delusively or otherwise) to be the last human being on earth, made of her vanquished dream, I know what I make of mine. I know that it was rotten. I know that Michael Cimino, who died peacefully in his bed in 2016 (of no known illness, and no assigned cause), and Hal Ashby, who died in 1988 of pancreatic cancer (like Warren Zevon, he had a lifelong phobia of doctors that did not serve him, and he sought care for an enigmatic symptom, a mysterious bruise traveling around his body, only when it was too late), were not protected by theirs. Even Ashby, gregarious Ashby—he might have lived like a hermit too, holed up at his place in Malibu Colony toward the end, but he welcomed a steady stream of visitors—would have been lonely, because nothing is lonelier than the final recognition that there is nothing one can do. Neither of these men had a family. Cimino lived alone, and Ashby had the company of a girlfriend, the last of a long line, and so they both approached their end in a certain type of futureless isolation: two people who'd given their lives to the movies, which in turn now had little use for them. Ashby had been plotting a comeback. He'd been close to getting *The Hawkline Monster*, that gothic western he'd been stalking now for fifteen years, off the ground at long last, and he'd been working, too, to set up a foundation, an outfit that would cultivate young filmmakers outside the studio system and give them the unfettered encouragement he'd once received from Norman Jewison, in his long-ago apprenticeship as an editor. Cimino claimed a few years before his death to have written fifty unproduced scripts. He insisted he felt animated by the writing of his novels, which were acclaimed in France (*Big Jane*, the story of a six-and-a-half-foot-tall female motorcycle enthusiast who escapes the dullness of 1950s Long Island to fight in the Korean War, won the Prix Littéraire Deauville in 2001), but never gained any traction in the States. Neither director ever gave up. But each came to his finish prematûrely, even if that prematurity would have been something he had to experience privately. Tinseltown itself had had enough.

◎

Maybe I have too. These meditations on people who soared and then collapsed—and on those who barely even "soared," who were dropped to the ground almost before they left the runway—all end in the same way, in grief and isolation. Whatever benediction exists comes from outside, that order that imposes itself only as we tell the stories of the dead, and from those moments, thankfully there are many, that lift up and out from the films themselves: Harold capering to safety, away from his final "suicide," to the strains of Cat Stevens; the maimed survivors of *The Deer Hunter* breaking into that spontaneous chorus of "God Bless America" while tucking into their eggs, or crooning "Can't Take My Eyes Off of You" to one another almost coquettishly as they dance around a pool table, on the eve of their shipping off to ruin. Ashby's vision of the world was a humanist one—acerbic and a little cranky, but largely convinced that individual lives contained agency and value—where Cimino's was, instead, a fatalist's. (There's a reason he was so attached to his Russian writers; see "Vronsky" and "Pushkov," a portmanteau that seems to allude pointedly to both Pushkin and Chekhov, in *The Deer Hunter*.) "What one loves about life are the things that fade," ran United Artists' advertising copy for *Heaven's Gate*, copy I suspect was scripted by Cimino himself, but what *I* love about life are the things that fail, that crash and burn without any particular fanfare. Not because I relate to them, but rather because they relate to me, me and every other inhabitant of this spectacular—and now itself failing—American experiment, the one created by immigrants like my grandfather and Puritans like my mother's ancestors, which only ever pretended to rest upon any bedrock of "success" anyway. We're all going to the same place, and this business of imagining ourselves insulated by accomplishment, or money, grows a little wearisome, after all . . .

◎

I write these lines in a notebook on El Matador State Beach, where I've come to escape—myself. I can't do it, of course, my restlessness is always with me, but from where I sit, fifteen minutes north of the Colony, where Hal Ashby died, I can almost see it: my taciturn grandfather, a man who looks old in every photograph I've ever been shown, a man I can barely picture outside of his everyday navy-colored suit and tie, without his omnipresent cigarette—a slow fuse for the cancer that would eventually kill him—stripping down to his briefs to wade into the water. Perhaps I am conflating him with Bob Hyde, in *Coming Home*. Those long-ago days of playing with Bruce Dern's dog took place in the Colony also. The day is overcast, the air clotted with the fabled "June gloom" that affects this city every year between May and August, that seems to start with the jacaranda trees bursting into purple blossom and end only on that date one rolls over to see the sun pushing, unexpectedly, through the blinds at 7:00 AM. It is late morning, and I am squinting out at a sea that is agate-colored, practically gray, scanning the waves to pick out the form of my daughter swimming between them. I have run for so long: like Cimino and like Ashby, I have attempted to outrun my family's history; have evaded—even during those times I was also a participant in it—the industry that made them. But there is no evasion left for me. I belong to the movies, and to that world of unfinished dreams. Maybe V does too. She is a teenager now, and some nights we sit together and watch movies: Hitchcock, Fincher, Tarantino . . .

I stare out across the water. For a moment, she disappears, but I'm not worried: she has learned to surf, and these days might be more comfortable in the water than on land. A breeze stirs, and I close my eyes to absorb all of it: gulls, human chatter—the wind-tossed voices of children—the distant drone of a helicopter overhead, the smell of salt air. I hold my eyes shut, and she could be right next to me, the mother who died so disappointed, who caused me—but much more importantly, suffered, herself—such pain. I wish she were. I wish I could tell my mother what I've come to know: that life is disappointment, but it is not *all* disappointment, and even that—the letdowns, pains, and distresses that afflict everybody— amount to a kind of gift. I open my eyes. The world blurs—sun is cutting through the fog, and it takes a moment for my eyes to adjust—and then I blink and seek out again the one I love and who loves me back, my V, who is walking out of the water now, long-limbed and summer-bronzed, smiling so broadly I can see it from forty feet away. She is coming toward me, and toward her future, this beautiful amphibian who does not run, and I—an amphibian too: half cinema and half literature, no longer torn between them—sit still, not dreaming of anything for once, but waiting.

Here she comes . . .

VIII

the age
of crime

renata adler

But from the highest public matters to the smallest private acts . . . from the alley to the statehouse, behind the darkened window or the desk; this is the age of crime.

—RENATA ADLER, *Pitch Dark*

"WHO'S THIS?"

The phone rang, and I'd picked up. This was more recently, a few years ago when I was—fittingly enough—organizing my bookshelves, unboxing my belongings in the apartment I live in now. The phone rang and I'd answered it, out of habit. I didn't recognize the number, just lashed into my pocket and picked up. "Hello?"

"This is Renata calling." The voice on the other end was patrician, a little plummy. It took me a moment to sift through the very narrow set of possibilities.

"Renata . . . Adler?" I said. "That Renata?"

"Well I think so," she said, and I could hear it, that unmistakable undertow that was already familiar to me: skeptical, amused, a little sharp. "There are times I might not be so sure."

I laughed, and then—after she explained that she'd been looking for me ("I'm supposed to be a reporter," she sighed, vexed that it had taken a while for her to turn up a telephone number)—we . . . what is the line from F. Scott Fitzgerald's *This Side of Paradise*, that book that made me want to become a writer, all those decades ago? "They slipped briskly into an intimacy from which they never recovered." So it was. I sat down and collapsed into a friendship with one of my favorite living writers, one I'd been reading regularly for the previous decade and a half, although her spirit had presided, in various ways, over earlier iterations of my life too. She was calling in response to an article I'd written for the magazine the *Believer*, an essay about her and her work. And if it was weird, of course, to hear from one of my heroes—it can be surprising, at times, for a writer to hear from anyone at all—it was weirder still that she felt, immediately, like a friend. Yet she did. We talked for a half hour or so, about what—books, gossip, the sorts of small, domestic tidbits people used to exchange, routinely, over the phone—I no longer wholly remember. But we've spoken occasionally since, and these conversations always evoke my mother, for some reason, and that world of my earliest childhood: a world of rotary phones and televisions whose channels you'd change by twisting a dial, adults holding burning cigarettes and rooms smelling always of weak coffee, or tonic water and smoke. Not because Adler seems old or antique, but rather because the frame of reference within which "Renata Adler" had been created, for me, *was* that world: my mother indeed had a copy of *Speedboat* on those shelves that had been so influential when I was a kid, those ones on which I'd found McGuane, Didion, Cheever, and others. When I was a teenager I'd sat in the dark with her at the Monica Twin in Santa Monica and watched Woody Allen's not-yet-problematized *Manhattan*, a film the internet would tell me, years later, contained a scene that was based on a conversation between Allen and Renata Adler. This was back in the era when Allen was still paired with Diane Keaton, when he represented the culture's nebbishy, cartoon version of a

New York intellectual, but I didn't need to know Adler's work then in order to feel what I did intuitively, passionately. *Speedboat* glowed on that shelf like the promise of a world I wasn't ready for, a sophistication I didn't quite possess. But if our Brentwood neighbor Joan Didion represented that world I was so desperate to escape—Los Angeles, with its plagues of Santa Ana winds, of locusts and liquor and Hollywood calculation—then Adler represented high ground: Manhattan, that place to which I might fly to become something other than what I was. I did, of course, escape for a while; I did not, alas, become anything else. But Adler still represents something to me: the type of artist I'd hope to be, and/or the world I'd like to inhabit, the world not just of film and of literature but of a fine-tuned ethical skepticism. I didn't read Adler until I was into my midthirties, but my awareness of her would crystallize a year or two after I graduated from high school, when I heard the English musician Lloyd Cole sing a song called "Speedboat" and talk about her in interviews. Even then, I knew. There was the world of movies, and there was the one of books. There was Los Angeles, particularly of the 1970s and 1980s, the nation's sunstruck, hedonic shadow capital— shapely of form but empty of substance—and there was New York. You know, that other place. The place where anyone serious, or so I'd been told, needed to go to contend.

◎

Dust filled my lungs. My eyes squinted against the light, the late-day glow that was filtering in through the windows when I hung up the phone—Adler had called from Connecticut, where she now lives—and the air was full of that musty card-board scent that occurs when you unbox all your books and start Tetris-ing your volumes onto shelves. Receipts and makeshift bookmarks, scraps of paper with random names and phone numbers scrawled across them, decades old; faded cash register tickets toting up purchases from Moe's Books in Berkeley, or the Strand in New York City, were scattered across the floor. That smell, so fadedly sweet and faintly sour, so decidedly intox-icating for anyone who ever spent joyous childhood hours in a library, knocked me out. "Life passes into pages if it passes into anything," James Salter wrote. His books were in these boxes too, alongside Adler's, my mother's copies of *Speedboat* and *Pitch Dark* I'd inherited, alongside McGuane and Fitzgerald and El-eanor Perry, the hundreds and hundreds of others. This was where I wanted to live, inside this graveyard into which I, too, will eventually be filed. I set those copies of Adler's books aside as I slotted others onto their shelves. I needed to see again what that sophistication was, what precisely I'd been missing all those years ago, when I'd first noticed *Speedboat* and it represented to me something necessary but unobtainable. I'd been to New York but may have missed it: that thing that was greater, and far more important, than any other sort of "success." I watched the sun drop, that rueful red orb hanging over the flats of West Hollywood, filling my apartment with the last of its light, be-fore I gave up my shelving—and my writing—for the day and settled into a corner, instead, to read.

◎

Renata Adler never really did time in Hollywood. Not *really*.
Neither of her novels has ever been adapted—given their pointillist, discontinuous narrative style, it would take a maniac or a
genius to try—and her journalism, though it's frequently just
as sinuous and witty as her fiction, lacks the first-person thrust
that would invite the movie business to come calling. She has
written (like Woodward and Bernstein) about Watergate; she
has written (like Joan Didion) about the Sunset Strip and the
flower children of the sixties; she has written about Cuba, and
about Biafra, and about the civil rights march in Selma; she has
written about G. Gordon Liddy and—most blisteringly—about
the Kenneth Starr report. The relentlessness of her intelligence,
her keen eye for the specific, coupled with both a high-grade
moral sense and a feeling for the absurd, can be a little exhausting. It's one thing to read *The Starr Report*, and quite another
to follow Adler's well-stropped mind on a hairpin tour of its
inanities. So while her writings upon these topics are among the
more interesting political writing of the era, the studios have
never turned to her takes on these events, nor has she ever, to
my knowledge, written a screenplay. Even so, Adler's career has
nevertheless been tied up at key points with the movies: for instance, there was her stint as a film critic for the *New York Times*
in 1968, which came early on in Adler's literary career, after she
had served for just a few years as a staff writer at the *New Yorker*.
If Adler's nonfiction has a flaw (the sort of "flaw" one might
hesitate to designate as such), it's a propensity toward a certain
style of outrage, an outrage not like our contemporary, social
media–fed variety, but one that is more existential and arguably
proportionate. It is more like a novelist's than a prosecutor's,

though Adler does have a pair of law degrees, one from Yale and an honorary doctorate from Georgetown, and it is bracing to encounter in a contemporary context. Reading Adler's fiction and nonfiction alike, I am reminded sometimes of those Eastern European writers especially—Kafka, Broch, Thomas Mann even—who tend to set their people against impenetrable and implacable systems. She is a moralist, like almost all great writers, but not a moralizer, like so many lousy ones, and she had no more admiration for most of the so-called New Journalists, the Norman Mailers, Tom Wolfes, and Gay Taleses among her contemporaries, than she did for the more traditional investigative reporters, the Bob Woodwards and Carl Bernsteins, who would have seemed to her institutionally compromised. Because this is the thing about Adler: she never lets herself off the hook. For anyone who's ever served time in Hollywood, all of us who've ever participated in its hypocrisies—which could mean everyone, even if you've never left Wisconsin—Adler's writing is a pointed reminder that one's smallest choices count. And even now, years after I first read them, I still turn to Adler's books to answer the question not just of how a person ought to be (which most good books tend to address, even if often by a kind of negative implication), but of what a person might, even still, become. I *like* people, like Adler, who aren't hypocrites. I say this as someone not free from hypocrisy himself. And if writing is, for me, a way of leaching myself of it, a chance to burn away the slippages that occur in daily life, well, the movies have rarely offered such a chance to anyone. The movies, American ones at least, tend to be much more about what people *wish* (or fear) they were. Which explains why Adler had such an agonal relationship with them, why she had in her writings a more congenial one—charged with irony, but also sincere—with soap operas and quiz shows. Melodramas might be sentimental, but they are not, in a venal or an ethical sense, dishonest. You could look into those things, as a moralist, and see in them your own reflection. Whereas the movies would seem almost inevitably distorting. You would hate them, more or less, as Snow White's stepmother hated her magic mirror, albeit for precisely the opposite reason.

◎

Renata Adler went to work as the *New York Times*' daily film critic in January 1968. She replaced Bosley Crowther, the staid, straitlaced critic who'd presided over the paper's movie reviews for twenty-seven years, and who'd shot himself in the foot by panning the previous fall's *Bonnie and Clyde*. That film, at first hammered by critics and then almost immediately reappraised, served as a shot across the bow to announce the arrival of a new style of American cinema, the so-called New Hollywood of the 1970s. A review like Crowther's, in which he'd called the film "cheap," "sleazy," "moronic"—the damning adjectives piled up—quickly came to look ridiculous, and the critic was shown the door. The *Times* must have thought they were doing what needed to be done: replacing a hopelessly out-of-touch member of the old guard with someone likely to be more suited to the requirements of the cultural moment, someone they perceived to be young and hip. Adler had been a staff writer, and occasional book critic, at the *New Yorker* when she was approached at a party and almost blindly offered the job. She was an outside-the-box selection, not having been a film writer previously—and being, also, the first woman the *Times* had ever hired for such a position—but she was not, in the sense that would have been prevalent at that time, "hip."

She approached her new gig filled with that same spirit that fills her writing from one end of her career to the other: a spirit of vibrating ambivalence, a dialectical churning. "The job came to me at an odd time," is how Adler puts it in her introduction to *A Year in the Dark*, the book that compiles her fourteen months' worth of *Times* columns and reviews. She'd started as a book reviewer for the *New Yorker*, she explains, but had quickly turned away from reviewing, because she didn't feel a sufficient number of books she was assigned warranted the attention. "I do not believe in professional criticism . . . as a way of life," she notes, which seems an odd admission for a, well, professional critic, and yet it was true. She didn't have the patience, the too easily renewable enthusiasm the job requires. (I'm no more a "professional critic" than Adler was, but I know what she means. It's hard to maintain an edge that isn't a hatchet's blade, that isn't both sharpened by irritability and dulled by overuse.) She wasn't a film critic—she wasn't really a "critic" at all, which explains why a number of film enthusiasts I know dislike her reviews. But *A Year in the Dark* is pretty engaging reading, almost more like a travel journal in certain respects than like "film criticism." The dutiful reviews of the year's more forgettable pictures are skimmable, though worth picking over for their satisfyingly pointy barbs ("Even if your idea of a good time is to watch a lot of middle-aged Germans . . . reddening, grimacing, perspiring, and falling over Elke Sommer, I think you ought to skip *The Wicked Dreams of Paula Schultz*," begins one, in fact the first of Adler's tenure), but as the year goes on, and the writer begins to consolidate her aesthetic, her sense of what's happening in Hollywood and elsewhere—there are pieces on the film festival at Cannes, which was disrupted that spring by student demonstrations and general strikes, and on the Venice Film Festival, which was shaken by a group of dissidents led by the director Pier Paolo Pasolini—the book grows more interesting. There are sharp meditations on empathy in the movies, and on audience laughter; there are thoughtful asides on criticism itself. And there are searching, intelligent responses in the moment to those high-water marks in the year's cinema, a year that is routinely considered among the modern era's best.[30]

The critic David Ehrenstein, to name one of Adler's prominent non-fans, has been known to propose her in conversation as the worst film critic in history. (In a 2004 listserv post, he refers to her as "unspeakable.") He's not alone, but I think Adler's detractors might be looking at her criticism through too narrow a lens. In her introduction to *A Year in the Dark*, an introduction that has the faint feel of someone wiping her muddy boots—as if the year had been spent not just in the

---

30. 1968 gave us *2001: A Space Odyssey* and *Rosemary's Baby*; it gave us *Yellow Submarine* and *Night of the Living Dead*, *Planet of the Apes* and *Faces*; it gave us movies for audiences high and low (and, uh, high and sober), and for people of all ages. To be fair, it also spewed forth a lot of junk: pictures like *A Place for Lovers* and *The Wicked Dreams of Paula Schultz* and *The Green Berets*. There is an unintentional comedy in Adler suggesting that "this has been the worst year in a long time for ... movies," but the films she holds up for approval are mostly those that have stood the test of time.

dark, but in the muck, of criticism—upon a doormat, Adler describes how she prepped for the job: by reading volumes on film by James Agee and Rudolf Arnheim, and by reading contemporary critics of different stripes (she doesn't name them, but refers to "the angry trash claimers . . . the brave commercialism deplorers . . . the giddy adjectivalists," and so on), and then by immersing herself in the movies. "In those months, I also began to go to the movies all day long, drive-ins, Spanish theaters, Chinese, Forty-Second Street, museums," she writes. "It began to produce a sensation of interior weightlessness, of my own time and experience drifting off like an astronaut's. It was not at all like the private reading binges that take place at home. It was more like travel, dislocating, among strangers, going into a public dark for dreams and controversy." I love this passage, but I suspect no serious film critic, nobody for whom the movies are a native art form, would describe it in this way: comparing moviegoing to space travel. But that's what makes Adler-the-critic interesting. She drags Wittgenstein into her reviews more often over the course of a year than most film writers will over a lifetime—that is to say, twice—but her slightly outside take on the movies is, for me, weirdly revelatory. She's no James Agee, no Manny Farber or David Thomson or Nick Pinkerton or Geoffrey O'Brien, no Molly Haskell or Penelope Gilliatt or James Baldwin, even, when it comes to taking the pulse of the movies. But she's fascinating, recording feelings and ideas that aren't commonplace, and that have a weight that goes far beyond that of just "opinion."

Indeed, Adler doesn't seem to care that much about opinions. Not about her own or about anyone else's, which is, also, an interesting position for a critic to take. "There is probably no more . . . valueless kind of communication than everyone's always expressing opinions about everything," she writes. "Not ideas, or feelings, or information—but opinions, which amount to little more than a long, unsubstantiated yes or no on every issue." Even as I smile to think of this idea being loosed into the lion's den of Twitter, I don't think she's wrong. And if it seems contrary—what is a newspaper critic's job, if not to opine on things?—what Adler is actually advocating for is something more along the lines of judgment: responses that are more interior, and less hyperbolic. She knows what every honest person does, which is that most of us don't *know* what we think most of the time, and that an opinion can be a way of preventing ourselves from ever finding out.

Still. Even if her assessments are largely on point, why do we care? Beyond our interest in Adler's judgment—she goes in for Godard and Cassavetes, for *Rosemary's Baby* and *Belle de Jour* and *Petulia* and *Bullitt* and *Yellow Submarine*—what difference does it make what a newspaper critic thought fifty years ago? The films themselves, I can understand reckoning with, but aren't the reviews, literally, just yesterday's papers? Why give those foxed, browning pages a second glance?

◎

Sometimes, when I am stuck, I get up to take a walk. When I am hashing out a problem in a novel or a script, when I cannot find my way clear inside a scene, I go up the street to Santa Monica Boulevard and head west. I live now not far from where I grew up, and when I really get going, I can travel for miles until I find myself confronting a storefront at 10559 Santa Monica Boulevard, which is presently called Frank's Wine & Spirits. When I was a boy, my grandparents owned this store, and my father used to take me here every Saturday afternoon to visit them. This was around the time—a year or two after, perhaps—Adler was reviewing movies for the *New York Times,* or when she had just departed and was back at the *New Yorker* again. I was just a kid, not even yet grade school age, and the country was still teetering in that space between radicalism's failure and revanchist right-wing corruption, that era—it felt like an age, but it was really just a moment—of macramé, gasoline lines, and warmed-over hippie slogans ("Go climb a rock"; "War is not healthy for children and other living things"), when the Vietnam War had been effectively lost but not abandoned, and Watergate was still on the horizon. This was the furnace in which I was forged, not just as a human being but as a political entity, and as a fledgling reader. The stories I cut my teeth on, the ones that enchanted me—*The Adventures of Tom Sawyer*; *The Boy's King Arthur: Sir Thomas Malory's History of King Arthur and His Knights of the Round Table*; *D'Aulaires' Book of Greek Myths*—were all essentially moral tales, ones in which heroism was up for grabs but the terms of this heroism were always slightly murky. I was preoccupied, more even than most children I think, with right and wrong, with the question of how a person could be not one or the other but both. (How could Lancelot be "good" if he was chasing his best friend's wife? How could Arthur if he was too blind to do anything about it? What did it mean that Hermes, that ethically questionable but always delightful figure, was my favorite of the pantheon?) These afternoons with my father were among my childhood's shining hours. We'd cruise this street in his long white Cadillac convertible, with the ragtop dropped and the Beatles blaring in the California sun; have lunch at the Brown Derby; stop at Brentano's bookstore in Century City. My mother's alcoholism hadn't destroyed her yet; my dad was present and attentive. They were ethical people themselves—like Adler, members of the silent generation, with political views that had been forged by contact with the hard-line leftism of the fifties: Pete Seeger, the Wobblies, and the like—but they weren't saints, and still they tried to teach me these things: how to be a decent person, how to suss out right from wrong, how to (maybe they knew I'd need it someday) forgive. Like all people, or like many, at least, they were at war with their own parents: my father's Saturday visits to the liquor store were for him grudging, whatever they were for me. His parents were immigrant small-business owners, custodians of the American dream, and we'd sit with them awhile as my grandpa Ruby taught me bits of Hebrew, and once he'd satisfied himself that he'd instilled some of the culture I was not getting anywhere else (my father did not take me to synagogue, or enroll me in Hebrew school), he would give me a small bag of candy that was intended to last the week. "Use your judgment," he would tell me, and this word, "judgment," had an ethical ring, a ring that, though it was spoken over M&M's and Pixy Stix, couldn't help but retain that decidedly *other* connotation, a judgment not merely of appetite but of (like that Pesach fable of the wise son, the simple son, the wicked son, and the one who does not know how to ask) morality. Ridiculous, I know, to read so much into a bag of candy. But my grandfather—Grandpa Ruby, the same one who'd once tried to drown himself in the Pacific—was an ethical man himself, and for all his difficulties parenting his own children (a Ukrainian refugee who'd needed to flee Stalin's pogroms when he was a small boy, he wasn't a great communicator with anybody), I knew what he was trying to tell me, in that way children always know. I knew he was trying to show me how not to be a monster. If only by trying to constrain—it's not so ridiculous, when you think on it—my greed.

I lay my palm on the side of that building as gently as if it were the flank of an animal, as if it were the Wailing Wall itself. Then turn and begin that long walk back along Santa Monica Boulevard, which is in fact Route 66, that mythic American road that runs all the way from Chicago to Pacific Park, terminating only as it reaches the sea. This road is as much a part of the national imagination as Sunset Boulevard; it factored prominently in the Dust Bowl migrations, has been mythologized both in song and on television, and it runs, through much of this city, parallel to Sunset and just a stone's throw south. When I was a boy, I didn't know that if I wanted to escape, as I did, all I would have needed to do would be to lean against one of the palm trees in Beverly Hills and start hitching east. But this Via Dolorosa would have taken me nowhere, if there were not human beings who could show me how to be, and what to become. My grandfather was one of those people. So, too, is Renata Adler, even if, quite honestly, my friendship with her is sporadic. It's all there on the page anyway, what I'm looking for from her. I don't know that I would want her life, as illustrious and enduring as the work it has produced remains.

This is the trouble with those who show you how to live, unfortunately. They don't necessarily know how to do it themselves. Then again, what a nightmare it would be if they did. Who wants to live under an Old Testament God, after all?

◎

The first glimpse of what would become *Speedboat*, Adler's first novel, appeared in April 1971 in the *New Yorker*. That book would show up in pieces, as a whole series of its chapters appeared in that magazine as short stories, before it was published in 1976. A lot, maybe too much, has been written about that novel, some of it by myself. By which I mean only that the attractions of *Speedboat*'s style are limitless—she is as clean and lethal a writer as Joan Didion, and also a good deal funnier—but the novel's content is so fiercely concentrated that writing "about" it feels frustrating. One winds up flaking off passages at random, pointing at these aphoristic bits of prose ("aphoristic" is not quite right; they don't philosophize so much as observe things so brightly they feel incandescent, quotable even at their most offhand) until one feels one might be losing the forest for the trees. "The simplest operations of life," she writes, "—voting in a booth, filling out returns, remembering whether or not one has just taken a pill—are very difficult." She writes, "The radical intelligence in the moderate position is the only place where the center holds. Or so it seems." She writes, "That 'writers write' is meant to be self-evident. People like to say it. I find it is hardly ever true. Writers drink. Writers rant. Writers phone. Writers sleep. I have met very few writers who write at all." The narrator is a reporter named Jen Fain, who, let's face it, shares more than a few characteristics with her creator. (There is also a tirade against what Jen refers to as the "assault mode" of contemporary criticism: the tendency to refer to work approvingly as "gut-wrenching" or "bone-crunching," to fall back on drab imperatives: "See it." "Read it." I'll come back to that.) I love *Speedboat*. My own copy of the book is so lived-in that even the stranger's name penciled across the flyleaf—the "Jane T. Shaw" who presumably was the book's original owner—feels like part of the furniture, of a piece with the dog-ears and annotations, the miscellaneous scraps of paper that still serve as bookmarks throughout. But whether or not Adler and Jen Fain are identical in their characterological outlines, or are even very much alike (by Adler's own admission, writing comes no more easily for her than it does for Jen; her own affinity for the "moderate position" is articulated in her second nonfiction collection, 1970's *Toward a Radical Middle*; and as for executive function, that ability to navigate the simple day-to-day that seems so difficult for the novel's narrator, well, I've never met a writer, myself very much included, who truly excelled at such things), I've become a bit more interested in *Pitch Dark*. Which is the last novel Adler published, in 1983, though there is at least one (or so she has told me, and so she has noted in interviews) written since. *Pitch Dark* is a sadder, darker, I think even a stranger book than *Speedboat*, although there are commonalities, not just of style and approach—the narrator, Kate Ennis in this case, is likewise a journalist—but of metaphor. "A rowboat, without oars. An outboard motor," she writes, before describing how, in this case, that motor won't start. Her interest, in *Pitch Dark*, is in the sputtering. Those periods of inanition, in which life doesn't seem entirely itself.

◎

What makes a writer fall silent? It is a funny question to ask, at the end of this book which is about writers, and filmmakers, actors, and musicians who have done exactly so, whose careers have been aborted or abridged by one thing and the next. Of course, we all fall silent eventually, but as anyone who's ever attempted to write a novel, or even a mildly challenging email, knows, there are times when the words just won't come together, when one's creative energies simply—fail. I suspect Adler has known this on a greater scale than most, not because she has ever suggested to me as much but because she has taken this feeling at least occasionally as her subject, because she has admitted it in interviews ("I guess," Adler told the *New York Times* in 1983, speaking of the hesitation that had preceded *Speedboat* but which evidently persisted on some level even after she was publishing fiction, "you could just call it lack of confidence"), and also because—I just do. I, too, have lost stretches of my writing life to this "lack of confidence," and so did my mother. For a period when I lived in San Francisco in my early twenties, I didn't write for *years*, or rather my attempts to do so ended, every single time, in frustration. I would crumple up the document, whether analog or digital, and push myself away in a spasm of misery and disgust, in a self-hatred so violent it began, at its worst, to seem like a cousin to a suicidal impulse. It *hurt*, not writing, and so when I read *Pitch Dark* (which does not, exactly, suggest evidence of writer's block—it is after all a book—but which codes some of the same feelings and inhibitions), I cannot help but recognize that despair I am sure Adler knew, and which I suspect we all know something of. Where would any of us be without the moderating effect of our failure, without those experiences that, however unpleasant, may be the only ones that hold us back from being monsters? Elizabeth Hardwick, whose own 1979 novel *Sleepless Nights* owes quite a bit to Adler—a similar pointillist style, a restless mosaic in the place of "plot"— opened her 1976 review of *Speedboat* with a meditation on guilt, which she suggested had effectively disappeared from American literature, as it had from American life. (What she called a "literature of paranoia" had effectively displaced it, she argued—a reasonable claim for a reviewer living under the tall shadows of writers like Thomas Pynchon and Don DeLillo, as well as the Watergate-era specter of Richard Nixon.) *Pitch Dark*, however, is *filled* with a consciousness of guilt. The narrator, Kate Ennis, has done something wrong. Or thinks she has. Or *feels* she has, what is worse. She cannot seem to escape it, this feeling of remorse, even if the incident that sparks it, that drives, in a literal sense, the "action" of the book, is so tiny: a fender bender on a remote Irish road between the narrator in her rental car (at the airport, she has just declined the liability coverage) and a lorry driver who just . . . doesn't want to be bothered. *It's nothing. Just a scratch. Why is this American woman getting so worked up?* The more the lorry driver shrugs her off—eventually, he agrees to go find a police officer but then disappears—the more paranoid Kate becomes. What's happening here? Has she done something wrong? The entire novel amounts to the narrator's attempt to outrun, literally and figuratively, the consequences of an event no one else seems to know or care about. That's it. That's the plot, so to speak, of *Pitch Dark*, bracketed by other things—the narrator's breakup with a married man, which is what sends her to Ireland in the first place—but really, it's just Kate's agitation over this minor incident. If that sounds "small" or unexciting, "plotless," to use one adjective that has affixed itself persistently, if not accurately, to Adler's work, it isn't: the interest, as in just about anything that's worth reading more than once, is in the gyre of the consciousness telling the story. But Adler also knows something that much contemporary writing (and contemporary living) seems to have forgotten: that there *are* no "minor" incidents, not of this kind anyway. A small moral violation, the kind that lets the self off the hook ("Oh, everybody does it"), is just as bloody as a larger one in a sense. And if this seems draconian, a little Old Testament, I refer you to Kafka, with whom Adler shared this ingrained awareness of guilt, but who believed, even further, that a crime didn't even have to be *committed* to stain a person somehow. I refer you to your Twitter feed, where the consequences of a million small frauds are written out daily, scrawled across the mortal body of contemporary America.

◎

That's *Pitch Dark*. And while I'm interested in it for reasons and in ways that have nothing at all to do with criticism (or Kafka: consider such my Wittgenstein-mentioning quota reached), I still find the novel useful as a signpost, a book that (far more than any number of others I, likewise, love) offers something a bit more explicit about how to live, what to do.

"We were running flat out," the book begins: with a short, declarative sentence that, in actuality, could as easily begin a novel called *Speedboat*. "The opening was dazzling. The middle was dazzling. The ending was dazzling. It was like a steeplechase composed entirely of hurdles," the paragraph continues, and the sense of sheer velocity, of open air, is deliriously inviting, like light on water. Even before you know what she's talking about ("It"? The "opening," the "middle," the "ending" of what?), *Pitch Dark*'s narrator seduces you with the rhythm and feel of those sentences, which turn out to be something of a feint ("It" is, naturally, a love affair—what else?—and she gets to the sputtering, the hesitation, the grief before the paragraph is even finished), but this *joie* stains the novel, it lurks even as Kate, troubled by guilt, raddled with grief, doesn't exactly experience it. "This is the age of crime," Adler writes (forty years later, I think, *You can say that again*). "And recently, I think the truth is this, over a period of days and nights some weeks ago, I became part of it." Kate is fleeing the scene—the country, on her way from a place called Cihrbradàn to Dublin in the middle of the night—once those feelings of guilt have grown too strong. "How else account for the fact that I found myself, at three am on a dark November night, haring in a rented car through the Irish countryside, under a sickle moon? At times it rained. Sometimes the sky was black and clear, with the moon and stars precise and perfect overhead. It was cold." She describes the road, the fields, the invisible landscape ("It was pitch dark"), the rare set of headlights headed the opposite way, the "small, dark, widely separated towns." Because she is herself, she imagines pay phones ringing from town to town even at this hour as her headlights are spotted: cops, a "sleepy but eager informer." Because it is Ireland in the late twentieth century, she imagines a truck driver she encounters might be a terrorist, possibly carrying gelignite. And as she knifes through the dark, as the day finally begins to break, she feels it: "If not real joy, at least a waning trepidation." Alone under the stars, "I felt what every vandal must feel as he races through the night: dawning exhilaration."

This is the age of crime. And this is it, I think, what *Pitch Dark*—and ultimately what Adler—is all about. If you find yourself in the dark, and if the guardrails—the state, the cops, the bureaucratic institutions, the journalistic beacons, any- and everything that might be expected to keep your moral compass in working order—are all crumbling and can no longer be counted on to guide you, *if your own conscience can't even be counted on anymore,* now that people leave and betray and wound each other for no reason, just because they are bored or, y'know, can't deal . . . what then? Because there are always extenuating circumstances ("The surgery. My state of mind. . . . All the little steps and phases and maneuvers, stratagems, of trying to leave him now"), "everybody has their reasons," as Jean Renoir put it, in *The Rules of the Game.* So, if this is the case . . . what then?

◎

We're a long way from Hollywood, aren't we? If you assume that the movies are just a symptom and not the actual disease (personally, I'm not sure), and if all these crashes and collapses I've described aren't just artistic misfortunes but ethical failures; if you assume that human hope (because that's all the movies are, really, in the end: in the broadest possible sense that's what they have to offer) is itself a crime, well, then, sure: Renata Adler's fiction has everything to do with Tinseltown. But even if it doesn't, other than in the notion that we are all, everywhere, implicated in this spirit of the age, *Pitch Dark* and *Speedboat* are useful to me. They offer a morality that isn't moralistic, a finger that does not point outward, at *you*, but instead prods gently at the abscesses of the self. Hollywood may or may not be its own moral ecosystem, but those books are with me every hour as I sit in my office, hammering away, or when I am beset by career disappointment. For too long I lived like the gambler, one of those sad-sack figures in Ashby's *Lookin' to Get Out*, who stagger out of the casino only after they have lost every last thing. Adler's books are like the raw shock of daylight, that first lungful of fresh air. Even if what is lost stays lost: I can't bring my mother or my marriage back to life, can't make those old dreams, of reward and renown, live either. But I can mourn them. There's more to California, and more to Los Angeles, than literature and the movies anyway. Though I am doomed to wander those precincts for the rest of my days, and so, doomed to fail. But though there are nights this shakes me from my sleep in a panic—the house odds arrayed so implacably against me—most of the time, I am glad. You play to win; you play to lose. You play because the game itself, and only that, allows you to feel alive. And only the presence of the other gamblers, the committed ones who aren't sharpies or cheats, only that lets you know you aren't alone.

Those who are familiar with Adler's work probably know this story too: how the writer's ostensible "takedown" of Pauline Kael in the August 14, 1980, edition of the *New York Review of Books* presaged the ruin of her career. Never mind that it predated the publication of *Pitch Dark* by three years, or her appearance on the cover of *New York* magazine—an article headlined "The Quirky Brilliance of Renata Adler" that encapsulated the peak of her celebrity—the *NYRB* piece is invoked regularly as The Place Where It All Went Wrong, where Adler's hurtling vehicle somehow cracked up. Her review of Kael's *When the Lights Go Down*, one of the legendary film writer's multiple compendiums of her *New Yorker* columns, could on the one hand be construed as yet another example of Adler's knack for making enemies, for chomping the paw that still has the scrap of food cupped within it. But it could also, on the other, be considered an exercise of the essential practice of criticism: to address, in a way that is both thoroughgoing and honest, the flaws of a work that is meretricious. Whichever view you prefer, Adler's piece is these days held forth, unreasonably I think, as proof that Adler was unnecessarily cruel, and that she had an ax to grind. As evidence that her life as a critic culminated in her becoming nothing more than a hatchet lady.

Truth be known, I have never loved Pauline Kael's writing. As much as her criticism is gospel, still, for a certain breed of enthusiast, I have always found that criticism a little hectoring, and her judgments hit or miss. Even at her very best, as in *Going Steady* (a book that compiles her writings from 1968 and 1969, and which overlaps in its subjects quite a bit with *A Year in the Dark*), there is something just a little off, a way in which her writing seems to play dirty when it comes to conscripting the reader. In "Trash, Art, and the Movies," for example, one of her best, and best-known, essays, Kael describes movies as "a tawdry corrupt art for a tawdry corrupt world" and as "the sullen art of displaced persons." She's not wrong, not in the context she's describing—that of our modern sense of dislocation, and the way that movies, even "bad" movies, can speak to that—but the hard-boiled rhetoric is disingenuous: it at once flatters us and intimates that we might be rubes if we question any of her assumptions. Adler's aesthetic and Kael's couldn't be any further apart. It's no surprise to see them at odds over Cassavetes's *Faces*, for example, and some of this may come down to class differences: for the Italian-born, Bryn Mawr–educated Adler, trash—a movie like *Wild in the Streets*—was *trash*, even when it was enjoyable; for Kael, the daughter of a California chicken farmer, trash was often more effective than "art" when it came to communicating the energies of the moment. As I say, she's not wrong, and the simple act of putting together a nervy argument along these lines was, especially at that time, a vital political gesture. But Kael had another side—there is a famous story about her having dinner one night at the director Sidney Lumet's apartment, and, asked what a critic's job was, gesturing toward her host and saying, "My job is to show *him* which way to go"—and by the time she published *When the Lights Go Down*, her career had taken a steep turn. Invited to Hollywood in 1979 to work as a producer, she'd clashed with her benefactors, Warren Beatty and the director James Toback, and then with almost everyone on the Paramount Studios lot. She was cut loose, and soon found herself back in New York, with her house critic's job no longer waiting. In other words, Adler's review happened to arrive at a vulnerable moment (and, it must be noted, Adler was one of a few writers who'd covered for Kael at the *New Yorker* while she was gone, taking over the Current Cinema column for a few months), but also at one where Kael's work seems to have declined, where she might have been corrupted by access, and by a sense of her own cultural importance.

Adler's essay (which ran in the *New York Review of Books* under the title "The Perils of Pauline" but was subsequently retitled "House Critic" for its inclusion in her 2001 collection *Canaries in the Mineshaft*) is most often cited for its determination that Kael's book is "without . . . exaggeration, not simply, jarringly, piece by piece, line by line, and without interruption, worthless. It turns out to embody something appalling and widespread in the culture." It is, as those too frequently quoted lines make clear, unsparing, and—at eight thousand words in which she applies the full juridical force of her intelligence to pulling apart Kael's vocabulary, syntax, and rhetorical tics—almost certainly longer than it needs to be. But it is not, and this is the presumption I think people tend to make, *gratuitous* in the slightest. She starts off by arguing that house criticism, this business of being forced to review movies (or books, or anything at all) regularly, consistently, day in and day out as a matter of course, because it is your *job*, is, itself, inevitably corrupting. "No serious critic can devote himself, frequently, exclusively, and indefinitely, to reviewing works most of which inevitably cannot bear, would even be misrepresented by, review in depth," she writes, underscoring that a writer as vivid and intelligent as Kael—a writer she had long followed with enthusiasm (Kael "seemed to approach movies with an energy and a good sense that were unmatched at the time in film criticism," Adler notes of the critic's earlier days)—might, indeed, be particularly vulnerable to such corruption. The piece doesn't stint: she takes Kael to task for her writing's rhetorical bullying, for its imprecision, and—above all—for its extreme taste for visceral metaphor, for crudely sexualized or scatological description. "The degree of physical sadism in Ms. Kael's work," Adler writes, "is, so far as I know, unique in expository prose. . . . Guts appear a lot, in noun, verb, or adjective form." It's a passage that recalls the one in *Speedboat* where she mocks the vogue for "assault-mode" criticism, for "eye-popping" hyperbole, and after she has spent some thousand-odd words decrying Kael's limited descriptive capability, it's easy to feel Adler is being cruel, only—

Is she? The piece isn't really about Kael; it's about her language, and even more, about the foreshortened, inadequate vernacular of modern commercial critical discourse. It's about the perils and limitations of a vocabulary that bends almost reflexively toward hyperbole—that mimics the movies, in this respect—and so distorts reality in its wake. Which could seem hyperbolic itself (once Kael's book has been pronounced "without interruption, worthless"—other than that, Mrs. Lincoln, how did you like the play?—7,900 additional words seems a lot to expend), but Adler actually has her sights set on much bigger game. After taking a tour through the rhetorical follies of Kael's prose—she cites the critic's reviews of *The Deer Hunter* and *Coming Home* in so doing—Adler winds the piece down on a quieter note, one that, I think, tends to get missed when people cite it as too aggressive, or as a personal attack. "Criticism will get over" Kael's critical style, she writes, but "what really is at stake is not movies at all, but prose and the relation between readers and writers, and of course art."

This statement is so abrupt, so low-key that it's easy almost to glide past it. But not only is the piece not really about Kael, it's not even about criticism: it's about the corruption of language in the institutional sphere, about how power—the kind of "power" Kael had accrued in her role as the *New Yorker*'s esteemed in-house film reviewer—destroys, and had turned a gifted writer into something more like a cop. (Any critic who thinks it's part of the job to "show [any artist] which way to go," to attempt this not by articulating persuasive aesthetics and ideas but by operating prescriptively, should probably get out of the business.) The piece is long, but it isn't unreasonable. It isn't even genuinely cruel, because it hinges, as ever with Adler, upon that larger point: of how small slippages in even a regional context—in the crumbling precision and rhetorical dishonesty of a weekly periodical's film reviews section—are symptomatic of something much larger and more important. If a language can't do anything but inflate ("huge!" "wonderful!" "the best!") or condemn in the bluntest of terms ("trash!" "dumpster fire!" "monster!"), if the terms of the argument become disingenuously *squalid*, then what's left of reality, that middle that may never have been too "radical" or desirable to begin with, but which nevertheless remains all we've got?

◎

What makes a writer fall silent?

Adler's piece on Kael didn't end the former's career, but it sits on a curve: what one might call the moral arc of a personality that never lets itself off the hook, but never lets well enough alone, either. It's what happens, maybe, when you meld a novelist's temperament with a lawyer's training and a journalist's mind. Since 2001's *Canaries in the Mineshaft*, there has been nothing new: only a reprinting of the two novels and a rounding up of her nonfiction's cream in *After the Tall Timber*. But while writing has always been difficult for Adler—in the *New York* magazine profile, she describes the act of doing so as "always a problem in every which way and from every direction"—I suspect the reason for her silence has more to do with the broken machinery of publishing than it does with creative ability. "I don't really suffer from writer's block," she said to me once. "But publication block . . ."

I haven't seen Renata now for a few years. At the time of this writing, I haven't done better than to trade a few telephone messages and stray, short emails (her emails seem to me, in their distilled and lightly quizzical perfection, like fragments of a novel, observations culled from the pages of *Speedboat*). Like so many writers who find themselves snagged on the prongs of a great hesitation, she seems in reality not to have lost a thing: her writing is as sharp and tensile as it has always been. A couple of summers ago I drove with a friend to see her in Connecticut, where she lives. I was visiting New England, as I rarely do anymore, and as we drove down from central New Hampshire, passing through the town of Hanover, where N and I once lived, and where our V was born, winding our way beneath lowering July skies through the cragginess of Vermont into the more manicured greenery of the Connecticut exurbs where we were meeting for lunch, it kept threatening to rain. The air was dense and humid, the landscape oddly ominous—we passed the redesigned site of an elementary school where there had been, a few years back, a notorious shooting[31]—and by the time we arrived I was drenched in sweat. We sat together and I didn't ask any questions about her work, or about literature or the movies; I just drank a martini, because it was an occasion, a holiday of sorts, and talked with a writer who made me, who is both my hero and my friend. She looked as she does in the photographs, the famous ones taken by Richard Avedon—her long braid is white now, but still hangs down her back—and was dressed, that day, in an oxford shirt, or rather a pair of them, soft pink and royal, oceanic blue, one buttoned inside the other. At some point in our meal I snapped a photograph: of Adler's elbow, a bucket of french fries, a glass of vodka (or water, I can no longer remember which) that serves for me to commemorate the occasion. I like this picture because it is elliptical and private, more offhand than the photograph my friend took later—of Renata and me together, full-frame, smiling—in the parking lot. It feels accidental, like it might have been shot by an agitated toddler who just grabbed the device and pointed and clicked randomly, but it retains a documentary quality, revealing something, at once bright and ridiculous, at the center of an afternoon that would otherwise, like any other, have been lost.

I like it, too, because it is a photograph of someone I admire, because the angle of the elbow suggests a head cocked in thought, or tilted in repose, or laughter, and because the absurdity of the gesture (*I'll commemorate this meal by photographing—my friend's*

---

31. When my friend asked Adler about this site later, during our lunch, her response seemed characteristically—if mordantly—incisive. "The archaeologists of the future will see a school built on top of another school and wonder why we blamed the architecture," she said.

wrist!) itself reminds me of her somehow, of that day she describes in *A Year in the Dark* when she decided to rearrange the
letters on her office door at the *Times* (MOVIE NEWS) into
MOVIE SNEW: a droll, anagrammatic approach to reality that
feels uniquely hers. And because the day will someday come
when this fragment, this *glimmer*, is all I have left to join all

those other wet fragments of memory, those damp and erosive pictures—scraps—that are what I retain, too, of my mother, and of V when she was a small girl. That piercing feeling of loss that, it turns out, is the *only* thing that ever renders us anything close to complete, those gains of spirit that we only seem to make, ever, by losing.

◎

It's getting late. I find myself looking at one last picture, one my mother and I took thirty years ago on Orcas Island. It was on that trip, that fateful trip to the Pacific Northwest that occurred shortly before we stopped speaking. We are standing on a shore and we are laughing, smiling. You would never know to look at the photograph that there was anything wrong. We look like any other mother and son. And yet the landscape that surrounds us—a pebbled shore, whitecapped water, pale, wintry skies—looks frigid. As if it grasps something of our relationship I am not quite ready to accept. And if I study the image a little closer, the sharp glint in my mother's eye begins to appear less like amusement and more like—anger.

Maybe I deserved her resentment. I was insufferable in those days, so sure I understood how the world was supposed to work. But as my mother and I rode on a ferry and then drove across Orcas Island—fogbound, sparsely populated, thick with fir trees and madrones, and stone beaches—I can remember I felt the pull of that place too. Maybe *I* should move here, I thought, lean into the isolation, into this regal-looking landscape that seemed as conducive as anywhere else (truly, I knew nothing) to the act of becoming a writer. I didn't, of course. But in my mind that palace of tall trees, that citadel encircled, *fortified*, by cold Pacific water, seemed viable.

"Here I am, for the first time and yet again, alone at last on Orcas Island." This line is one of *Pitch Dark's* multiple refrains, and each time I come across it ("for the first time and yet again"), I want to ask Adler what happened to her there, or rather—I want to ask myself what would have happened if I'd done that instead of moving to San Francisco. Would any of my mistakes, would the whole lifetime of them that followed, have been averted? Probably not. *Certainly* not, and yet it's still a dream: the dream of a life unblemished, of the first love affair that never ends, of the world that recognizes your—yes, *your*—gifts and opens its palm to offer everything you ever desired.

I already know how that story ends: with a rude awakening. As, of course, it should, and it must. But these days, as the world shudders along so horribly, and as I make my way through a life that feels more fortunate, maybe, than I deserve, I wonder whether "success" was ever even the object to begin with, or if "failure," that spasmodic sequence of convulsive and sometimes brutal experiences that makes up the core of every honest person's life, mightn't have been the real pursuit all along. Perhaps not. Perhaps I am mistaken. But even so, as I walk along the wide avenues of Hollywood, California, that sun-plastered plain that squats somewhere between Silver Lake and the beach, that nebulous and largely notional geography that holds so many things (the Chateau Marmont! The Polo Lounge! Wherever it is the movers and the shakers meet these days), and so many people, so many hungry young dreamers who still want (a Netflix sale! A podcast!) the same thing such wishfuls have always wanted, in slightly different form, I am filled all the same with grief. Because what I miss are not the things that never came to pass but rather the illusion, the bright hope for the future that you know—in your heart of hearts, you *know*—is false, that even if you should somehow fulfill it, you will be left, in part, with a fistful of sand.

Here I am, however. I ran and I ran, yet most days it is like I never left. Sometimes, on Larchmont Boulevard, I run into N and R, and I stop to chat with them both, to pet their dog and trade words with their son, V's much younger half brother. Other days I am in a hurry to get home to my own partner, Samantha, and to our own dog and our shared future. Now and then at night I find I cannot sleep, battered by insomnia, and I do what any native-born Angeleno would do under such conditions: I get up and go for a drive. It is my favorite hour in the city, the one in which the streets are empty and the traffic lights flash yellow ("In a real dark night of the soul it is always three o'clock in the morning," Fitzgerald wrote in "The Crack-Up," but isn't the hour of one's secret joy, one's private elation, the same?), and the dawn waits somewhere unseen on the eastern horizon. At that hour, the Chateau Marmont is a drowsy shack hidden behind white walls and frowsy-looking palms; the Sunset Strip is nothing but a crummy road dotted with drunks and Uber drivers, boulevard of only the most stunted and abortive dreams. I blast up Crescent Heights and then follow Laurel, passing that apartment where I lived almost a decade ago, speeding up the hollow tunnel of the Canyon all the way to Mulholland, where I hang a left. It is so quiet now, almost impossibly silent as I wind along this street that is named after the city's legendary architect and water baron—the one whose possible crimes have been laid out and tried in the movies too—and which runs above Los Angeles like a ridged scar, or a spine. It winds roughly parallel to Sunset Boulevard, but high above it. As I run toward the Pacific—fittingly, this section of Mulholland will terminate into dirt before I can get there—I can see it all: the flat, sparkling wasteland of the Valley to my right, and, in spots, the glowing face of the city to my left, the southerly basin that shows, at that hour, its truest colors: its glittering night-lights and never-ending shine, ruffled by desert winds and rippling around the edges with surf. I pick up speed as I go. I reach for the stereo dial and turn it up. "Blue," the song goes, "blue." That's the color of the singer's room, David Bowie keeping me company as I drive. There's no traffic at this hour—not up here—and for brief moments, microseconds only, I close my eyes, strobing the road, reliving the idiocies of adolescence, haring along in blackness just like Kate Ennis fleeing her crime in Ireland. But what I feel isn't dwindling guilt or nervous trepidation: it is happiness, plain and simple. And as I look down on the city, that place where I was born and where my bones will someday—someday—come to rest, I think of my sleeping daughter and my beloved Sam, of my mother who was born here and my father who lives here still. I think of *you*, you excellent strivers, you wannabes and aspirants, you hopefuls young and old. Gazing down from Mulholland toward Sunset and the city, I can almost see your evergreen faces, your slumbering, yoga-toned bodies draped in sleep masks, your water glasses glistening, *burning* even in the dark, as you turn restlessly beneath the burden of your dreams. How radiant you all are, and how lovely; how innocent, in sleep, of every crime except wishfulness, how beautiful and how light-giving, how very much, indeed precisely, you are like—stars.

ENDNOTES

*page 12: They "[looked] as though they . . . "*Nancy Milford, *Zelda* (New York: Harper & Row, 1970), 67.

page 13: At fifteen, too, I'd read . . . F. Scott Fitzgerald, "The Crack-Up," *Esquire*, February 1, 1936, repr. March 7, 2017, https://www.esquire .com/lifestyle/a4310/the-crack-up.

page 16: All those portraits and self-portraits . . . Fitzgerald, "The Crack-Up."

page 16: You can take Hollywood for granted . . . F. Scott Fitzgerald, *The Love of the Last Tycoon* (New York: Scribner, 1994), 3.

page 17: "Suppose you were a railroad man . . ." Fitzgerald, *The Love of the Last Tycoon*, 20.

page 22: He wanted the pattern of his life . . . Fitzgerald, *The Love of the Last Tycoon*, 91.

page 22: the popular author whose novels . . . Maureen Corrigan, *So We Read On: How "The Great Gatsby" Came to Be and Why It Endures* (New York: Little, Brown, 2014), 12.

page 22: Fitzgerald described Stahr . . . Fitzgerald to Littauer, September 29, 1939, in *A Life in Letters* (New York: Charles Scribner's Sons, 1994), 409.

page 23: Writers aren't people exactly. . . . Fitzgerald, *The Love of the Last Tycoon*, 12.

page 23: To Stahr, the author donated . . . Fitzgerald, *The Love of the Last Tycoon*, 17.

page 24: Budd Schulberg, who would immortalize ... Budd Schulberg, "Old Scott: The Mask, the Myth, and the Man," *Esquire*, January 1, 1961, https://classic.esquire.com/article/1961/1/1/old-scott.

page 25: Hemingway, who'd repaid Fitz's ... Hemingway to Arthur Mizener, April 22, 1950, in *Selected Letters 1917–1961* (New York: Charles Scribner's Sons, 1981), 689.

page 25: Dorothy Parker, his friend for twenty years ... Dorothy Parker, "The Art of Fiction No. 13," interview by Marion Capron, *Paris Review*, no. 13 (Summer 1956), 15.

page 29: It looked a bit like an inverted wedding cake ... Evelyn De Wolfe, "DGA Headquarters Nears Completion in Hollywood," *Los Angeles Times*, November 13, 1988, http://articles.latimes.com/1988-11-13/realestate/re-191_1_dga-headquarters.

page 35: "With his plumped-out cheeks ..." Eleanor Perry, *Blue Pages* (Philadelphia: Lippincott, 1979), 31.

page 36: Now she stares through the taxi window ... Perry, *Blue Pages*, 35.

page 37: During the argument that kicks off **Blue Pages** ... Perry, *Blue Pages*, 13.

page 41: It was a natural adaptation for her ... Carol Lawson, "Eleanor Perry Dies; Wrote Screenplays," *New York Times*, March 17, 1981, https://www.nytimes.com/1981/03/17/obituaries/eleanor-perry-dies-wrote-screenplays.html.

page 42: Frank was so green that ... Ariel Schudson, "Frank & Eleanor Perry," *New Beverly Cinema* (blog), February 27, 2017, http://thenewbev.com/blog/2017/02/frank-eleanor-perry.

page 42: Frank would eventually find himself . . . Dana Lemaster, "Film Appreciation: *David and Lisa*," *Thinking Cinema* (blog), July 31, 2015, https://www.thinkingcinema.com/film-appreciation-david-and-lisa.

page 43: When we say an adaptation is good . . . Truman Capote, Eleanor Perry, and Frank Perry, *Trilogy* (New York: Macmillan, 1969), 41–42.

page 44: "Extrapolate it, but not violate it." . . . Perry, *Blue Pages*, 147.

page 47: In the end, it was Sydney Pollack . . . JB, "*The Swimmer*," *The Overlook* (blog), *F This Movie!*, March 3, 2015, http://www.fthismovie.net/2015/03/the-overlook-swimmer.html.

page 48: Writing about Christina Stead's blistering . . . Eleanor Perry, "Oh Dad, Poor Dad, the Family's Filled with Hatred and the Kids Are So Sad," review of *The Man Who Loved Children*, by Christina Stead, *Sydney Herald Tribune*, April 18, 1965, Book Week, 1, 15.

page 48: In her Life *review of Kaufman's* . . . Eleanor Perry, "Angry Mom Revolts, Writes Book About Dad," review of *Diary of a Mad Housewife*, by Sue Kaufman, *Life*, February 17, 1967.

page 52: The movie is excruciating to watch . . . Susan King, "'Last Summer' to Have Rare Screening from American Cinematheque," *Los Angeles Times*, January 18, 2012, http://articles.latimes.com/2012/jan/18/entertainment/la-et-last-summer-20120118.

page 60: "I honestly don't feel that the marriage . . ." Guy Flatley, "Don't Ask Them to Go on Daddy Sam's Yacht," *New York Times*, April 12, 1970, https://www.nytimes.com/1970/04/12/archives/movies-dont-ask-them-to-go-on-daddy-sams-yacht.html.

page 60: In New York *magazine, the Perrys* . . . Frank Perry and Eleanor Perry, "Can This Marriage Be Saved?," *New York*, September 1, 1969, 54.

page 62: "Please don't leave me," Lucia begs . . . Perry, *Blue Pages*, 11.

page 64: Barbara Goldsmith was younger . . . Andrea Chambers, "Author Barbara Goldsmith and Director Frank Perry Only Collaborate Off Camera," *People*, June 23, 1980, https://people.com /archive/author-barbara-goldsmith-and-director-frank-perry-only -collaborate-off-camera-vol-13-no-25.

page 65: In a 1974 recorded interview . . . Eleanor Perry, interview by Arthur Knight, *In Conversation* series, Gordon Skene Sound Collection, October 28, 1974, https://pastdaily.com/2018/03/25/eleanor-perry -discusses-writing-film-feminism-1974-past-daily-gallimaufry.

page 66: In 1979 she told an interviewer . . . "Eleanor Perry Finds a Novel Way to Surface," *Pittsburgh Press*, March 14, 1979, 57.

page 66: In an anecdote that would come to define . . . Charles Champlin, "Critic at Large: Memories of Writer Linger," *Los Angeles Times*, June 10, 1981.

page 66: "I adore Fellini," she told the cops. . . . Paula Mejia, "Summers and Swimmers," *Paris Review*, June 16, 2017, https://www .theparisreview.org/blog/2017/06/16/summers-and-swimmers.

page 68: "If Saul Bellow or Philip Roth complains . . ." "Knight at the Movies," *Hollywood Reporter*, April 20, 1979.

page 68: "I haven't read it," Frank sniffed . . . Chambers, "Author Barbara Goldsmith and Director Frank Perry Only Collaborate Off Camera."

page 68: the preposterous "Arnold Rivers," who sticks . . . Perry, *Blue Pages*, 132.

page 68: "EST convinced me . . ." Perry, *Blue Pages*, 38.

page 69: Philip was a perfect example of the affluent . . . Perry, *Blue Pages*, 37.

page 71: A **Washington Post** *profile from 1979 . . .* Megan Rosenfeld, "Perrying Men and Marriage," *Washington Post*, April 13, 1979, https://www.washingtonpost.com/archive/lifestyle/1979/04/13 /perrying-men-and-marriage/ea2c088a-f5cd-4df8-987e-610c7f58df5a /?utm_term=.61d6d5c5ab66.

page 73: She estimated that it had taken . . . Liz Smith, "Page Six," *New York Post*, April 28, 1979.

page 73: "Stop here. Look." She gestured . . . Ann Bayer, "After Death, Mementos That Mean a Life," *New York Times*, February 17, 1982, https://www.nytimes.com/1982/02/17/garden/after-death-mementos -that-mean-a-life.html.

page 88: an excellent online appreciation . . . Nick Pinkerton, "Bombast: Carole Eastman," *Film Comment*, November 21, 2014, https://www.filmcomment.com/blog/bombast-carole-eastman.

page 88: Biskind describes her in both books . . . Peter Biskind, *Star: How Warren Beatty Seduced America* (New York: Simon & Schuster, 2010), 198.

page 88: In **Easy Riders, Raging Bulls,** *Biskind adds . . .* Peter Biskind, *Easy Riders, Raging Bulls: How the Sex-Drugs-and-Rock 'n' Roll Generation Saved Hollywood* (New York: Simon & Schuster, 1998), 130.

page 89: Pinkerton offers a description from the screenwriter . . . Patrick McGilligan, *Jack's Life: A Biography of Jack Nicholson* (New York: W. W. Norton, 1994), 97.

page 89: Patrick McGilligan's Nicholson biography describes . . . McGilligan, *Jack's Life*, 89.

page 91: Born in Glendale, in 1934 . . . Ronald Bergan, "Carole Eastman: Screenwriter Famous for a Chicken Salad Dispute," *Guardian*, March 25, 2004, https://www.theguardian.com/news/2004/mar/26 /guardianobituaries.film.

page 91: Born in Glendale, in 1934... Dennis McLellan, "Carole Eastman, 69; Wrote Screenplay for 'Five Easy Pieces,'" *Los Angeles Times*, February 27, 2004, http://articles.latimes.com/2004/feb/27/local/me-eastman27.

page 91: The writer described herself as... McGilligan, *Jack's Life*, 94.

page 92: Eastman was first a model... McLellan, "Carole Eastman, 69."

page 93: the screenwriter Barry Sandler, who lived next door... Interview with author, October 17, 2018.

page 94: As one who reaches for her six-shooter... Dennis McDougal, *Five Easy Decades: How Jack Nicholson Became the Biggest Movie Star in Modern Times* (Hoboken, NJ: Wiley, 2008), 57.

page 95: Critics commonly praised Eastman's dialogue... McDougal, *Five Easy Decades*, 111.

page 97: If Eastman was, as Biskind claims... Biskind, *Easy Riders, Raging Bulls*, 306.

page 101: "It'll be like The African Queen *in the desert..."* Marc Eliot, *Nicholson: A Biography* (New York: Three Rivers Press, 2013), 45.

page 102: that famous coffee shop scene... McGilligan, *Jack's Life*, 111.

page 103: In the 1972 Time *article...* "Show Business: Behind the Lens," *Time*, March 20, 1972, 92–93.

page 103: She wears aviator shades and a T-shirt... Eliot, *Nicholson*, 46.

page 104: God knows where the "Adrien" came from... Eliot, *Nicholson*, 45.

page 109: All time is truly lost and gone... Torquato Tasso, *Aminta: A Pastoral Play*, trans. Charles Jernigan (New York: Italica Press, 2000), 13.

page 110: I have seen that it is because . . . Carole Eastman, Harry Ransom Center, Container 20.5, "Print material and notes on quiz kids, undated."

page 111: review from Vincent Canby in the New York Times . . . Vincent Canby, "Nichols's 'Fortune' Is Old-Time Farce," *New York Times*, May 21, 1975, https://www.nytimes.com/1975/05/21 /archives/nicholss-fortune-is-oldtime-farce.html.

page 111: a belated championing from the Coen brothers . . . "The 96th Best Director of All-Time: Mike Nichols," Cinema Archives, accessed September 12, 2020, http://thecinemaarchives.com/2019/08/13 /the-96th-best-director-of-all-time-mike-nichols.

page 112: According to the production designer . . . Biskind, *Easy Riders, Raging Bulls*, 509.

page 112: This was the period in which David Geffen . . . Christian Williams, "David Geffen's Touch of Gold," *Washington Post*, May 6, 1982, https://www.washingtonpost.com/archive/lifestyle/1982/05/06/david -geffens-touch-of-gold/0661d044-e596-4f01-883f-9d1857f0b9b9.

page 113: In 1991, a brief column in the Calendar section . . . Pat H. Broeske, "Three Easy Pieces," *Los Angeles Times*, March 3, 1991, F24.

page 116: She will be writing and directing a script . . . Carole Eastman, Harry Ransom Center, Container 2.3, "Interview with Betty Ulius, 1971."

page 120: In one of the letters . . . Carole Eastman, Harry Ransom Center, Container 20.6–7, "Correspondence, 1970–2000, undated."

page 122: The cause, one obit claimed . . . Bergan, "Carole Eastman," *Guardian*.

page 125: "Stranded beanless on the boulevard" . . . Carole Eastman, Harry Ransom Center, Container 20.8, "Poetry, undated."

page 137: "I was driving fast..." Thomas McGuane, "The Art of Fiction No. 89," interview by Sinda Gregory and Larry McCaffery, *Paris Review*, no. 97 (Fall 1985), https://www.theparisreview.org/interviews /2867/thomas-mcguane-the-art-of-fiction-no-89-thomas-mcguane.

page 137: "Suddenly you're standing in the middle of it..." McGuane, "The Art of Fiction."

page 138: Some say he saw a girl on a bicycle... William McKeen, *Mile Marker Zero: The Moveable Feast of Key West* (New York: Crown, 2011), 117.

page 140: McGuane describes his dad as hardworking... McKeen, *Mile Marker Zero*, 56.

page 142: Joyce Carol Oates, reviewing the book... Joyce Carol Oates, review of *The Sporting Club*, by Thomas McGuane, *New York Times*, March 5, 1969, Sunday Book Review, https://www.nytimes .com /1969/03/23/archives/the-sporting-club-by-thomas-mcguane -220-pp-new-york-simon-schuster.html.

page 146: and against the statistical ones too... Nancy Graham, "Racing with death on Sunset: Scenic Road Stirs Impulse to Speed," *Los Angeles Times*, February 3, 1985, https://www.latimes.com/archives/la-xpm -1985-02-03-we-13583-story.html.

page 147: "I saw an old drunk fall in front..." Thomas McGuane, *Panama* (New York: Farrar, Straus and Giroux, 1978), 43.

page 147: "There is a trigger that makes the day begin..." McGuane, *Panama*, 127.

page 150: A dark brown elevator cable... Thomas McGuane, *The Bushwhacked Piano* (New York: Vintage, 1994), 46.

page 152: In a 1985 interview... Beef Torrey, ed., *Conversations with Thomas McGuane* (Jackson: University Press of Mississippi, 2007), 95.

page 152: In 1988 he would tell Jean W. Ross . . . Torrey, *Conversations with Thomas McGuane*, 102.

page 154: "I don't feel the profound difference . . ." Torrey, *Conversations with Thomas McGuane*, 27.

page 155: When Kastner discovered . . . McKeen, *Mile Marker Zero*, 138.

page 156: I looked around and spotted . . . Elizabeth Ashley with Ross Firestone, *Actress: Postcards from the Road* (New York: Fawcett Crest, 1978), 163–64.

page 156: When Ashley met Becky McGuane . . . Ashley, *Actress*, 165.

page 157: "I don't fuck married men . . ." Ashley, *Actress*, 167.

page 158: "Any asshole can direct a movie . . ." McKeen, *Mile Marker Zero*, 145.

page 160: "Duval Street, crowded and Latin all day . . ." Thomas McGuane, *Ninety-Two in the Shade* (New York: Vintage, 1995), 64.

page 161: Becky felt guilty . . . Ashley, *Actress*, 200–201.

page 161: Peter Fonda had been agitating . . . McKeen, *Mile Marker Zero*, 147.

page 162: When she left her reading . . . Ashley, *Actress*, 204.

page 163: Whether it was Fonda's drug problem . . . McKeen, *Mile Marker Zero*, 148.

page 164: Things were swirling. . . . Larry McMurtry, *All My Friends Are Going to Be Strangers* (New York: Simon & Schuster, 1972), 22.

page 165: Jerry now knew with terrible . . . Don Carpenter, *The Hollywood Trilogy* (Berkeley, CA: Counterpoint, 2014), 531.

page 165: McGuane's Key West neighbor ... Tennessee Williams, "On a Streetcar Named Success," *New York Times*, November 30, 1947, https://www.nytimes.com/1947/11/30/archives/on-a-streetcar-named-success-tennessee-williams-on-a-streetcar.html.

page 168: McGuane put it this way ... Torrey, *Conversations with Thomas McGuane*, 134.

page 168: showing up in lasciviously titled ... Harmon Henkin, "Tom (McGuane) & Margot (Kidder) & Peter (Fonda) & Becky (McGuane) & Whoops," *People*, February 9, 1976, https://people.com/archive/tom-mcguane-margot-kidder-peter-fonda-becky-mcguane-whoops-vol-5-no-5.

page 169: John Leonard, in the New York Times ... John Leonard, "Books of the Times," review of *Panama*, by Thomas McGuane, *New York Times*, November 21, 1978, https://www.nytimes.com/1978/11/21/archives/books-of-the-times-dangerous-flowers.html.

page 169: while Jonathan Yardley ... Jonathan Yardley, "Thomas McGuane Reaches for the Big Sky," review of *Panama*, by Thomas McGuane, *Washington Post*, February 28, 1982, https://www.washingtonpost.com/archive/entertainment/books/1982/02/28/thomas-mcguane-reaches-for-the-big-sky/89e5d950-87b4-4f21-82f4-145cc84ce27c.

page 170: "Even in the sun ..." McGuane, *Panama*, 136.

page 171: I was a simple occupant ... McGuane, *Panama*, 120.

page 171: McGuane would later note ... Torrey, *Conversations with Thomas McGuane*, 46.

page 171: "The occupational hazard of ..." McGuane, *Panama*, 52.

page 173: In Joy Williams's guidebook ... Joy Williams, *The Florida Keys: A History and Guide*, 10th ed. (New York: Random House, 2003), 130.

page 173: In a sharp article published... Mark Kamine, "The Late Style of Thomas McGuane," *Believer*, no. 47 (September 1, 2007), https://believermag.com/the-late-style-of-thomas-mcguane.

page 183: Allegedly Stanley Kubrick's first choice... Guy Flatley, "Most of All, Tuesday Remembers Mama," *New York Times*, November 7, 1971, https://www.nytimes.com/1971/11/07/archives /most-of-all-tuesday-remembers-mama.html.

page 184: as film historian David Thomson wrote... David Thomson, *The New Biographical Dictionary of Film*, 6th ed. (New York: Knopf, 2014), 1105.

page 184: at least she tells Cavett... Rex Reed, *People Are Crazy Here* (Memphis, TN: Devault-Graves Digital Editions, 1974), loc. 2863 of 4233, Kindle.

page 185: In her 1968 review of **Pretty Poison**... Pauline Kael, *Going Steady: Film Writings, 1968–1969* (London: Marion Boyars Publishers, 1994), 169.

page 186: In a 1971 interview with the **New York Times**... Flatley, "Most of All, Tuesday Remembers Mama."

page 188: According to Conner, Weld's nickname... Floyd Conner, *Pretty Poison: The Tuesday Weld Story* (Fort Lee, NJ: Barricade, 1995), 10.

page 188: Per **If It's Tuesday** ... **I Must Be Dead!**... Samuel Veta and Yosene Ker Weld, *If It's Tuesday ... I Must Be Dead!* (Sherman Oaks, CA: Samuel Veta, 2002), 42.

page 197: Weld herself claimed to... Conner, *Pretty Poison*, 163.

page 202: "The eternal Los Angeles..." Sam Sweet, *Hadley Lee Lightcap* (Los Angeles: All Night Menu, 2017), 7.

page 205: She waived alimony... Flatley, "Most of All, Tuesday Remembers Mama."

page 205: I feel so misplaced ... Flatley, "Most of All, Tuesday Remembers Mama."

page 206: "I went to look at the ashes ..." Conner, *Pretty Poison*, 173–74.

page 206: Later, she said, "I'm suspended ..." Flatley, "Most of All, Tuesday Remembers Mama."

page 206: A Rex Reed piece ... Reed, *People Are Crazy Here*, loc. 2849 of 4233, Kindle.

page 213: In one of D's favorite novels ... Walker Percy, *The Moviegoer* (1961; repr., New York: Alfred A. Knopf, 1995), 13.

page 231: The singer's ex-wife ... Crystal Zevon, *I'll Sleep When I'm Dead: The Dirty Life and Times of Warren Zevon* (New York: Harper-Collins, 2007), 135.

page 235: His friend Tom McGuane ... Zevon, *I'll Sleep When I'm Dead*, 429.

page 235: The novelist William Gaddis wrote ... William Gaddis, *The Recognitions* (New York: Penguin, 1993), 95–96.

page 239: In the introduction to Kevin Avery's ... Paul Nelson and Kevin Avery with Jeff Wong, *It's All One Case: The Illustrated Ross Macdonald Archives* (Seattle, WA: Fantagraphics, 2016), v.

page 240: As Archer thinks in 1956's **The Barbarous Coast** ... Ross Macdonald, *The Barbarous Coast* (1956; repr., New York: Vintage, 2007), 119.

page 240: It was like a dream come true ... Kevin Avery, *Everything Is an Afterthought: The Life and Writings of Paul Nelson* (Fantagraphics, 2011), 390.

page 242: Wading in with the usual malarkey ... Avery, *Everything Is an Afterthought*, 362.

page 250: "My songs are all about fear ..." C. M. Kushins, *Nothing's Bad Luck: The Lives of Warren Zevon* (Da Capo, 2019), 332.

page 251: "You'd be so proud of me! ..." Zevon, *I'll Sleep When I'm Dead*, 392.

page 253: His friend Ryan Rayston ... Kushins, *Nothing's Bad Luck*, 332.

page 256: He died in the middle ... Zevon, *I'll Sleep When I'm Dead*, 104.

page 257: I cannot help but think of Ross Macdonald ... Avery, *Everything Is an Afterthought*, 394.

page 257: As he told Paul Nelson ... Nelson et al., *It's All One Case*, 61.

page 264: If "the function of freedom ..." Toni Morrison, "Cinderella's Stepsisters" (college commencement address, Barnard College, New York, May 13, 1979).

page 264: There is the famous story ... Biskind, *Easy Riders, Raging Bulls*, 141.

page 269: After the director told ... Peter Biskind, "The Vietnam Oscars," *Vanity Fair*, February 19, 2008, https://www.vanityfair.com / news/2008/03/warmovies200803.

page 269: The two men shared ... Nick Dawson, *Being Hal Ashby: Life of a Hollywood Rebel* (Lexington: University Press of Kentucky, 2009), 342.

page 272: What little he did offer ... Steve Garbarino, "Michael Cimino's Final Cut," *Vanity Fair*, April 15, 2010, https://www.vanityfair.com /hollywood/2010/04/ciminos-final-cut-200203.

page 275: When the director's method-acting star ... Dawson, *Being Hal Ashby*, 127.

page 278: "I feel like I have never ..." Dawson, *Being Hal Ashby*, 150.

page 278: Cimino's father died young . . . Garbarino, "Michael Cimino's Final Cut."

page 280: "Have you ever said no! . . ." Dawson, *Being Hal Ashby*, 117.

page 280: The director had "a self-assurance . . ." Steven Bach, *Final Cut: Dreams and Disaster in the Making of Heaven's Gate* (New York: William Morrow, 1985), 119.

page 281: Of Cimino's physical appearance . . . Bach, *Final Cut*, 118.

page 282: The writer Sean Fennessey . . . Sean Fennessey, "Hal Ashby's American Pictures: The Realistic Magic of the 1970s' Finest Director," *Ringer*, September 6, 2018, https://www.theringer.com /movies/2018/9/6/17826818/hal-ashby-documentary-harold-maude -last-detail-hollywood-shampoo-being-there-coming-home.

page 284: For a long time Eastman's reputation . . . Dennis McLellan, "Charles Eastman dies at 79; playwright and screenwriter," *Los Angeles Times*, July 10, 2009, https://www.latimes.com/archives/la-xpm-2009 -jul-10-me-charles-eastman10-story.html.

page 286: "You've treated me with more courtesy . . ." Dawson, *Being Hal Ashby*, 309.

page 287: "We would hear his Mercedes . . ." Dawson, *Being Hal Ashby*, 245.

page 293: most famously, Vincent Canby . . . Vincent Canby, "'Heaven's Gate,' a Western by Cimino," *New York Times*, November 19, 1980, https://www.nytimes.com/1980/11/19/arts/heavens-gate-a-western -by-cimino.html.

page 294: "Why isn't anyone drinking . . ." Bach, *Final Cut*, 360.

page 295: "Michael was a little crazy . . ." Bach, *Final Cut*, 400.

page 295: asked in 2015 if... Bach, *Final Cut*, 400; Seth Abramovitch, "Michael Cimino: The Full, Uncensored Hollywood Reporter Interview," *Hollywood Reporter*, March 2, 2015, https://www.hollywoodreporter.com/news/michael-cimino-full-uncensored-hollywood-778288.

page 296: "So why did you have the surgery...?" Garbarino, "Michael Cimino's Final Cut."

page 297: "When I'm kidding, I'm serious..." Garbarino, "Michael Cimino's Final Cut."

page 298: "Nobody lives without making mistakes..." Garbarino, "Michael Cimino's Final Cut."

page 299: "This is a lonely country..." Leticia Kent, "Ready for Vietnam? A Talk with Michael Cimino," *New York Times*, December 10, 1978, https://www.nytimes.com/1978/12/10/archives/ready-for-vietnam-a-talk-with-michael-cimino-cimino.html.

page 310: When I was a teenager... "Rate My Professor! Renata Adler: 'Hot for Goin on 70,'" *Observer*, November 16, 2006, https://observer.com/2006/11/rate-my-professor-renata-adler-hot-for-goin-on-70.

page 312: "Life passes into pages..." James Salter, *Burning the Days* (New York: Random House, 1997), 203.

page 315: A review like Crowther's... Bosley Crowther, "Run, Bonnie and Clyde," review of *Bonnie and Clyde*, directed by Arthur Penn, *New York Times*, September 3, 1967, https://www.nytimes.com/1967/09/03/archives/run-bonnie-and-clyde-run-bonnie.html.

page 315: Adler had been a staff writer... Jesse Kornbluth, "The Quirky Brilliance of Renata Adler," *New York*, December 12, 1983, 37.

page 316: "The job came to me . . ." Renata Adler, *A Year in the Dark: Journal of a Film Critic 1968–1969* (New York: Random House, 1969), xiii.

page 316: "Even if your idea of a good time . . ." Adler, *A Year in the Dark*, 1.

page 317: In a 2004 listserv post . . . David Ehrenstein, reply to "NYTimes critics any recommendations," Fred Camper's "A Film By" discussion group, May 10, 2004, https://www.fredcamper.com/afilmby/0009701.html.

page 318: "In those months . . ." Adler, *A Year in the Dark*, xv.

page 319: "There is probably no more . . ." Adler, *A Year in the Dark*, 82.

page 323: "The simplest operations of life . . ." Renata Adler, *Speedboat* (New York: Random House, 1976), 91.

page 323: "The radical intelligence in the moderate . . ." Adler, *Speedboat*, 40.

page 323: "That 'writers write' is meant to be self-evident. . . ." Adler, *Speedboat*, 28.

page 324: "A rowboat, without oars. . . ." Renata Adler, *Pitch Dark* (New York: Alfred A. Knopf, 1983), 22.

page 325: "I guess," Adler told the New York Times *. . .* Samuel G. Freedman, "Renata Adler Takes an Artistic Risk," *New York Times*, December 27, 1983, https://www.nytimes.com/1983/12/27/books/renata-adler-takes-artistic-risk.html.

page 326: What she called a "literature of paranoia" . . . Elizabeth Hardwick, "Sense of the Present," review of *Speedboat*, by Renata Adler, *New York Review of Books*, November 25, 1976, https://www.nybooks.com/articles/1976/11/25/sense-of-the-present.

page 327: "We were running flat out . . ." Adler, *Pitch Dark*, 3.

page 328: "This is the age of crime . . ." Adler, *Pitch Dark*, 43–46.

page 329: "The surgery. My state of mind. . . ." Adler, *Pitch Dark*, 42.

page 332: In "Trash, Art, and the Movies," . . . Pauline Kael, "Trash, Art, and the Movies," *Going Steady: Film Writings 1968–1969* (New York, London: Marion Boyars Publishers, 1994), 87.

page 332: there is a famous story about . . . Nathan Heller, "What She Said: The Doings and Undoings of Pauline Kael," *New Yorker*, October 24, 2011, https://www.newyorker.com/magazine/2011/10/24/what -she-said.

page 333: Adler's essay . . . Renata Adler, *Canaries in the Mineshaft: Essays on Politics and Media* (New York: St. Martin's, 2001), 329.

page 333: "No serious critic can devote . . ." Adler, *Canaries in the Mineshaft*, 327.

page 334: "Criticism will get over . . ." Adler, *Canaries in the Mineshaft*, 368.

page 336: In the New York *magazine profile . . .* Kornbluth, "The Quirky Brilliance of Renata Adler," 40.

page 337: I like it, too . . . Adler, *A Year in the Dark*, xvii.

WORKS

BOOKS

The Love of the Last Tycoon, F. Scott Fitzgerald (Scribner, 1994)

The Pat Hobby Stories, F. Scott Fitzgerald (Scribner, 1995)

I'd Die for You: And Other Lost Stories, F. Scott Fitzgerald, edited by Anne Margaret Daniel (Scribner, 2018)

"The Crack-Up," F. Scott Fitzgerald, *Esquire*, February 1, 1936

So We Read On: How "The Great Gatsby" Came to Be and Why It Endures, Maureen Corrigan (Little, Brown, 2014)

Zelda, Nancy Milford (New York: Harper & Row, 1970)

F. Scott Fitzgerald: A Life in Letters: A New Collection, edited and annotated by Matthew J. Bruccoli (Scribner, 1995)

"Old Scott: The Mask, the Myth, and the Man," Budd Schulberg, *Esquire*, January 1, 1961

Crazy Sundays: F. Scott Fitzgerald in Hollywood, Aaron Latham (Viking, 1970)

Some Time in the Sun, Tom Dardis (Limelight Editions, 1998)

The Disenchanted, Budd Schulberg (Allison & Busby Classics, 2013)

Blue Pages, Eleanor Perry (Lippincott, 1979)

Trilogy, Truman Capote, Eleanor Perry, and Frank Perry (Macmillan, 1969)

Diary of a Mad Housewife, Sue Kaufman (Seal Press, 2005)

The Stories of John Cheever, John Cheever (Ballantine Books, 1980)

Play It as It Lays, Joan Didion (FSG Classics, 2005)

The White Album: Essays, Joan Didion (FSG Classics, 2009)

"After Death, Mementos That Mean a Life," Ann Bayer, *New York Times*, February 17, 1982

"Bombast: Carole Eastman," Nick Pinkerton, *Film Comment*, November 21, 2014

Star: How Warren Beatty Seduced America, Peter Biskind (Simon & Schuster, 2010)

Easy Riders, Raging Bulls: How the Sex-Drugs-and-Rock 'n' Roll Generation Saved Hollywood, Peter Biskind (Simon & Schuster, 1998)

Jack's Life: A Biography of Jack Nicholson, Patrick McGilligan (W. W. Norton, 1994)

Nicholson: A Biography, Marc Eliot (Three Rivers Press, 2013)

Aminta: A Pastoral Play, Torquato Tasso, translated by Charles Jernigan (Italica Press, 2000)

The Sporting Club, Thomas McGuane (Vintage, 1996)

The Bushwhacked Piano, Thomas McGuane (Vintage, 1994)

Ninety-Two in the Shade, Thomas McGuane (Vintage, 1995)

Panama, Thomas McGuane (Farrar, Straus and Giroux, 1978)

Cloudbursts: Collected and New Stories, Thomas McGuane (Vintage, 2019)

Conversations with Thomas McGuane, edited by Beef Torrey (University Press of Mississippi, 2007)

Mile Marker Zero: The Moveable Feast of Key West, William McKeen (Crown, 2011)

Actress: Postcards from the Road, Elizabeth Ashley with Ross Firestone (Fawcett Crest, 1978)

All My Friends Are Going to Be Strangers, Larry McMurtry (Simon & Schuster, 1972)

The Hollywood Trilogy, Don Carpenter (Counterpoint Press, 2014)

Fridays at Enrico's: A Novel, Don Carpenter, Jonathan Lethem (Counterpoint Press, 2014)

"On a Streetcar Named Success," Tennessee Williams, *New York Times*, November 30, 1947

The Florida Keys: A History and Guide, 10th ed., Joy Williams (Random House, 2003)

Going Steady: Film Writings, 1968–1969, Pauline Kael (Marion Boyars Publishers, 1994)

Pretty Poison: The Tuesday Weld Story, Floyd Conner (Fort Lee, NJ: Barricade, 1995)

If It's Tuesday . . . I Must Be Dead!, Samuel Veta and Yosene Ker Weld (Samuel Veta, 2002)

Hadley Lee Lightcap, Sam Sweet (All Night Menu, 2017)

The Moviegoer, Walker Percy (1961; repr., New York: Alfred A. Knopf, 1995)

I'll Sleep When I'm Dead: The Dirty Life and Times of Warren Zevon, Crystal Zevon (HarperCollins, 2007)

The Recognitions, William Gaddis (Penguin, 1993)

The Barbarous Coast, Ross Macdonald (Vintage, 2007)

The Blue Hammer, Ross Macdonald (Alfred A. Knopf, 1976)

The Galton Case, Ross Macdonald (Vintage Crime/Black Lizard, 1996)

The Zebra-Striped Hearse, Ross Macdonald (Vintage Crime/Black Lizard, 1998)

The Instant Enemy, Ross Macdonald (Alfred A. Knopf, 1968)

Everything Is an Afterthought: The Life and Writings of Paul Nelson, Kevin Avery (Fantagraphics, 2011)

It's All One Case: The Illustrated Ross Macdonald Archives, Paul Nelson and Kevin Avery with Jeff Wong (Fantagraphics, 2016)

Nothing's Bad Luck: The Lives of Warren Zevon, C. M. Kushins (Da Capo, 2019)

Accidentally Like a Martyr: The Tortured Art of Warren Zevon, James Campion (Backbeat, 2018)

Warren Zevon: Desperado of Los Angeles, George Plasketes (Rowman & Littlefield Publishers, 2017)

Being Hal Ashby: Life of a Hollywood Rebel, Nick Dawson (University Press of Kentucky, 2009)

"Michael Cimino's Final Cut," Steve Garbarino, *Vanity Fair*, April 15, 2010

Final Cut: Dreams and Disaster in the Making of Heaven's Gate, Steven Bach (William Morrow, 1985)

"Michael Cimino: The Full, Uncensored Hollywood Reporter Interview," Seth Abramovitch, *Hollywood Reporter*, March 2, 2015

Burning the Days, James Salter (Random House, 1997)

A Year in the Dark: Journal of a Film Critic 1968–1969, Renata Adler (Random House, 1969)

Speedboat, Renata Adler (Random House, 1976)

Pitch Dark, Renata Adler (Alfred A. Knopf, 1983)

Canaries in the Mineshaft: Essays on Politics and Media, Renata Adler (St. Martin's, 2001)

After the Tall Timber: Collected Nonfiction, Renata Adler (New York Review Books, 2015)

FILMS

The Great Gatsby, d. Herbert Brenon, 1926

Three Comrades, d. Frank Borzage, 1938

Winter Carnival, d. Charles Reisner, 1939

The Women, d. George Cukor, 1940

The Great Gatsby, d. Elliott Nugent, 1949

Sunset Boulevard, d. Billy Wilder, 1950

The Many Loves of Dobie Gillis (TV show), created by Max Shulman, season 1, 1959–60

Wild in the Country, d. Philip Dunne, 1961

David and Lisa, d. Frank Perry, 1962

"Bad Actor," *Alfred Hitchcock Presents*, season 7, episode 14, d. John Newland, 1962

Soldier in the Rain, d. Ralph Nelson, 1963

Ladybug, Ladybug, d. Frank Perry, 1963

I'll Take Sweden, d. Frederick De Cordova, 1965

The Cincinnati Kid, d. Norman Jewison, 1965

Lord Love a Duck, d. George Axelrod, 1966

The Shooting, d. Monte Hellman, 1966

In the Heat of the Night, d. Norman Jewison, 1967

The Swimmer, d. Frank Perry, 1968

Pretty Poison, d. Noel Black, 1968

The Thomas Crown Affair, d. Norman Jewison, 1968

Model Shop, d. Jacques Demy, 1969

Midnight Cowboy, d. John Schlesinger, 1969

Last Summer, d. Frank Perry, 1969

Gaily, Gaily, d. Norman Jewison, 1969

The Landlord, d. Hal Ashby, 1970

Diary of a Mad Housewife, d. Frank Perry, 1970

The Lady in the Car with Glasses and a Gun, d. Anatole Litvak, 1970

Five Easy Pieces, d. Bob Rafelson, 1970

Puzzle of a Downfall Child, d. Jerry Schatzberg, 1970

I Walk the Line, d. John Frankenheimer, 1970

A Safe Place, d. Henry Jaglom, 1970

The Sporting Club, d. Larry Peerce, 1971

Tarpon (documentary), d. Guy de la Valdene, Christian Odasso, 1971

Harold and Maude, d. Hal Ashby, 1971

Play It as It Lays, d. Frank Perry, 1972

Silent Running, d. Douglas Trumbull, 1972

Magnum Force, d. Ted Post, 1973

The Last Detail, d. Hal Ashby, 1973

The Long Goodbye, d. Robert Altman, 1973

Thunderbolt and Lightfoot, d. Michael Cimino, 1974

Chinatown, d. Roman Polanski, 1974

The Great Gatsby, d. Jack Clayton, 1974

The Fortune, d. Mike Nichols, 1975

F. Scott Fitzgerald in Hollywood (TV movie), d. Anthony Page, 1975

Rancho Deluxe, d. Frank Perry, 1975

92 in the Shade, d. Thomas McGuane, 1975

Shampoo, d. Hal Ashby, 1975

Bound for Glory, d. Hal Ashby, 1976

The Missouri Breaks, d. Arthur Penn, 1976

The Last Tycoon, d. Elia Kazan, 1976

Looking for Mr. Goodbar, d. Richard Brooks, 1977

Who'll Stop the Rain, d. Karel Reisz, 1978

The Deer Hunter, d. Michael Cimino, 1978

Coming Home, d. Hal Ashby, 1978

Being There, d. Hal Ashby, 1979

Second-Hand Hearts, d. Hal Ashby, 1980

Heaven's Gate, d. Michael Cimino, 1980

Tom Horn, d. William Wiard, 1980

Serial, d. Bill Persky, 1980

Thief, d. Michael Mann, 1981

Author! Author!, d. Arthur Hiller, 1982

Lookin' to Get Out, d. Hal Ashby, 1982

Let's Spend the Night Together (documentary), d. Hal Ashby, 1982

Once Upon a Time in America, d. Sergio Leone, 1984

Year of the Dragon, d. Michael Cimino, 1985

8 Million Ways to Die, d. Hal Ashby, 1986

The Sicilian, d. Michael Cimino, 1987

Heartbreak Hotel, d. Chris Columbus, 1988

Desperate Hours, d. Michael Cimino, 1990

Man Trouble, d. Bob Rafelson, 1992

Feeling Minnesota, d. Steven Baigelman, 1996

The Sunchaser, d. Michael Cimino, 1996

South of Heaven, West of Hell, d. Dwight Yoakam, 2000

Warren Zevon: Keep Me in Your Heart (documentary), d. Nick Read, 2003

The Great Gatsby, d. Baz Luhrmann, 2013

SOUNDTRACK[32]

Chinatown, OST, Jerry Goldsmith, 1974

The Long Goodbye, OST, John Williams, 1973

The Doors, The Doors, 1967 ("The End")

Forever Changes, Love, 1967 ("Maybe the People Would Be the Times or Between Clark and Hilldale")

Live at the Café Carlyle, Bobby Short, 2007 ("Out of My Mind")

For Ladies Only, Steppenwolf, 1971 ("Ride with Me")

Pretties for You, Alice Cooper, 1969 ("Reflected," "Levity Ball")

Harvest, Neil Young, 1972 ("A Man Needs a Maid")[33]

On the Beach, Neil Young, 1974 ("Revolution Blues," "Motion Pictures," "On the Beach")

Younger Than Yesterday, The Byrds, 1967 ("Everybody's Been Burned")

---

32. These songs can be found (as many of them as possible) in a public playlist on Spotify: "Always Crashing in the Same Car (OST)."

33. This song, which has occasionally been upbraided for its ostensible sexism, was in fact written in sympathy with Carrie Snodgress's character in *Diary of a Mad Housewife* after Neil Young saw the movie.

The Notorious Byrd Brothers, The Byrds, 1968 ("Artificial Energy," "Draft Morning," "Wasn't Born to Follow," "Triad")

Head, The Monkees, 1968 ("Porpoise Song")

Rancho Deluxe, OST, Jimmy Buffett, 1975 ("Rancho Deluxe (Main Title)," "Livingston Saturday Night"[34])

Low, David Bowie, 1977 ("Always Crashing in the Same Car," "Speed of Life," "Sound and Vision," "A New Career in a New Town")

Lust for Life, Iggy Pop, 1977 ("Success," "Turn Blue," "Sixteen")

Adolescent Sex, Japan, 1978 ("Adolescent Sex")

Girlfriend, Matthew Sweet, 1991 ("Girlfriend")

Lord Love a Duck OST, Neal Hefti, 1966 ("Lord Love a Duck")

Thief OST, Tangerine Dream, 1981

Remain in Light, Talking Heads, 1980 ("The Great Curve")

Mott, Mott the Hoople, 1973 ("I'm a Cadillac/El Camino Dolo Roso")

Countdown to Ecstasy, Steely Dan, 1973 ("Bodhisattva," "Show Biz Kids")

Good Old Boys, Randy Newman, 1974 ("Marie")

On the Radio – Greatest Hits Volumes I & II, Donna Summer, 1979 ("On the Radio")

---

34. If you happen to catch the movie, Thomas McGuane can be seen working a mandolin as part of Buffett's band during a barroom sequence in which they play "Livingston Saturday Night."

Where the Action Is! Los Angeles Nuggets: 1965–1968, various artists, 2009 ("(You Used to) Ride So High," The Motorcycle Abilene, "Splendor in the Grass," Jackie DeShannon with The Byrds)[35]

Solid Zinc: The Turtles Anthology, The Turtles, 2002 ("Like the Seasons," "Outside Chance")

Warren Zevon, Warren Zevon, 1976 ("Mohammed's Radio," "Carmelita," "Join Me in LA," "Desperados Under the Eaves")

Excitable Boy, Warren Zevon, 1978 ("Accidentally Like a Martyr," "Excitable Boy," "Werewolves of London")

Bad Luck Streak in Dancing School, Warren Zevon, 1980 ("Bad Luck Streak in Dancing School")

Stand in the Fire, Warren Zevon, 1980 ("Lawyers, Guns and Money," "Frank and Jesse James")

The Envoy, Warren Zevon, 1982 ("The Overdraft," "Jesus Mentioned," "Ain't That Pretty At All")

Sentimental Hygiene, Warren Zevon, 1987 ("Trouble Waiting to Happen," "Detox Mansion," "Reconsider Me")

Transverse City, Warren Zevon, 1989 ("Splendid Isolation," "They Moved the Moon," "Nobody's in Love This Year")

Mr. Bad Example, Warren Zevon, 1991 ("Angel Dressed in Black," "Things to Do in Denver When You're Dead")

Mutineer, Warren Zevon, 1995 ("The Indifference of Heaven," "Jesus Was a Cross Maker")

---

35. "(You Used to) Ride So High" is an early Zevon song, but really this entire compilation embodies the sound of the Sunset Strip in the sixties spectacularly.

Life'll Kill Ya, Warren Zevon, 2000 ("I Was in the House When the House Burned Down," "For My Next Trick I'll Need a Volunteer," "Dirty Little Religion," "Don't Let Us Get Sick")

My Ride's Here, Warren Zevon, 2002 ("You're a Whole Different Person When You're Scared")

The Wind, Warren Zevon, 2003 ("Dirty Life and Times," "Disorder in the House," "Keep Me in Your Heart")

The Landlord OST, Al Kooper, 1970 ("Brand New Day," The Staple Singers)

Mona Bone Jakon, Cat Stevens, 1970 ("Trouble")

Footsteps in the Dark: Greatest Hits, Vol. 2, Cat Stevens, 1984 ("If You Want to Sing Out, Sing Out")

Pet Sounds, The Beach Boys, 1966 ("Wouldn't It Be Nice," "Let's Go Away for Awhile," "Pet Sounds")

Sunflower, The Beach Boys, 1970 ("All I Wanna Do," "It's About Time")

Surf's Up, The Beach Boys, 1971 ("Feel Flows," "'Til I Die," "Surf's Up")

Aftermath, The Rolling Stones, 1966 ("Out of Time")

Rattlesnakes, Lloyd Cole and the Commotions, 1984 ("Speedboat")

LIST OF ILLUSTRATIONS

MONKEYBITCH:

F. Scott Fitzgerald in a photo booth. Courtesy of and copyright © the Fitzgerald Papers, Manuscripts Division, Department of Rare Books and Special Collections, Princeton University Library.

POLISH STAR:

The Directors Guild of America, 7920 Sunset Blvd. Copyright © Matthew Specktor.

View of the Ferris wheel at Santa Monica Pier. Photo by Matthew Specktor, copyright © Matthew Specktor.

Eleanor Perry on the jury of the Berlin Film Festival, 1972. Photo by Konrad Giehr, licensed by Age of Photo Stock.

THE INTERVALS:

Easter Sunday, 1970. Copyright © Frederick Alan Specktor.

Small doodle in Carole Eastman's handwriting, undated. Courtesy of the Harry Ransom Center at the University of Texas at Austin.

THE SLOWEST MOMENT OF YOUR LIFE:

Author photo of Tom McGuane. Courtesy of Tom McGuane, copyright © Laurie McGuane.

Tom McGuane, Truman Capote, Tennessee Williams, and James Kirkwood in the 1970s. From the Key West Art and Historical Society. Licensed under the Creative Commons.

QUASIMODO PLAYS HERSELF:

Still from *Play It as It Lays*, 1972. Courtesy of and copyright © Universal Studios.

Tuesday Weld publicity photo, circa 1963. Licensed under the Creative Commons.

THE CADAVER AND THE SEARCH:

Vanity license plate, 1982. Copyright © Matthew Specktor.

Ross Macdonald, Paul Nelson and Warren Zevon at the Coral Casino Beach and Cabana Club, Santa Barbara. Courtesy of and copyright © Crystal Zevon.

KINGS, KILLINGS, ETC.:

The author in Malibu, circa 1971. Copyright © Frederick Alan Specktor.

Surfer girl at the beach. Copyright © Virginia Specktor.

THE AGE OF CRIME:

Frank's Wine and Spirits, 10559 Santa Monica Blvd, formerly owned by Reuben and Stella Specktor. Copyright © Matthew Specktor.

Still Life: Renata's Elbow with Fries. Copyright © Matthew Specktor.

KEY ADDRESSES

1448 N. Hayworth Avenue—Narrator's address at the beginning of the novel

1443 N. Hayworth Avenue (aka The Fitzgerald House)—Sheilah Graham's apartment, where F. Scott Fitzgerald died

1403 N. Laurel Avenue—Fitzgerald's own residence at the time of his death

7920 Sunset Blvd—The Directors Guild of America (site of narrator's fateful teenage argument with his mother)

551 ½ Westmount Drive—Carole Eastman's address while writing *Five Easy Pieces*

8221 Sunset Blvd (The Chateau Marmont)—Carole Eastman's occasional address in the mid-1970s and Tom McGuane's Los Angeles bivouac, when he was in town

1230 Horn Avenue—Warren Zevon's famed "Cat Piss Manor," where he lived in the late 1980s/early 1990s

1801 Grace Avenue (The Princess Grace Apartments, formerly The Hollywood Hawaiian Hotel)—the site of Zevon's great "Desperadoes Under the Eaves"

Malibu Colony Road—address of both Bruce Dern and Hal Ashby in the late 1970s[36]

---

36. Exact house numbers unknown, but it's a small private road (and probably would fall on the "Here Be Dragons" side of a much larger map, but depending on how much geography we want to cover . . .)

ACKNOWLEDGMENTS

My deepest thanks to Cathy Henderson and Steve Wilson at the Harry Ransom Center at the University of Texas at Austin, and to Louise Hilton at the Margaret Herrick Library in Beverly Hills, for their assistance as I was researching the lives of Carole Eastman and Eleanor Perry, respectively. Also, of course, to Tom McGuane, Crystal Zevon, and Renata Adler.

I am grateful for those friends who offered insight, assistance, and various forms of moral and/or editorial support: Malerie Willens, Maryse Meijer, Deb Shapiro, Ivy Pochoda, Lili Anolik, Julia Ingalls, Barry Sandler, Jane Halloran, Jonathan Lethem, Sean Howe, John Hilgart, Will Sheff, Dean Wareham, Britta Phillips, Deborah McGaffey, Marge McGaffey, Stacey Sher, David Manson, Sam Sweet, Matt Sumell, Catherine Park, Tyler Malone, Brian and Veronica Grazer, Andrew Winer, D. Foy, Kevin Avery, Christine Sneed, Merle Ginsberg, Jerry Schatzberg, Monte Hellman, Bret Easton Ellis, Gary Fisketjon, Michael C. Hall, Katherine Taylor, Kim Morgan, Rachel Cusk and Siemon Scamell-Katz, Gillian MacKenzie, Isabel Mendia, Laura Anderson, Abigail Sims, Eva Katz, Anne Margaret Daniel, and Anne Horowitz.

Allison Devereux, my agent, is an essential creative partner, the sort of ally every writer dreams of having. This book simply would not exist without her. The same of everyone at Tin House: Craig Popelars, Tony Perez, Masie Cochran, Nanci McCloskey, Becky Kraemer, Elizabeth DeMeo, Diane Chonette, Jakob Vala, and Yashwina Canter.

And to my family, present one way or another for every step: Fred Specktor, Johanna Specktor, Nancy Heller, Jonas Heller, Candace Culp, and Katherine Howe. Above all to my wife, Samantha, and my daughter, Virginia, who are, and always will be, everything.

AUTHOR PHOTO © JULIE PATTERSON

MATTHEW SPECKTOR is the author of the novels *American Dream Machine* and *That Summertime Sound*; a nonfiction book, *The Sting*; and the forthcoming memoir, *The Golden Hour* (Ecco/HarperCollins). His writing has appeared in *The New York Times*, *The Paris Review*, *The Believer*, *Tin House*, *Vogue*, *GQ*, *Black Clock*, and *Open City*. He has been a MacDowell fellow, and is a founding editor of the Los Angeles Review of Books. He resides in Los Angeles.

www.matthewspecktor.com